Political enthusiasm

Manchester University Press

Political enthusiasm

Partisan feeling and democracy's enchantments

Andrew Poe

MANCHESTER UNIVERSITY PRESS

Published by Manchester University Press
Oxford Road, Manchester M13 9PL

www.manchesteruniversitypress.co.uk

British Library Cataloguing-in-Publication Data
A catalogue record for this book is available from the British Library

ISBN 978 1 5261 5691 4 hardback
ISBN 978 1 5261 9568 5 paperback

First published 2022
Paperback published 2026

The publisher has no responsibility for the persistence or accuracy of URLs for any external or third-party internet websites referred to in this book, and does not guarantee that any content on such websites is, or will remain, accurate or appropriate.

EU authorised representative for GPSR:
Easy Access System Europe – Mustamäe tee 50,
10621 Tallinn, Estonia
gpsr.requests@easproject.com

Typeset by Newgen Publishing UK

Contents

Enthusiasm is par excellence the weapon of the weak.
– Frantz Fanon, *Black Skin, White Masks* (1952)

Introduction: enthusiasm's strange confusion

Animated by the heat of the struggle, pushed beyond the natural limits of one's own opinion by the opinions and excesses of one's adversaries, each loses sight of the very object of their pursuits and takes up a language that corresponds poorly to true sentiments and secret instincts.

– Alexis de Tocqueville, *Democracy in America* (1835)

Beginning enthusiasm

Enthusiasm has long been perceived as a fundamental danger to democratic politics.[1] Regarded as a source of threatening instabilities manifest through political irrationalism, enthusiasm appeared as a direct threat to the reason and order on which democracy was nobly thought to depend. It was once upon a time taken for granted that, in order for democracy to function well, it required "a touch of anomie."[2] Many believed that too much political excitement and partisan sentiment would lead to antidemocratic closures and the rise of despotisms.[3] And one can certainly understand this modern political anxiety, especially in the wake of fascist uprisings, and in clear view of the toxic rancor in democracies today. But such a desire for a sober and moderate democracy is also dangerously misleading, ignoring the emotional basis on which democracy depends and thrives.

Recent large-scale democratic ruptures – from Black Lives Matter protests in the United States, to impeachment counterdemonstrations in Brazil, an attempted *coup d'état* in Turkey, and prodemocracy rallies in Hong Kong – have evinced the significance of political enthusiasm as a real force in contemporary mass political movements. Indeed, counter Isaac Taylor's once-classic thesis that "(w)here there is no error of imagination, no misjudging of realities, no calculations which reason condemns, there is no enthusiasm," contemporary democratic movements display enthusiasm as a necessary affective force, beyond the erroneous imaginary to which it was once so often relegated.[4] And yet, for all the seeming potency of recent public passions, it remains unclear whether or how enthusiasm might operate as a specific political affect in a continuing democratic project.

Previous historical reflections on enthusiasm might make us suspicious of any such feelings in politics.[5] Alexis de Tocqueville, for example, anxious regarding enthusiastic partisanship in late eighteenth-century democratic France, understood the enthusiast as one "animated by the heat of the struggle."[6] By his accounting, enthusiasm does not just fuel commitment, it exaggerates it – with the result that reaction becomes the basis for malformed political action, rather than our own deeply held values and beliefs. Such an awakening of enthusiasm produced what Tocqueville described as a "strange confusion," leaving democratic citizens paralyzed by their own affective delusions. Indeed, enthusiasm has long been associated with delusion – religious self-possession, superstition, and various other modes of irrationality have all been used to characterize this phenomenon. For modern political liberalism, enthusiasm has served as the limit to what is permissible, both ideationally and affectively. In fact, Scottish Enlightenment thinkers once imagined a science of liberal politics devoted solely to the main problem of curing enthusiasm. For all the anxiety enthusiasm seems to produce though, we might rightly wonder whether enthusiasm can even serve as the foundation for sustained political engagement. Or is such an affect merely momentary and episodic – a dangerous and chaotic uprising of political energy?

This book traces the changing ways enthusiasm has been understood politically, illustrating how this affect has been manifest in democracy's modern history. By political enthusiasm, I mean a form of the affect of extreme conviction, and the particular political force of that conviction as it manifests itself in radically transforming political structures.[7] I argue that enthusiasm in democracy works to identify and foster progressive change. We feel enthusiasm at precisely those moments of new beginnings, when politics takes on new shapes and novel structures. Being clear about how we experience enthusiasm, and how we recognize it, is thus crucial for democracy, which depends on progression and the alteration of ruler and the ruled. Not all feelings encourage a healthy democratic politics, and identifying how enthusiasm works within political worlds can make sense of these lingering dangers. I work to uncover enthusiasm from its confused history, examining this affect as a radical contemporary political phenomenon, and exploring how enthusiasm operates in modern politics through logics of possession, including occupation and the general strike.

Enthusiasm is derived from the Greek ἐνθουσιασμός, "being possessed by a god." It is often regarded today as a deeply intense feeling, a passionate conviction for a cause, and an overwhelming emotion of excitement. But earlier histories of this feeling hint at slightly more insidious tones.[8] It was once thought, for example, that enthusiasm was a psychological condition without *logos*, and thus the boundary between reason and sentiment. By this view, to be *in* enthusiasm was to be *in* a frenzy, totally out of one's own control. It was also once thought that enthusiasm was a religious feeling. To feel enthusiasm was to be taken with divine inspiration, to be possessed by a spirit. In premodern theological debates, such possessions were sometimes seen as heretical threats to existing orthodoxies, signs of more dangerous conflictual fragmentations yet to come. Indeed, as an affect once associated with abstraction and testimony to divine inspiration, enthusiasm has its historical origins in Western religious experience.[9] In the early history of this phenomenon, it was generally thought that the only real measure of humanity's access to divinity could be confirmed by the expression of something named "enthusiasm."

Over time, a series of religious reformations, coupled with modern social and political enlightenments, transformed enthusiasm from a religious affect into a political danger. And, by the end of the eighteenth century, enthusiasm seemed to have become a centerpiece of revolutionary, rather than religious, experience. Such descriptions of this extreme affect do not quite make sense of how we might ordinarily experience enthusiasm in modern democracies today, or how we might distinguish such feelings from other heightened affective responses. But, while contemporary discourse may regard enthusiasm as having lost some of these potencies, there is much evidence that this feeling still lingers as a serious affective force. Calling our attention back to the genealogy of enthusiasm, paying attention to it as a distinct social and political phenomenon, should allow us to begin to encounter its unique political powers. Here we can be clear about when enthusiasm is useful and when it may be dangerous to a more contemporary politics.

Building on wide-ranging theoretic engagements with democracy, religion and politics, affect, revolution, and protest, we can focus in on the idea of enthusiasm itself as a resource to make sense of the grammar of democratic transformations – that is, the connections that link and organize political thought and action. The arguments I put forth in this book on political enthusiasm are both descriptive and normative. I investigate how political actors use enthusiasm to motivate allegiances, how we have come to think on the dangers of enthusiasm in democratic politics, and how else we might think about enthusiasm today. I examine the challenges enthusiasm poses to democracy, especially in the context of neoliberalism and neofascism, but also consider ways of reconstituting this crucial political affect to motivate democratic resistance to authoritarian rule. From its inception, democracy has relied on a constant affective energy of renewal. And, by tracing the way this emotional energy is made manifest in political actions – from ancient times to the present – this book sheds light on the way enthusiasm has been understood by political scientists, philosophers, and political activists, as well as its implications for contemporary democratic politics.

Today, enthusiasm seems pervasive. Christian evangelicals, Islamic fundamentalists, the fascist Right in Europe, and the global anarchist Left, have all been named enthusiasts; but so too have Greta Thurnberg and the "Skolstreijk för klimatet," the Black Lives Matter protesters in the summer of 2020, the *Gilets jaunes* in Paris in 2018, the masses of ordinary Brazilians who boycotted increased bus fares in 2013, and activists in the Oakland general strike of 2011. The political organization known as HAMAS takes the very name of "enthusiasm" as a moniker.[10] Political leaders, from Barack Obama to Vladimir Putin, Silvio Berlusconi, Geert Wilders, Jörg Haider, Marine Le Pen, Recep Tayyip Erdoğan, and Donald Trump have all been derided and/or celebrated as an "enthusiast." On both the left and the right, enthusiasm has become a crucial affect, used to confirm the efficacy of political positions, and to motivate partisan allegiance. I follow these transformations and their consequences, addressing the puzzle of how a phenomenon that once seemed so dangerous to Western conceptions of politics could become so commonplace.

Much of contemporary political history points to the need to rethink political enthusiasm. Presently, democracies face a fundamental paradox with regards to political affect. The rise of authoritarianism through democratic elections seems motivated by polarized and extremizing electorates. In such a climate, political parties and social movements alike have deep incentives to generate enthusiasm. As if to testify to this new condition, former US president Donald Trump recently exclaimed, "We are doing something very special. People are feeling it. The enthusiasm in this country has never been higher."[11] And yet, in order to resist the frameworks of these dangers, democratic subjects must also muster energies that seem already to be directed into the legitimation of fascist logics.[12] For all the attention paid to the rise of fascist or quasi-fascist paradigms, too much political theory scholarship takes enthusiasm as a passive or empty phenomenon, ignoring the unique content of specific affective logics, and the agency made manifest in such political feeling.[13] We need to understand the changing ways enthusiasm has been understood politically, exploring how political actors use enthusiasm to motivate allegiances, how we have come to think on the dangers of enthusiasm in democratic politics, and how else we might think about enthusiasm today.

To contest

The framework for this book comes from the once popular Enlightenment practice of the essay contest. As Foucault reminds us, "Today when a periodical asks its readers a question, it does so in order to collect opinions on some subject about which everyone has an opinion already; there is not much likelihood of learning anything new. In the eighteenth century, editors preferred to question the public on problems that did not yet have solutions."[14] This is Foucault's opening to his own belated answer to the 1784 essay-contest question "What is Enlightenment?" In 1775,

Christoph Martin Wieland, editor of *Der Teutsche Merkur*, offered up a less well-known essay contest: "Can we distinguish between fanaticism (*Schwärmerei*) and enthusiasm (*Enthusiasmus*)?"[15] At stake in this contest's question is whether and how affect becomes political. And it is to this particular essay contest that contemporary democratic theory might lend a close ear.

At issue in this contest are the forms of public feeling. Of special interest is whether all public sentiment poses a threat to democratic politics, or if there are certain manifestations of public feeling that democracy might depend on. Two feelings at issue in this once-historical contest were *Schwärmerei* and *Enthusiasmus*. Sometimes translated as "fanaticism," *Schwärmerei* was thought to be a particularly disturbing public feeling. The word *Schwärmerei* is of German origin, and generally thought to be an onomatopoetic derivation of the sound of swarming insects; referring to a swarm of bees, the *shhhhhh* and *buzz* echoed in the word resemble the sounds of a swarm as it mixes together. *Enthusiasmus*, by contrast, was thought by Wieland and his contemporaries to have more radical potentials for Enlightenment rationality. Here was an affect that might commingle with reason, maybe even turning reason into a new kind of god. Indeed, there was a general anxiety underlying Enlightenment discourse that rationality itself might be fanatical – that Enlightenment was impossible to represent to someone that had not already received its unmediated truth. Keeping this context in mind, Wieland posed the question of whether or how we might distinguish between fanaticism and enthusiasm to help get at this anxiety, and to untie the knot that it formed in Enlightenment political thought. Just as Foucault offered up his own answer to the question "What is Enlightenment?" I work to explore Wieland's question regarding whether we can distinguish between fanaticism and enthusiasm, and offer up a new answer.

Foucault's thinking is equally important to this story. He was also deeply interested in the distinction between fanaticism and enthusiasm, and was haunted by what he referred to as his "enthusiasm" for the Iranian revolution. Foucault arrived in Iran in 1978 amid much political turmoil. He was there to report on the growing unrest and resistance to the Shah. Less in the events, and more in the live forces of opposition, Foucault found a manifestation of a renewed political spirit. In that spirit to resist – to resist the Shah, to resist capitalism, to resist Americanism, to resist imperialism – Foucault uncovered what he thought of as a new form of politics, commingling traces of the Islamic tradition, Marxist critique, and Enlightenment publicity. Foucault's interest was particularly directed at those moments before history could judge – before there was a difference between the witness and the judge – when no one yet knew what would result from these resistances. Paying attention to such moments, Foucault insisted, was an opening into how we might understand the affective forces of the political. How does revolution appear when it begins? What affective pathways need to be opened in order for a political revolution to initiate? What looks so obvious from the ideological stance of the historical judge was, Foucault claimed, far from clear in the spirit of the crowds of protestors who resisted what they perceived as the malformed politics of a corrupt regime.

As many, including Foucault himself, have noted, this stance echoes Immanuel Kant's own reflections on the French Revolution. As Kant famously exclaimed,

> The recent revolution of a people which is rich in spirit may well either fail or succeed, accumulate misery and atrocity, it nevertheless arouses in the heart of all spectators (who are not themselves caught up in it) a taking of sides according to desires which border on enthusiasm and which, since its very expression was not without danger, can only have been caused by a moral disposition within the human race.[16]

This admiration for a spirit, an adoration that almost "borders on enthusiasm," has been read as Kant's politics of sympathy, where an equivalence between political actors gets drawn through rationalized feeling for the ideals another commits to.

I offer a different reading of this famous passage, paying close attention to the effect the form of Wieland's question has on Kant, and anyone who would work to distinguish between enthusiasm and fanaticism. Using the frame of the contest that asks whether we can distinguish between enthusiasm and fanaticism, I show how the very question of distinction works to malform enthusiasm and fanaticism. Wieland and other Enlightenment thinkers worried that, without being able to distinguish between enthusiasm and fanaticism, there could be no affective basis for moral progress – that all claims of progress would simply be political. And, while this anxiety seems to form the basis of this essay contest's question, it need not – I argue – form all its answers.

Instead, I offer a post-secular reading of enthusiasm. In this line, we might better say that enthusiasm is a "leftover" of religion in secular thinking, a concrete means of following the link between secular and pre-secular ideas.[17] The secular is itself a particular formulation that appears with specific religious imagination as its limits. Enthusiasm, I argue, crosses that boundary, and carries religious thinking. Being clear about those limits and the counter of Enlightenment rationality can make sense of this aporia – the vessel that allows for a remnant of what we can sustain. Historically, that remnant provoked a desire that could not always be met, but this book aims to engage not political authority, but the affect that allows us to authorize the political. Beneath the classical Enlightenment faith in progress is an anxiety that never really goes away, and enthusiasm helps us see how this anxiety appeared, what happened to it over time in political thought and practice, and why we still need to account for it today.

Kant's reading of the spectator's enthusiasm for revolution, and the insurgent possibility of their own political action, point the way to the force of enthusiasm and its reason. But the metaphysical dimensions of early enthusiasms seem to have contributed long-lasting tones to enthusiasm's derogations, especially in Enlightenment thought. As Simone Weil once worried,

> The real stumbling-block of totalitarian regimes is not the spiritual need of men for freedom of thought, it is men's inability to stand the physical and nervous strain of a permanent state of excitement, except during a few years of their youth. And it is in connection with this inability that the problem of freedom arises, for people feel free in a totalitarian regime to the precise extent that they feel enthusiastic ... But enthusiasm is a machine that wears out, and then a man begins to be aware of coercion, and the sense of being coerced is enough to produce in his mind that combination of docility and rancour which is typical of slaves.[18]

When the energy of enthusiasm runs out, political agents may not like what they see. Moreover, they may not be able to change the politics they helped initiate. This is a serious concern, especially if enthusiasm only belongs to spectators. If only enthusiasm could last, so Weil suggests, it would be a welcome associate to freedom. But when that enthusiasm exhausts itself, all that is left is a dangerous admixture of reason and faith, all of which supports the delegated authority of the dictator. This is similar to Jacob Talmon's concern that democracy can decline into "a dictatorship based on ideology and the enthusiasm of the masses ... the synthesis between the eighteenth-century idea of the natural order and the Rousseauist idea of popular fulfilment and self-expression. By means of this synthesis rationalism was made into a passionate faith."[19] Here we find an anxious mode of enthusiasm, different from what Kant proposed; enthusiasm is the irrationalism of the masses, driving politics by ideology against their democratic interests. Such anxiety generates an important malformation of enthusiasm, obscuring what might be read as the "positive" of this phenomenon. Taking Weil seriously, I want to consider how similar the radical form of enthusiasm we might pull out of Kant's thinking compares to hers. I worry that the negative that frames Weil's critique enthusiasm does not precisely enunciate the terms of enthusiasm itself.

I read Kant's enthusiasm as the posing of the question of opening – an affective sign that all systems of order have the capacity to be (re)opened. This was once a dangerous claim, both politically and philosophically. Kant was asserting that it might be possible, through the enthusiasm of spectators, to define the moral progress of humanity. Implied here was that not all states would necessarily find themselves in line with such progress; a serious critique indeed.

Enchantments

This book provides a distinctive perspective on how to think about enthusiastic political acts and affects, one that uses a variety of theoretical and empirical examples to ask new questions about civic attachment and democratic politics.[20] Foundational here is Jane Bennett's *The Enchantment of Modern Life: Attachments, Crossings, and Ethics*, a text that has been instrumental in drawing attention to the topic of affect within the context of modern political attachments, paying close attention to the dangers faced in evacuating enchantment from modern politics. As Bennett explains,

"To be enchanted is to be struck and shaken by the extraordinary that lives amid the familiar and the everyday."[21] I'm especially interested in the ways in which that experience of enchantment becomes political, and how it helps us navigate in turn the extraordinary and eventful. By providing a historical grounding for the transformations of philosophical rhetoric surrounding enthusiasm, and bringing these debates to bear on more contemporary political phenomena (including general strikes and suicide protest), this book not only fills a critical gap in this existing scholarly effort, but also breaks new ground on key issues that future scholars can build upon.

Here I follow closely on new developments in the theoretical literature that hope to make sense of the potentialities of these recent political changes. Especially useful here is Benjamin Moffitt's *The Global Rise of Populism: Performance, Political Style, and Representation.*[22] Moffitt takes aim at the pervasive prejudice that pathologizes populism, arguing that "underlying some of these arguments is a version of the social psychology of the late nineteenth century, in which 'the people,' associated with uncontrollable crowds, masses or mobs are considered an unruly remainder of 'politics as such,' and as a result, populism is seen as a phenomenon that should be viewed with fear and concern."[23] Paying attention to enthusiasm as the affective force that underlies democracy should help contemporary democrats move past such aristocratic anxieties.

My argument specifically elaborates on the insights of several key texts in the recent literature on enthusiasm. In his influential *Fanaticism: On the Uses of an Idea*, Alberto Toscano draws our attention to the degradation of fanatics – the relegation of fanaticism to, as he puts it, "the domain of psychopathology."[24] Building on Toscano, I pay close attention to the distinction between enthusiasm and fanaticism. If fanaticism moves towards radical egalitarianism, it does so through a productive inequality with enthusiasm. Reflecting on the history of enthusiasm as a religious passion, Jordana Rosenberg's *Critical Enthusiasm: Capital Accumulation and the Transformation of Religious Passion* has argued: "This informal integration of religious and civil abstractions makes its appearance not only in the ideology of the sovereign state, but also in the historicization and aestheticization of this state in the discourse of enthusiasm."[25] Set in the context of eighteenth-century England, Rosenberg's critique was a critical contribution to understanding the literary and economic routes of these energies. However, her work does not address the following political consequences, an omission that remains within the broader scholarly discourse. Building on her argument, my book fills that gap.

My argument directly contrasts with Mac Kilgore's, who, in *Mania for Freedom: American Literatures of Enthusiasm from the Revolution to the Civil War*, makes the claim that enthusiastic events highlight the key component of the lived experience of enthusiasm – a mania for freedom.[26] Focused on early American rhetorics of enthusiasm, Kilgore is especially attuned to the affective grammars of enthusiasm in modes of resistance. In this way, our texts come close together. Where we differ is in our account of how to understand the precise qualities of enthusiasm. Kilgore claims the name "enthusiast" "described any person who preached a democratic authority invested in the people or the individual rather than in the institutional mediations of government or church, and who claimed the right (by heaven or by natural law) to throw off or resist governments and laws when they fail to affirm said authority."[27] While Mac Kilgore focuses on enthusiasm as the search for liberty, my reading emphasizes enthusiasm as a sign of political change. Without being clear on enthusiasm's processes, the dangerous exaggerations Tocqueville described as afflicting France may – I argue – become a regular democratic pathology.

Such anxieties have often resulted in efforts to motivate allegiance with what might be termed "neutral" objects – from the "civic nation," to constitutions, and universal human rights. These approaches have had significant advantages, allowing theorists and policymakers alike to construct locations for political identities, presenting clear boundaries regarding who can and will ally themselves together. Especially important here has been the theory of "constitutional patriotism," which assumes that national particularism – fueled by Romantic political psychologies – encourages attachments that stand in the way of more democratic (even postnational) political configurations.[28] Instead, this theory aims to encourage the formation of group identities around shared norms and values rather than the civic or ethnic allegiances of a nation. Accordingly, as Jürgen Habermas has attempted to demonstrate,

"On the basis of universalistic norms, no particular entity possessing an identity-forming power (such as the family, the tribe, the city, state, or nation) can set up bounds to demarcate itself from alien groups. If this place is not filled, universalistic morality, in the same way as the ego structures consistent with it, would remain a mere postulate."[29] Habermas and others have worked to construct a patriotism that would allow for cohesion among a collective political body, without basing this cohesion on biological or pre-political justifications.[30] Such efforts are directed towards supporting a civic allegiance, without succumbing to the dangers of relativism, thus allowing for a universal, rational morality to determine norms within a republican civic body.

Enthusiasm becomes a crucial orientation point in struggles over differing conceptions of who "the people" are. Ethnic nationalism defines itself according to an *ethnos*, where belonging to the nation, and enjoying the rights of citizenship, comes only from biological ties to an ethnic group that holds majority rule within the state. As Seyla Benhabib explains, the *ethnos* is "a community bound together by the power of shared fate, memories, solidarity, and belonging. Such a community does not permit free entry and exit."[31] Civic allegiances, by contrast, afford rights to those who are part of the *demos*, that is, to the body of persons who (at least) tacitly accept the duties of citizenship. The distinction between *ethnos* and *demos* is often held in stark contrast.[32] As Margaret Canovan observes, "Modern critics of nationalism believe that by recovering features of classical republican tradition we can reinterpret what it is to be a people in ways that detach it entirely from ethnic Romanticism."[33] For Canovan and others, the distinction between the people as Romantic Volk (pre-political) and the people as republican populous (political) is central for articulating the strengths and limits of "political will." This "will" proves necessary to maintain collectivity in republics, a mechanism ignored by Romantic political thought, which instead relies on "natural" allegiances to substantiate collectivity. But we might wonder what feelings join this will.[34]

Recently, "political will" has become an increasingly fraught concept.[35] If we consider events such as January 6th, 2021, we can understand why. Democracy's advocates have aimed at overcoming the limitations of affect associated with ethnic nationalism, and the preliminary reflections associated with the uninspired resources liberalism so often employs in its attempts to bind communities together. Some democratic theorists want to believe the binding of community can be achieved without requisite recourse to pre-political attachments, redefining "political will" in terms of neutral objects of attachment. And, while such efforts are important for thinking through who "the people" are, these theories offer no clear answer for what binds the polity together. Constitutional patriotism and similar efforts to explain what motivates democratic allegiances fail to offer coherent accounts of affective motivations because it ignores the function of political enthusiasm.

Political enthusiasm poses what might be named the question of "opening." It acts as an affective sign that whatever order has proceeded it has the capacity to be (re)opened. If legitimate sovereign agency is the question of modern politics, how we access that question, how we keep it open as a question, requires enthusiasm as an operative concept.

Passages to democracy

In what follows, I trace a critical genealogy of enthusiasm. Here I ask three questions: (1) What do we mean by enthusiasm? (2) Why has it been hollowed out, especially in contemporary politics? (3) What problems do we face with and without the concept? The first part of this book explores the question of how it was that enthusiasm became a political concept – what the history of the transformation of that concept was, from religious enthusiasm to the "secularization" of that concept. With this early genealogy in place, I then examine the covering over of this concept – how ideology, coupled with the rise of liberalism, helped to construct and magnify the dangers of enthusiasm. A crucial thread to this part of the genealogy is manifest in some unusual inheritances of Kant's political thought. While some have relied on Kant's thinking to depoliticize the concept of enthusiasm, I show how some radical theorizations of collective action have also relied implicitly on a Kantian notion of enthusiasm. Then, focusing on more contemporary uses of enthusiasm, including political suicide, general strikes, and the mobilization of crowds, I conclude by offering a diagnosis of the pathologies requisite to the misunderstanding of political enthusiasm, and the resolutions that should result from its clarification. In this way, I offer an alternative narrative of enthusiasm, working to be cognizant of both its dangers and its radical political potential.

The opening chapter of this book brings to focus the different varieties of enthusiasm. I recall C. M. Wieland's question about how to distinguish between enthusiasm and fanaticism and examine it from a more contemporary vantage point. I begin with Wieland's own articulation of the problem and his working definitions, as well as the place he saw for enthusiasm in an increasingly rationalized world. Wieland himself considered his essay as a kind of "gathering" (a way of initiating, rather than precluding, debate). Much of this chapter follows Wieland's lead, contextualizing the previous articulations of enthusiasm on which his definitions and arguments rely. Further, in order to help place Wieland's essay into the existing literature on this topic, I divide Wieland's concise history of enthusiasm into three categories: religious enthusiasm, enthusiasm as a bodily disease, and moral enthusiasm. I discuss how these conceptualizations differ and why such differences are important for elucidating the concept of enthusiasm itself. The chapter concludes by noting how this context clarifies how enthusiasm can be reconceived as a political concept.

As Kant famously exclaims, "The recent revolution … arouses in the heart of all spectators … desires which border on enthusiasm."[36] This admiration for a revolutionary political spirit has been read as Kant's politics of sympathy, where equality is drawn through rationalized feeling for the ideals another commits to. In Chapter 2, I offer a different reading, one that pays close attention to the effect the form of Wieland's question has on Kant, and anyone who would work to distinguish between enthusiasm and fanaticism. I offer here a distinct counter-reading of Kantian enthusiasm that moves past the purified spectator, immune to political engagement. This reading of enthusiasm makes sense of Kant's own anxiety regarding this "most dangerous" political idea, where Kant gives us the terms to think through how to cross the boundary between actor and spectator, and the place of enthusiasm in constructing that pathway. While Kant struggled to come to terms with the significance of enthusiasm, this chapter argues that we see the grounds for a radical reading of enthusiasm within his thinking.

And, while Kant would later disavow this position, we need not draw the same conclusions. This chapter presents Kantian political enthusiasm as a performance that motivates revolutionary action.

Turning to more contemporary discourse, Chapter 3 illustrates how enthusiasm can become both ideological and apolitical. As enthusiasm developed from a religious to a political phenomenon, the result was a bifurcation of its meanings, where enthusiasm was sometimes experienced as an affect that accompanied zealotry, and at other times as a more benign swooning. Focusing on the political thought of Hannah Arendt, this chapter pays particular attention to the affective basis of zealotry. It examines the role of the spectator in democratic politics, and the place of the spectator's enthusiasm in public discourse. While sympathetic to Arendt's aims, this chapter also presents a critique, noting that she inherits a binary notion of enthusiasm, one that turns political enthusiasm into a depoliticizing affect. Paying attention to this contrasting logic, this chapter shows how certain readings of enthusiasm can fuel an exclusionary and secularized affect, while vacating the concept of its potency. The aim of the chapter is to highlight and push against the binary logic underlying much thinking on enthusiasm, and the culmination of that logic in a kind of depoliticization. By delineating varieties of the binaries of enthusiasm, this chapter works to form a new ground for the rethinking of enthusiasm.

In Chapter 4, I explore what happens when enthusiasm starts to become enmeshed in ideology, and how to begin to distinguish it in action. Here I highlight an alternative pathway for a more radical manifestation of political enthusiasm. Considering Walter Benjamin's essay *Critique of Violence* (1921), this chapter explores acts of enthusiasm, and especially the general strike. Benjamin's discussion of the general strike draws the political imagination to what he named a "pure" politics, beyond mediation. This chapter reads the strike as a principle of political intrusion – one that is a lurking, though sublimated, enthusiasm. This reading productively problematizes the force of the strike. It extends Benjamin's thesis, beyond any historical imagination of the general strike as the mere force of labor, instead reading the strike as an act of enthusiasm that extends and complicates Kant's thinking, and in different ways from the Arendtian inheritance. This chapter also moves to more contemporary examples of enthusiastic acts, considering immolations, hunger strikes, and other "suicides" as similarly "general" politics, rupturing the violence of the state according to its own pathways of power.

In Chapter 5, I offer a refocusing on enthusiasm in democracy, and especially the contemporary affective strategies and conditions faced in democratic life. As an entry into the contemporary view of democracy, this chapter explores Rancière's book *Hatred of Democracy* as a site to begin to consider these affective dimensions. At the heart of this affective life, according to Rancière, is the condition of hatred. This chapter shows how Rancière, sometimes explicitly and sometimes implicitly, deploys a "democratic" rhetoric that does not seek to destroy this logic of hatred. Rather, his thinking seeks to find a means of existing in a world where hatred(s), including hierarchies and xenophobia, are a profound reality to be resisted, but also exist as a spring to take energy from. This move, from the hatreds that plague democratic life (hatred of democracy), to a political engagement with hatred that acknowledges its reality (hatred for democracy), depends on developing a grammar that begins to reflect these democratic forces between subjectivities. This chapter shows that, at the heart of this grammar of hatred, there lurks a persistent enthusiasm. Making sense of political hatreds, and the specific ways they damage democracy, requires a deep understanding of political enthusiasm.

The danger in most present understandings of enthusiasm is this: The very logics that can lead to fascism and undemocratic authoritarianism may in fact also be necessary for the preservation of democracy. Hence the facile assimilation of enthusiasm and fanaticism is dangerously misleading – precisely for democracy as a way of life. My conclusion offers an examination of the most contemporary manifestations of enthusiasm, and the confusions they entail. Accompanying the recent rise of populist movements in Western democracies has been the analogous aura of fascism. While once it would have been unnecessary to ask, one might now have to inquire what historical relation, if any, continues to persist between fascism and democracy. The early histories of fascist movements, and their defeat, are well known. My conclusion explores what happened to the subterranean political effect of fascism once unleashed – the "excitation" of fascism as it carries through the genealogy of this political from, even in its exhausted condition.

The result of this analysis is a tracing of the affective boundary between fascism and democratic politics, one that distinguishes excitation from enthusiasm. This chapter shows both how understanding the affective logics raised through fascism might be necessary for preserving democratic forms of life, as well as the risks posed in mixing these forms of politics together. Special attention is paid here to democratic resistances to fascism. My conclusion uncovers a mechanism for identifying the affective boundary that lies between fascism and democracy, and the costs of confusing fascist excitation and democratic enthusiasm.

Enthusiasm has always been crucial to democratic politics. My aim in this book is to make sense of that significance, as well as the threats posed in misunderstanding it. How are we committed to our politics? Does that commitment lead to or away from partisanship? Kant was asserting that it might be possible, through enthusiasm, to define the moral progress of humanity. Implied here was that not all states and governments would necessarily find themselves in line with such progress. I read enthusiasm as a performance of an opening, a resistance within hierarchical power that acts as a release of authority.[37] This opening "between" was originally that space that religious experience perceived as opening *between* the human and divine, but it has now taken on very different forms and masks.[38] Can we imagine enthusiasm before fanaticism, as it is without its consequence? Is there a way of resisting fanaticism that transforms enthusiasm into its full potential? These questions shape my rereading of acts of enthusiasm and their political affect.

The reader should note, my entry into these analyses is through a series of shortcuts[39] – scenes that present enthusiasms in moments of time. This may be disorienting at first, which is why I signal it upfront. These scenes should highlight the dyads that lurk beneath various political imaginaries, including the struggle between actor and spectator, the contrast between actor and thinker, the distinctions between determinative judgment and reflective judgment, and ultimately the tropes of the human and inhuman. In their own way, I think we can see how each dyad traps enthusiasm. Attention to these scenes should offer a re-narration of some crucial moments in the history of modern political thought, and the historical frames on which these ideas are based.

Many have worried that contemporary moments of enthusiastic partisanship signal the requiem of democracy. But partisanship itself – as opposed to toxic enmity – may in fact be necessary to a well-functioning democracy. Political enthusiasm appears wherever there is a fierce struggle to steer politics in new directions. As a vibrant force of conviction, political enthusiasm allows us to identify commitments to transforming political structures. In this way, we can use it to denote when and how partisanship begins to collapse into vicious hostilities. Paying attention to why political actors feel enthusiasm may then be the most vital means to track pathways to new political beginnings and new democracies.

Notes

1 Comprehensive reviews on the concept of enthusiasm include R. A. Knox, *Enthusiasm: A Chapter in the History of Religion* (Oxford University Press, 1950); Susie Tucker, *Enthusiasm: A Study of Semantic Change* (Cambridge University Press, 1972); and Michael Heyd, *"Be Sober and Reasonable": The Critique of Enthusiasm in the Seventeenth and Early Eighteenth Centuries* (E. J. Brill, 1995). For a literary perspective on the place of enthusiasm, see John Mee, *Romanticism, Enthusiasm, and Regulation: Poetics and the Policing of Culture in the Romantic Period* (Oxford University Press, 2005). For the most recent historical revaluation of enthusiasm, especially for Enlightenment discourse, see Lawrence Klein and Anthony La Vopa, eds., *Enthusiasm and Enlightenment in Europe, 1650–1850* (Huntington Library Press, 1998). Alberto Toscano usefully explores the origins of this concept in his *Fanaticism: The Use of an Idea* (Verso, 2010), see, for example, chap. 3, "Raving with Reason." While Toscano explores the framework of fanaticism in relationship to enthusiasm, my argument follows the mirror logic of tracing enthusiasm's multiple manifestations. Other recent explorations of enthusiasm include Jordana Rosenberg, *Critical Enthusiasm: Capital Accumulation and the Transformation of Religious Passion* (Oxford University Press, 2011); John Mac Kilgore, *Mania for Freedom: American Literatures of Enthusiasm from the Revolution to the Civil War* (University of North Carolina Press, 2016); and Lea Ypi, "On Revolution in Kant and Marx," *Political Theory* 42, no. 3 (2014): 262–87.
2 Robert Lane, *Political Ideology: Why the American Common Man Believes What He Does* (Free Press, 1962), p. 208.

3 See, for example, Simone Weil, "Cold War Policy in 1939," in *Selected Essays, 1934–1943: Historical, Political, and Moral Writings*, trans. Richard Rees (Oxford University Press, 1962), pp. 177–94; Jacob Talmon, *The Origins of Totalitarian Democracy* (Beacon Press, 1952); and, more recently, Jonathan White and Lea Ypi, *The Meaning of Partisanship* (Oxford University Press, 2016).

4 Isaac Taylor, *Natural History of Enthusiasm* (Holdsworth & Ball, 1829), p. 7.

5 See Tucker, *Enthusiasm*; and Heyd, *"Be Sober and Reasonable."*

6 Alexis de Tocqueville, *Democracy in America*, ed. Harvey Mansfield and Delba Winthrop (University of Chicago Press, 2000), p. 10.

7 See Toscano, *Fanaticism*, esp., chap. 3.

8 For a comprehensive review of this problematic, see Klein and La Vopa, *Enthusiasm and Enlightenment in Europe, 1650–1850*.

9 See, for example, Knox's classic *Enthusiasm*.

10 HAMAS is an acronym – Harakat al-Muqawama al-Islamiya – which translates as "The Islamic Resistance Movement," but the word *hamas* itself can be translated directly as "zeal," "courage," or "enthusiasm."

11 Donald Trump, "Thanksgiving Day Message," November 23, 2017, www.youtube.com/watch?v=iQE1ZFWJMcM (accessed 2 June 2018).

12 William Connolly, *Aspirational Fascism: The Struggle for Multifaceted Democracy under Trumpism* (University of Minnesota Press, 2017).

13 Cheryl Hall, *The Trouble with Passion: Political Theory Beyond the Reign of Reason* (Routledge, 2005).

14 Michel Foucault, "What Is Enlightenment?" in *The Foucault Reader*, ed. Paul Rabinow (Pantheon Books, 1984), p. 32. For further context on the essay contest, see, for example, James Schmidt, ed., *What Is Enlightenment: Eighteenth-Century Answers and Twentieth-Century Questions* (University of California Press, 1996).

15 From Christoph Martin Wieland's "Schwärmerei und Enthusiasmus," which originally appeared in the fourth issue of *Der Teutsche Merkur* in 1775 (pp. 151–5). The *Merkur* was a significant monthly literary and cultural journal for the German *Aufklärung* (Enlightenment), and Wieland served as both publisher and editor. It was his intent that this journal should serve as the voice of his generation, forming the ground for a sort of public education that had never before existed in Germany. Regarding Wieland's place in classical Weimar culture, and in German "high culture" generally, see W. H. Bruford, *Culture and Society in Classical Weimar, 1775–1806* (Cambridge University Press, 1962), pp. 39–48. For a general review of Wieland's political thought, see Frederick Beiser, *Enlightenment, Revolution, and*

Romanticism: The Genesis of Modern German Political Thought, 1790–1800 (Harvard University Press, 1992), esp. chap. 13, "The Political Philosophy of C. M. Wieland."

16 Immanuel Kant, "A Renewed Attempt to Answer the Question: 'Is the Human Race Constantly Improving?'" excerpted from *The Conflict of the Faculties*, reprinted in *Kant: Political Writings*, ed. H. S. Reiss (Cambridge University Press, 1970), p. 182.

17 Judith Butler, "Is Judaism Zionism?" in *The Power of Religion in the Public Sphere*, ed. Eduardo Mendieta and Jonathan van Antwerpen (Columbia University Press, 2011).

18 Weil, "Cold War Policy in 1939," p. 189.

19 Jacob Talmon, *The Origins of Totalitarian Democracy* (Beacon Press, 1952), p. 6.

20 This work fits closely with a growing literature that rethinks political affect, including Sara Ahmed, *The Cultural Politics of Emotion* (Edinburgh, 2004); Corey Robin, *Fear: The History of a Political Idea* (Oxford, 2006); Michael Frazer, *The Enlightenment of Sympathy* (Oxford, 2010); Sonali Chakravarti, *Sing the Rage: Listening to Anger after Mass Violence* (University of Chicago, 2014); Jodi Dean, *Crowds and Party* (Verso, 2018); Kevin Duong, *The Virtues of Violence: Democracy against Disintegration in Modern France* (Oxford University Press, 2020); and William Davies, *Nervous States: Democracy and the Decline of Reason* (Norton, 2019), among others.

21 Jane Bennett, *The Enchantments of Modern Life: Attachments, Crossings, and Ethics* (Princeton University Press, 2001), p. 4. In addition to Bennett's work, Lars Tønder's *Tolerance: A Sensorial Orientation to Politics* (Oxford University Press, 2013) caused scholars to rethink critical elements of attachment, especially as they applied to toleration and the embodied elements of political affect. Similarly, Libby Anker's influential and much cited work *Orgies of Feeling: Melodrama and the Politics of Freedom* (Duke University Press, 2016) brought needed attention to collectivity of affect, and the narrative pathways such affect travels on. These works have become central to political theory in their engagement with affect and its practical consequences for political attachments.

22 See esp. Benjamin Moffitt, *The Global Rise of Populism: Performance, Political Style, and Representation* (Stanford University Press, 2016), chap. 8, "Populism and Democracy."

23 Ibid., p. 135.

24 See Toscano's preface to *Fanaticism*.

25 See Rosenberg's further discussion of this point in her introduction to *Critical Enthusiasm*, p. 5.

26 Kilgore, *Mania for Freedom*.

27 Ibid., p. 5.

28 Jürgen Habermas, *Between Facts and Norms: Contributions to a Discourse Theory of Law and Democracy* (MIT Press, 1998); Jan Müller, *Constitutional Patriotism* (Princeton University Press, 2016).

29 Jürgen Habermas, "*Können komplexe Gesellschaften eine rationale Identität ausbil- den*" [Can complex societies form a rational identity] (1974), in *Zur Rekonstruktion des his-torischen Materialismus* (Suhrkamp, 1976), p. 101; cf. fn 11 in Patchen Markell, "Making Affect Safe for Democracy? On Constitutional Patriotism," *Political Theory* 28, no. 1 (2000): 38–63 (and this is his translation).

30 See Habermas, *Between Facts and Norms*.

31 See Seyla Benhabib, *Another Cosmopolitanism* (Oxford University Press, 2006), p. 65.

32 Ibid.

33 See Margaret Canovan, *The People* (Polity, 2005), p. 49.

34 Ibid., p. 50.

35 See Habermas, "Popular Sovereignty as Procedure," first published in *Forum für Philosophie Bad Hamburg*, ed., *Die Ideen von 1789* (Frankfurt am Main, 1989), reprinted as appendix I in *Between Facts and Norms*.

36 Kant, "A Renewed Attempt," p. 182.

37 Lyotard has argued that the concept of "passage" is crucial to Kant's idea of enthusiasm, but for Lyotard the passage is between phases of critique. Lyotard is helpful here, for he finds in Kant a speculative rationality at odds with the old Kant so often identified with the first critique and what Nietzsche reflected on as the cold rationality of the Enlightenment imaginary. The "new" speculative Kant, Lyotard explains, thinks according to the "as if." Jean-Francois Lyotard, *Enthusiasm: The Kantian Critique of History* (Stanford University Press, 2009), p. 12.

38 In his late lectures at the Collège de France, Foucault claims "the pastorate was formed against a sort of intoxication of religious behavior" (p. 195). Michel Foucault, *Security, Territory, Population: Lectures at the Collège de France, 1977–1978*, ed. Michel Senellart, trans. Graham Burchell (Palgrave Macmillan, 2007).

39 Many thanks to Bill Connolly for his suggestions that shortcuts – like scenes from a film – would perform this problem for the reader. Henri Bergson uses similar language to describe one possible experience of temporality in *Creative Evolution* (Henry Holt, [1907] 1911). For Bergson, the cinematic view that denies the shortcut, misunderstands the constant interruption of mediation and representation. I take Connolly's point, that my reading on enthusiasm may depend on shortcuts, so as not to collapse into the logic of capture I mean to critique.

1

Igniting politics: from enthusiasm to fanaticism

The fury flies from face to face, and the disease is no sooner seen than caught ... Such force has society in ill as well as in good passions, and so much stronger any affection is for being social and communicative.

> – Anthony Ashley Cooper, Third Earl of Shaftesbury,
> *A Letter Concerning Enthusiasm* (1708)

New political spirits

From October 10–19, 1977, the Kanun-e nevisandagan-e Iran – the left oppositional group, known in English as the Writers' Association of Iran – hosted a series of poetry readings. Every evening, beginning around 8 p.m., authors and poets and students and workers and all manner of ordinary Iranians gathered as an audience at the Goethe Institute and German Cultural Center, on what was then Pahlavi Avenue. This was arguably the finest street in central Tehran, designed to display the potency of the Shah's regime. Tree-lined and pristine, this street, with its vast shades of green, miraculous life, stood in resistance against the desert. The first of these readings at the German Cultural Center was so overcrowded, with thousands of people having turned out to listen on a rainy evening, that the audience spilled into the surrounding neighborhood. Sounds and voices echoed through the crowd, spilling around street corners and over buildings and walls. By one witness's account, this moment might best be described as the "peak of emotional communion" in Iran, so excited were the people gathered. These communions are now referred to as the "dah sab" (the ten nights).[1]

What began during these ten nights are now often referred to historically as the spiritual beginning of the Iranian revolution. These readings proved a significant event for the Iranian people, beginning a social and political movement that would eventually cast them upon the stage of world politics in a spectacle of mass participation. The fervor that manifested in the ten nights seemed to have unified a diverse constellation of political actors, all set on a fundamental transformation. The early moments of the revolution in Iran were unique, seemingly combining leftist organizational methods of protest with religious intensity as a bulwark. Against the forces of imperialism, colonialism, capitalism, and the logics of Western domination, the Shiite revolution was to provide a substantive alternative to the modalities of liberalism and communism that then set the political landscape. With a new incarnation of political spirituality as the driving force, this revolution appeared as though a new form of emancipation might be possible, and one that could both resist the hyper-individualism of Western democracies, as well as the bureaucratic vacancies of Soviet communism.

The history of Iran that runs from October 1977 to April 1979 might not be so easily recognizable today. What Iran became through this revolution was not necessarily what the Iranian people might have imagined possible, or even desirable. As Melinda Cooper reminds us, "In early 1979, a tenuous coalition of Iranian Marxists, leftists, and Shiite clerics brought down the secular oligarchy of the American-backed Mohammad Reza Shah Pahlavi, instituting in its place the equally authoritarian and theocratic rule of Khomeini."[2] What was dreamt of in "the ten nights" was more than a new government, more than a liberation from the Shah; what was dreamt of was, as Michel Foucault reflected, "the introduction of a spiritual dimension into political life, in order that it (political life) would not be, as always, the obstacle to spirituality, but rather its receptacle, its opportunity, and its ferment."[3] Before the revolution became a violently oppressive force, there was a latent promise that the orbit of that revolution might be a new spirit for cooperation, one as yet all but impossible in Iran or anywhere in the modern world.

History has not confirmed this thesis. While Iran has become a source of anti-imperialism and anti-Western capitalism, once led primarily by left-leaning Marxist student groups and various Islamic Mujahedin, it has often done so through repressive statist tactics. While the revolution itself may have begun in response to the forces of capitalism and modern Western Christianity, the transition to the new regime seems to have internalized this violence, becoming equally brutal.[4] This turn in the trajectory of the revolution, away from once-emancipatory futures, has cast a pall over those who saw promise in the early moments of a political turning. Foucault, in particular, has long been haunted by what he named his "enthusiasm" for the Iranian revolution.[5]

Foucault arrived in Iran amid much political turmoil. Early September 1978 was a moment of extreme political tension in Tehran, especially between the Confederation of the Iranian Students' National Union and other protests groups in conflict with the Shah. In the midst of these conflicting voices, a dangerous spark flashed at the end of the Ramadan feast that year. In response to swelling crowds of protestors, the Shah – seeming to fear a decline of the power of the state – declared martial law. The specific order called for the killing of all protestors that refused to disband. As one report explains, "A massive demonstration on Jaleh Square in Tehran was violently crushed, and between 2,000 and 4,000 demonstrators were killed. This massacre seriously reduced the chances for reconciliation, and henceforth the popular rallying call was for the shah's departure, rather than for reforms."[6] It was in the midst of such tumult that Foucault arrived to report on the growing unrest.[7]

While many in the liberal West saw the growing violence in Iran as unnerving, Foucault's reporting for the Italian newspaper *Corriere della sera* took a more nuanced view. Less in the events, and more in the live forces of opposition, Foucault found a manifestation of a renewed political spirit. In what he described as the "spirit to resist" – to resist the Shah, to resist capitalism, to resist Americanism, to resist imperialism, to resist colonialism – Foucault uncovered what he thought of as a new form of politics, commingling traces of the Islamic tradition, Marxist critique, and Enlightenment publicity. In Tehran, in 1978, Foucault believed he had found a form of what he named "political enthusiasm" – a new spiritual politics, formed by igniting shared resistance.

The idea that a new politics had formed in the Iranian revolution in September 1978 was not a popular one. Indeed, Foucault was accused of a sort of "revolutionary conservatism" – what one critic described as a call for

a complete revolution of progressive modernism ... Reading the pro-
phetic, futural philosophy of the later Heidegger back into the Shiite
eschatology of the twelfth Imam, Foucault describes the political
ideal of divine law as a kind of groundless ground, "something very
old and also very far into the future," a "light that is capable of illu-
minating the law from the inside."[8]

While after the revolution, many historians have come to see this
"groundless ground" as the opening of a power vacuum that
allowed for precisely the violent repressions for which the Iranian
revolution would so often be condemned, Foucault's interest was
in the moments before history could judge – before there was a
difference between the witness and the judge, when no one yet
knew what would result. Paying attention to this moment, Foucault
insisted, would help us to better understand the affective forces of
the political. How does revolution appear when it begins? What
affective pathways need to be opened in order for a political revolution to initiate? The "groundless ground" that looks so obvious
from the ideological stance of the historical judge was far from
clear in the spirit of the crowds of protestors who resisted what
they perceived as the malformed politics of a corrupt regime.

As many, including Foucault himself, have noted, this stance
echoes Kant's reflection on the French Revolution. As Kant famously exclaims:

> The recent revolution of a people which is rich in spirit may well
> either fail or succeed, accumulate misery and atrocity, it nevethe-
> less arouses in the heart of all spectators (who are not themselves
> caught up in it) a taking of sides according to desires which border
> on enthusiasm and which, since its very expression was not without
> danger, can only have been caused by a moral disposition within the
> human race.[9]

This admiration for a spirit, an admiration and adoration that
almost "borders on enthusiasm," has been read as Kant's political
spectatorship – a politics of sympathy based on the ideals perceived
in another's actions. As one critic explains it, "What matters is not
the miserable reality that followed the upheavals, the bloody con-
frontations, the new oppressive measures, and so on, but the enthusiasm that the events in Iran stimulated in the external (Western)
observer, confirming his hope in the possibility of a new form of

spiritualized political collective."[10] The difficulty here is whether we should judge Foucault for supporting what obviously became such a violent politics, or if there is more to be learned from what he hoped for, even despite what happened in the unrest of revolution. Foucault reveals an important desire to think through the possibility of a new political spirituality that would release the West from its own intellectual exhaustion. Paying close attention to that release, how it gets mobilized, and the dangers political actors face in doing so, become the main terms on which to evaluate this "political enthusiasm."

Answers to the question: "What do we mean by enthusiasm?"

In 1775, Christoph Martin Wieland, then editor of *Der Teutsche Merkur*, perhaps the most prominent literary journal of the German Enlightenment, proposed an essay contest on the question of what we might mean by enthusiasm.[11] While essay contests were a common means of editors to propel scholarly and public debate on issues of social significance, Wieland was especially worried about the place of enthusiasm in social and political life, and this question was of great significance to him. The purpose of this contest, he argued, was to address the growing concern that Enlightenment philosophy could not distinguish itself from ideology and partisan subjective reflection. Nowhere, according to Wieland, was this mental confusion more obvious, or the stakes of such confusion higher, than in the conceptual distinction between *Schwärmerei* and *Enthusiasmus*, fanaticism and enthusiasm.

Schwärmerei has its origins in biological classification, originally used to refer to swarms of bees. The word was meant to imitate the sound of swarming insects, the shhhhhh and buzz of their motions and communications mixed together.

Enthusiasmus, by contrast, derives – as in English – from the Greek ἐνθουσιασμός, which is best read as "being possessed by a god."[12] Enthusiasm is defined in common English usage as "rapturous intensity of feeling in favour of a person, principle, cause, etc.; passionate eagerness in any pursuit, proceeding from an intense conviction of the worthiness of the object."[13] Also, less commonly, we might now read enthusiasm as inspiration, a spirit within, being possessed by a demon or a god. Enthusiasm has been linked to poetic imaginaries, as well as religious fantasy. And, more recently, the affect has come to signify both an irrationalism and a frivolity.

If we consider enthusiasm's long history, the term was originally used to describe priestly behavior in ancient Greece, especially the perceived heightened condition of consciousness during religious practices.[14] Enthusiasm was what witnesses were said to perceive happening to priests and oracles as "gods entered inside" them, divinity speaking through mediation. In this originary history, enthusiasm and inspiration are almost synonymous. So too is madness. As Plato describes it, "The best things we have come from madness, when it is a divine gift. The prophetess of Delphi and the priestesses at Dodona are out of their minds when they perform that fine work of theirs for all of Greece, either for an individual person or for a whole city, but they accomplish little or nothing when they are in control of themselves."[15] Here we see that, at least in this early narration of the phenomenon, enthusiasm was not a common experience, but rather part of the interaction between divinity and humanity – a rare madness inspired therein. In this way, enthusiasm was more commonly witnessed than experienced directly. Because a "divine presence transfigured consciousness" of the priests, a particular form of religion was made possible, whereby divinity and humanity came together in a performance of their unity.[16] Such mediations by priests and seers was important as a boundary between the human and the divine, and a hierarchy between those humans who could reside on this boundary.

The history of *Schwärmerei*, despite its biological referent, is perhaps more modern in its common usage. While best translated as "swarm" or even "swoon," *Schwärmerei* was also quickly adopted as a common phrasing of fanaticism, where *Schwärmerei* and *Fanaticismus* become interchangeable. The German "*Fanaticismus*," like the English "fanaticism," derives from the Latin "*fanum*," meaning temple.[17] It is defined in English usage as "the condition of being, or supposing oneself to be, possessed," and "the tendency to indulge in wild and extravagant notions."[18] While the word *Schwärmerei* may be more modern, the link to *fanum* points to a more ancient history, and a historical portrait of the original "fanatics" – those who occupied the temple to which "*fanum*" refers – gets at a more precise rendering of the concept.[19] The ancient historian Lactantius provides the following account: "In honor of Virtus, whom [the Romans] call Bellona, the priests make offerings not with the blood of another victim, but with their own. Cutting their shoulders and thrusting forth drawn swords in each hand, they run towards each other, they are beside themselves, they are frantic."[20] As one contemporary historian explains it, "These priests, who were known as *fanatici*, indulged in armed dances of bloody frenzy. Their hair flying, they pirouetted brandishing their two-edged axes. At the height of the dizziness excited by the beating of timbrels and the sinister wailing of the trumpets, they hacked their arms to sprinkle the idol with red splashes, before predicting the future to the dumbfounded spectators."[21] Adding to this, as Tibullus describes it: "Once set in motion by the action of the Bellona, neither the bite or fire, nor blows from a whip frighten this distracted woman [the priestess]. With her own hands she wounds her arms with an axe, and her flowing blood sprinkles the goddess, yet she feels no pain. Standing, her side pierced by a spear, her bosom torn, she chants the future as told to her by the powerful goddess."[22] We know such exhibitions were themselves incorporated into Roman military practices, where priests – both men and women – staged these abuses before soldiers marching to war. Fanaticism takes on an entirely different and more violent meaning in this history. In the original instantiation of the concept, the experiences of the priests were meant to provoke and enrapture witnesses, literally transposing their mind towards violence, all this in preparation for the coming battle. Unlike the ancient Greeks' experience of enthusiasm, these witnesses were themselves supposed to be transfigured, entering into a mimicked and then shared state as those that initiated the frenzied process.

Returning to Wieland's question, the problem with any conceptual confusion between fanaticism and enthusiasm – at least as Wieland suggests it – was that it would leave little conceptual space for any positive form of excitement and conviction. "*Schwärmerei*," he worried, "is a disease of the soul – a real 'soul fever'; *Enthusiasmus* is the real *life* of the soul. What a difference essential nature in cause and effect can make!"[23]

For Wieland, there was as much danger in understanding enthusiasm as a purely religious phenomenon as there was in letting it remain synonymous with fanaticism. While it might certainly feel like God was "inside us," enthusiasm might actually be a necessary corollary to the right use of reason (moral enthusiasm) or political conviction (political enthusiasm). Consequent to this worry, was the concern that moral, political, and religious transformations of the world would all – at least without enthusiasm – be left to mold a dull, lifeless, and false world. Thus, Wieland posed a question that came to transform debate in late eighteenth-century Germany, and far beyond: Is there any difference between fanaticism and enthusiasm, and what does it matter if there is?

Wieland's question, and the contest that ensued, may be an unfamiliar form of academic and literary discourse today. But Wieland was one of several prominent academic editors who could stimulate academic discourse on a subject that did not yet have clear resolution. The essay contest was a clear means of initiating this discourse. Such a contest would give the reading public the chance to survey transformations in the different varieties of enthusiasm that contributed to Wieland's question, and to make sense of the intellectual and political significance in distinguishing between fanaticism and enthusiasm.[24]

Wieland himself considered his essay as a kind of "gathering" – a way of initiating, rather than precluding, debate. Much of the discussion in this chapter follows his lead, collecting the previous articulations on which his definitions and arguments seem to rely. I take up the opportunity to present the reader with a survey of those various conceptions of enthusiasm, setting the stage for a more contemporary investigation of enthusiasm. Following from this survey, we will have the chance to ask Wieland's same question again from a more contemporary vantage point.[25] Following on the literature that examines this topic, I divide this concise history of enthusiasm into three categories: religious enthusiasm, enthusiasm as disease, and moral enthusiasm. I conclude with a discussion of how this context, in which Wieland is himself responding, opens up the possibility of reconceiving enthusiasm as a political concept.

Contesting emotion

Wieland's "Schwärmerei und Enthusiasmus" essay initiates a contest, rethinking enthusiasm as a divided concept. Instead of enthusiasm being described by two synonymously interposed concepts, Wieland worried that the words themselves may in fact reflect two distinct experiences of related, but separate phenomena. Here the binary of secular rationalism and a religious imaginary seems to reproduce a binary regarding healthy and unhealthy forms of affect. At issue for Wieland was whether a "healthy" form of Enlightenment rationalism did or did not depend on some feeling for truth, whether by inspiration or allegiance. If one could not feel one's way to truth, how could one have access to it? How open was the Enlightenment conception of reason, and who was it open to? The trajectories of such anxieties run in myriad directions. From the deformation of the concept of progress, to the reservation of Enlightenment for a minority elite, Wieland became concerned that, without a serious answer to the question of whether there was a distinction between enthusiasm and fanaticism, it might never be clear whether Enlightenment discourse was itself anything beyond a fanatical belief in the value of pure reason.[26] Human life, by Wieland's view, depended on the "head" and the "heart."[27] As Enlightenment rationality moved further and further away from affective experiences of the world, the very viability and functionality of reason was itself at risk. How, Wieland wondered, could reason find its way through concepts in the world without emotions to guide it? Could the Enlightenment fantasy of reason simply be a myth?

Yet Wieland was worried about more than a mere abstract guide for reason. Of significance here was the historical inheritance of philosophic thought, and thus Wieland's own place in intellectual history. If the likes of Horace and Petrarch, to use his examples, could both be described interchangeably as enthusiasts or fanatics, then Enlightenment thinkers like him might also be susceptible to such confusion.[28] If philosophy could be confused with superstition, then the Enlightenment itself might have inadvertently created – even in its ardent defense of rationality – the basis for its own demise into irrationality.[29] Without a clear mechanism for

distinguishing between different kinds of affective states, and especially enthusiasm and fanaticism, thought itself had no parameters
from which to measure its own health and sickness.[30]

The only means Wieland found for navigating past this dilemma
was the employ of reason to distinguish between different concepts in their use. While his excavation of the functional differences
between fanaticism and enthusiasm are, even by his own account,
merely cursory, it is still worth reviewing them here, as his essay initiates a debate that drove to the heart of Enlightenment discourse,
revealing a pathology of reason that continues to hold relevance for
how motivations – especially political ones – might be normatively
justified today.[31]

The first concept Wieland sought to delineate in his essay was
Schwärmerei. Wieland describes this state as "a disease of the soul,"
"a soul fever."[32] By his reading, *Schwärmerei* is a kind of infestation
of the soul, but one that is not inspired by nature, or beauty, or
the good. Instead, so Wieland argued, the soul becomes deformed,
especially in its isolation from nature and its own essential self. The
logic of *Schwärmerei* is a logic of division, breaking the person who
experiences it apart from themselves, and introducing a binary of
actual and ideal self, divided by an ideational gulf that can never
be transcended.

Wieland's view of *Schwärmerei* as a mental sickness was not
uncommon. The Grimm brothers define *Schwärmerei* as the mental
state of heresy, a foggy confusion of concepts.[33] Adelung defines it
as something caught in a swarm (a swarming thing). *Schwärmerei*
referred to fanatics and dreamers, anyone who might mistake confusion for truth, as well as one who abandons oneself to debauchery.[34]
As Wieland himself worries, *Schwärmerei* often retains a derogatory, slanderous nature. Certainly, it was no compliment to refer to
someone as suffering from *Schwärmerei*.[35]

Quite literally, we might best read *Schwärmerei* as referring
to the experience of being part of a swarm – the phrase reads as
"swarming-ness," or the capacity to swarm.[36] Only later does
the phrase enter into common German discourse as a means to
describe, and assault, one's fellows. To describe a person as being
a *Schwärmer* was to consider them as being incapable of maintain-
ing composure; lost to mental delusions and confusing them for
the truth. To be a *Schwärmer* meant that that a person was caught

up in a swarm, unable to deliberate and reason about the world around them. The latent rhetoric in this word invites us to consider both what it would be like to locate oneself in a swarm, but also how a swarm appears outside itself to witnesses.[37] This division is crucial. Calling someone a *Schwärmer* means that *they* are themselves lost to the swarm, and *you* are not. It can also mean that they have somehow given up their humanity. For to be in a swarm can mean to become like an insect. This is part of the insult latent in the term. Yet, as Peter Fenves observes, it also means a kind of divinity imparted on the swarmer:

> *Schwärmerei* points toward something more and less than human – less than human because animals, not human beings, aggregate into swarms; and more than human because the only animals whose multitudes turn into swarms are those that, like the gods, are able to take leave of the earth. A desire to depart from the earth … is implied in every use of the term *Schwärmerei*, just as, *ordine inverso*, the decent of a god to the earth is implied in Socrates' use of the term *entheos*. And "swarmers associate with one another precisely because they desire more than terrestrial society … " By disassociating themselves from civic society, swarmers collect into non-civic (if not uncivil), non-social (if not anti-social), non-natural if not un-natural), and always temporary, multiplicities.[38]

The swarm, even if momentarily, dissolves each member's individuality and humanity, empowering them through their allegiance to the extra-terrestrial collective. And, while we might find emancipations here, for Wieland, such allegiance was dissolving of the human self. For this reason, Wieland explains *Schwärmerei* is a sort of disease. It is central that it be seen this way, because Wieland believes a *Schwärmer* could not be held responsible for their actions and can also be cured from this state of impairment. Only if both conditions prove true, can *Schwärmerei* lose its derogatory label.

Wieland presumed that within any unhealthy body there was a healthy person that could be rescued. To this end, he argued that philosophy's course was to identify causes and cures for diseases of the mind, both of the individual and the collective. In proposing a contest over how to think on the human mind, Wieland issued a challenge to the reading public to disentangle the two terms, so as to gain clarity on the problem of *Schwärmerei*, as well as the benefits of enthusiasm. The means of curing this disease, so Wieland hoped, was *Enthusiasmus* – a necessary recourse to reason, and also a kind of moral inspiration.[39]

But, as Foucault reminds us, while an eighteenth-century editor might hope for one answer, the questions posed for these essay contests were only ever asked of subjects where no clear opinion could be garnered. Indeed, if we think on the very origins of the word contest – a shared witnessing – Wieland may have hoped to develop a discourse that would form a shared opinion, and one that would be witnessed by all.

Enthusiasm, at least as Wieland seemed to envision it, was that "state, where our soul is ignited," it "is itself god-like." He was especially interested in the secularization of the divine experience. As he explains, "It is as though [so many claim] the enthusiast effuses that which they received by contact with God. Such deeply infused love of truth and beauty and goodness is the very real influence of the deity; it is [as Plato says] God within side us."[40] Adding, it is "the real *life* of the soul."[41] If the swarm is a delusion, enthusiasm is – so Wieland hoped – an amplified reality. Read this way, Wieland hoped for a thorough witnessing of enthusiasm as the means by which reason receives direction; the feeling of inspiration that accompanies rational thought. Enthusiasm could thus work on the diseased soul as a kind of salve, warming and soothing those mental drives that might agitate persons towards extra-terrestrial and supernatural encounters. It could be the means by which we *feel* we know what is good in the world. Thus, "to be an enthusiast, well ... this is to be the most loved, the noblest, and the best that any human could be."[42] Or so he hoped. Wieland placed so much hope in the concept of enthusiasm, we might even argue that he was becoming fanatical for it, and the universal logics of reason he fantasized it might secure.[43]

Possession

What is the source of derogation in *Schwärmerei*? Where is the intended harm in comparing a person, not just to an insect, but to a swarm? It turns out that the historical origins of this slight run deep within early modern European discourses on another contest – the struggle for supremacy of preachers within the early manifestations of European Protestantism. As Adelung and Grimm both confirm, the initial use of *Schwärmerei* to derogatorily refer to humanity originates in accusations of heresy levied by Martin Luther against his opponents.[44] Luther moves the definition of this term from an articulation of beastly swarms – especially of bees – to *Schwärmerei* as religious fanatics. Luther worried that there was no means of distinguishing true and false prophets (presaging Wieland's concern that there was no way to distinguish between true and false reason). As Protestant Christianity was beginning to transform (a process that Luther himself was initiating), there was simultaneously a space for true and false revelations of the new faith. As one historian explains,

> When Luther wanted to castigate the mobs that followed self-appointed field preachers or rampaged through churches smashing statues, the verb *Schwärmeren* was ready to hand. It evoked bees swarming around the hive; a flock of birds zigzagging across a field; a pack of hounds straying off the scent. One could hear an ominous buzzing and flapping (or murmuring) and imagine the erratic movement of an aggregate, a kind of perverse order in frenzied disorder. The epithet derived much of its force from this cluster of metaphors, evoking all sorts of implications about deviance and conformity, selfhood and collectivity, private fantasy and public authority.[45]

Luther held his opponents up as those who instigated the crowds, drawing them this way and that. He saw these "field preachers" – here Luther locates his enemies in the rural, labored, and uneducated mindset – as instigating such frenzied crowds beyond all reason or religiosity. For Luther, *Schwärmerei* was faith gone horribly awry. It was the consequence of false prophets employing the authority of true religious leaders, and in doing so, using faith to transform humanity into the inhuman.[46]

Importantly, Luther himself was not immune to accusations (or concerns) that an inner voice had corrupted him. Many of Luther's substantive critics used this same language of *Schwärmerei* against him.[47] The risk of accusing others of false thoughts or an overheated imagination was that such indictments might be inverted, and the accuser would find themselves having to defend against similar claims. This is precisely the problem with religious enthusiasm – in attempting to justify objects of faith, the inner voice, that which only a single individual can hear and justify, often becomes the basis for proclamations on external objects as true or false for the faith. Indeed, Luther may have had his own complicated history with such an inner voice, and its use to legitimate or undermine his authority. As one analyst observers,

> Three of young Luther's contemporaries (none of them a later follower of his) report that sometime during his early or middle twenties, he suddenly fell to the ground in the choir of the monastery at Erfurt, "raved" like one possessed, and roared with the voice of a bull: "*Ich bin's nit! Ich bin's nit!*" or "*Non sum! Non sum!*" ... Reporters agree only on the occasion which upset him so deeply: the reading of Christ's *ejecto a surdo et muto daemonio* – Christ's cure of a man possessed by a dumb spirit.[48]

Luther was desperately worried that *his* god was the provocation of *his* fear, rather than a consolation to his humanity.

Still, Luther did find it helpful to utilize such mechanisms in order to define his opponents in terms of such naturalized language. The image of "the swarm" was terrifying in its dehumanization of worshipers. Luther hoped to distinguish such groups as heretics. Moreover, it also gave a vehicle for "true believers" to temper themselves, lest they fall under the categorization of "*Schwärmer*." Such dialectical distinctions – of true and false faith, of good and bad feelings, of well-composed mental faculties and corrupted reason – plagued the discourse that surrounds *Schwärmerei* throughout its history. Indeed, it seems to be part of its categorization as an epithet that it can be used to clearly delineate boundaries between desirable and un-desirable behavior.[49]

Still, such accusations against deformity in worldview sometimes had the anathema effect of bolstering support for a counter cause. The Anabaptists, for example, were one group who often received Luther's condemnation of promoting "swarming" behavior.[50] Anabaptists defined faith through baptism, arguing that true faith in Christ was only ever demonstrated through freely chosen baptism. At stake in the struggle between the Anabaptists and Luther was the direction of the Reformation movement.[51] The Anabaptists firmly believed that anyone could serve as a true prophet and thus preach the teachings of the Gospel.[52] In this sense, there was a radical openness to their understanding of the faith. What distinguished their faith was how crucial they understood the second baptism to be, and the extreme practices they came to associate as necessary for the profession of true faith through that baptism. By the Anabaptists' account, divine inspiration was made available only to those who suffered through a "second baptism"; and this inspiration could (and did) take any variety of physical, verbal, and psychological form.[53]

Luther saw the authority structure of Anabaptism to be a malformed alternative to his methods, where so much authority rested in their conversion at the second baptism that it created a "swarm" mentality among the congregation in favor of more and more radical confessions (and real violence if they were withheld). In some sense, Luther's accusation against the Anabaptists helped further confirm the boundaries of their swarm, and may have encouraged even greater radicalness in their practices. Indeed, their struggles with Luther and his followers gave them much identity.

The culmination of this struggle was the Anabaptist rebellion at Münster. There, religious elites of the movement attempted to found a "New Jerusalem" in 1534. This short-lived theocracy relied on public baptisms and readmission of true faith by all citizens. All manner of violence was employed to foster admissions of true faith or heresy, and citizens were encouraged to work collectively to admonish the guilty and sinful at all costs.[54] The gruesomeness of these attacks, coupled with the public spiritedness of the mobs' efforts to force faith through violence, left an indelible image on the movement and it remains a palpable example of religious fanaticism to this day. In fact, it is hard to disassociate the term *Schwärmerei* from Anabaptism, at least in a religious context.

But, even despite the violence, such problems of condemnation of dissent were broadly present within diversifying religious communities of Protestantism generally. The various English protestant sects that emerged in the seventeenth century suffered a similar condemnation as religious zealots.[55] With so many voices competing for legitimacy as that of the one true faith and light, rhetorical mechanisms of exclusion and condemnation became crucial. Enthusiasm was, because of its vagueness, precisely the best vehicle for accomplishing such divisions. As John Pocock rightly observes, in such a pluralist spiritual and intellectual environment, "the mind could intoxicate itself with the phantasmata of these unreal entities, and fancy itself

possessed by them."[56] The greater the possession, and the demonstration of that possession, the greater the display of faith.

Thus, religious enthusiasm (as *Schwärmerei*) came to mean the
dissolution of true faith at the costs of fantasies created through
the mechanisms that the originary faith seemed to rely on. It was
quickly becoming impossible, both conceptually and historically, to
distinguish between true enthusiasm and its malformation.

In fervor and fury: enthusiasm as disease

Where enthusiasm was, primarily in the seventeenth century, viewed
as a wholly religious experience, eighteenth-century European thinkers came to consider it as an object of serious scientific analysis.[57]
In particular, enthusiasm came to be viewed as central to the course
of burgeoning studies in scientific medicine.[58] Though this medical
outlook on enthusiasm did little to distinguish it from fanaticism, at
least initially (here fanaticism came to be considered as the suffering from enthusiasm), much definition was given to the experience
of enthusiasm itself. It was alternatively described as a disease, an
overheating of the body that confused the mind, or even a mania.[59]
The depths of the effects consequent to this shift in discourse present
themselves in several significant reconsiderations on the functioning
of the human mind and its social consequences. Attention to familiar
voices that we might associate with this shift (particularly Locke,
Shaftesbury, and Hume), allow us to see the entryway by which
enthusiasm started to become more than just a religious problem.

John Locke – himself a trained physician – was one of the first to
appropriate this medical rhetoric for a revaluation of enthusiasm.[60]
Because enthusiasm was still primarily a religious term during the
composition of his essay on the subject, Locke had to work hard to
conceptually distinguish religious behavior from the medical condition he was interested in describing (and, strangely, also interested
in condemning).[61] As he puts it:

> Immediate revelation being a much easier way for men to establish
> their opinions and regulate their conduct than the tedious and not
> always successful labour of strict reasoning, it is no wonder that
> some have been very apt to pretend to revelation, and to persuade
> themselves that they are under the peculiar guidance of heaven in

their actions and opinions, especially in those of them which they cannot account for by the ordinary methods of knowledge and principles of reason ... Whatever groundless opinion comes to settle itself strongly upon their fancies is an illumination from the Spirit of God, and presently of divine authority: and whatsoever odd action they find in themselves a strong inclination to do, that impulse is concluded to be a call or direction from heaven, and must be obeyed: it is a commission from above, and they cannot err in executing it.[62]

For Locke, enthusiasm as a religious experience was a kind of mental laziness, an excuse to not do the hard work of reasoning through the complexities of faith and its objects. Here, Locke begins to develop the discourse that contrasts the divine revelation received by the fanatic and the philosopher's self-reasoned arguments. Revelation, because filled with a void of authorship and authority – at least from a secular perspective – can be applied and reapplied to any object and interpretation of that object.

But what causes this laziness, by Locke's account, is not entirely clear. When considered as either a result of divine revelation or of reason, how does laziness disrupt the well-functioning of the mind? Imagining that such an experience could be located in the body or the brain, Locke argues: "This I take to be properly enthusiasm, which, though founded neither on reason nor divine revelation, but rising from the conceits of a warmed or overweening brain, works yet, where it once gets footing, more powerfully on the persuasions and actions of men than either of those two, or both together."[63] For Locke, enthusiasm is a physical impairment consequent to overheating. This results in a real readjustment of behavior, the loosening of "persuasions" and character. By Locke's view, such delusions of divine presence were merely the easiest discourse to fit enthusiasm. In actuality, he thought it to be a psychical state, and one to be avoided and condemned.

Locke, in a foreshadowing of Wieland's concerns, sees the concept of enthusiasm as significant for undermining the functionality and mechanisms of reason. As he explains, "Reason is lost upon [enthusiasts], they are above it: they see the light infused into their understandings, and cannot be mistaken; it is clear and visible there, like the light of bright sunshine; shows itself, and needs no other proof but its own evidence: they feel the hand of God moving them within, and the impulses of the Spirit, and cannot be mistaken in what they feel."[64]

By this view, even the religious experience itself is a kind of delusion set upon by the imagination's inability to (quite literally) cool itself.

Yet problematic in Locke's understanding seems to be the failure to explain how enthusiasm, in whatever form it takes, spreads between people, and seems to function as a source of social disorder. This, according to Shaftesbury, was Locke's significant mistake.[65] While Locke may have been right to shift the discourse away from the religious experience that prejudiced its analysis, his understanding of it as a disease was too fixed in the body and the individual's experience of enthusiasm once active on the mind.

How does enthusiasm begin? How does it spread? Is it an individual or a social phenomenon? These were the questions that plagued Shaftesbury in his subsequent investigations of enthusiasm. As he explains:

> One may with good reason call every Passion Panick which is rais'd in a Multitude, and convey'd by Aspect, or as it were by Contact or Sympathy. Thus popular Fury may be call'd Panick, when the Rage of the People, as we have sometimes known, has put them beyond themselves; especially where Religion has had to do. And in this state their very Looks are infectious. The Fury flies from Face to Face: and the Disease is no sooner seen than caught. They who in a better Situation of Mind have beheld a Multitude under the power of this Passion, have own'd that they saw in the Countenances of Men something more ghastly and terrible than at other times is express'd on the most passionate occasion. Such force has Society in ill, as well as in good Passions: and so much stronger any Affection is for being social and communicative.[66]

Here Shaftesbury reveals the affective quality of human experience. Enthusiasm for him is a "disease" that effects social orders, and is consequent to social structures. Such feelings arise because individuals are immersed in a social world that would make them vulnerable to such feelings.

Importantly, Shaftesbury builds a more detailed and lucid bridge between accounts of enthusiasm as religious experience and enthusiasm as a medical phenomenon. As he continues his accounting:

> Religion is itself also Panick – for it is when Enthusiasm of any kind gets up; as oft, on melancholy occasions, it will. For Vapours naturally rise; and in bad times especially, when the Spirits of Men are low, as either in publick Calamitys, or during the Unwholesomeness

of Air or Diet, or when Convulsions happen in Nature, Storms, Earthquakes, or other amazing Prodigys: at this season the Panick must needs run high.[67]

The social phenomenon of panic explains how individuals become susceptible to both the exterior conditions, as well as the internal reactions to those conditions. Enthusiasm is not simply something one feels alone; nor is it entirely social. Rather, like fear of any disaster that might affect a community generally, individuals come to recognize the spreading affection in others. This ignites a personal experience of the affection. The two experiences – one social, the other personal – are thus related, but indistinguishable.

But Shaftesbury, despite offering a more nuanced view of the experience of enthusiasm, still does not do any work at distinguishing whether enthusiasm might, in certain circumstances, be desirable (or whether there might even be multiple forms or expressions of enthusiasm). In response to this large lacuna in Shaftesbury's thinking, Hume offers up a distinction between a positive and a negative experience of competing forms of inspired affection, between enthusiasm and what he labels as its counter, superstition.[68]

For Hume, superstition fills a void created by fears that seem produced from unaccountable causes. He describes it as such:

> The mind of man is subject to certain unaccountable terrors and apprehensions, proceeding either from the unhappy situation of private or public affairs, from ill health, from a gloomy and melancholy disposition, or from the concurrence of all these circumstances. In such a state of mind, infinite unknown evils are dreaded from unknown agents; and where real objects of terror are wanting, the soul, active to its own prejudice, and fostering its predominant inclination, finds imaginary ones, to whose power and malevolence it sets no limits. As these enemies are entirely invisible and unknown, the methods taken to appease them are equally unaccountable, and consist in ceremonies, observances, mortifications, sacrifices, presents, or in any practice, however absurd or frivolous, which either folly or knavery recommends to a blind and terrified credulity. *Weakness, fear, melancholy, together with ignorance, are, therefore, the true sources of superstition.*[69]

Hume argued that a collection of subjective affects were themselves conditioned on experiences of social phenomena. Superstition arises because our experiences of all social phenomena may not be good.

We may suffer feelings of impotence, or fear, or melancholy, and in that suffering, if we remain ignorant of the causes of these problems, or refuse to investigate and take stock of possible solutions, we risk opening ourselves to the feats of superstition.

Of course, not all experiences need be malignant, or need prey on our weaknesses. Though we may not always know why good things are happening to us (and, indeed, we may not want to), we can still find pleasure and inspiration in their occurrence. As Hume elaborates,

> But the mind of man is also subject to an unaccountable elevation and presumption, arising from prosperous success, from luxuriant health, from strong spirits, or from a bold and confident disposition. In such a state of mind, the imagination swells with great but confused conceptions, to which no sublunary beauties or enjoyments can correspond. Every thing mortal and perishable vanishes as unworthy of attention. And a full range is given to the fancy in the invisible regions or world of spirits, where the soul is at liberty to indulge itself in every imagination, which may best suit its present taste and disposition. Hence arise raptures, transports, and surprising flights of fancy; and confidence and presumption still encreasing, these raptures, being altogether unaccountable, and seeming quite beyond the reach of our ordinary faculties, are attributed to the immediate inspiration of that Divine Being, who is the object of devotion. In a little time, the inspired person comes to regard himself as a distinguished favourite of the Divinity; and when this frenzy once takes place, which is the summit of enthusiasm, every whimsy is consecrated: Human reason, and even morality are rejected as fallacious guides: And the fanatic madman delivers himself over, blindly, and without reserve, to the supposed illapses of the spirit, and to inspiration from above. Hope, pride, presumption, a warm imagination, together with ignorance, are, therefore, the true sources of enthusiasm.[70]

By this account, enthusiasm is that feeling that what is going to happen to us, coming from the future (so to speak), is that which has been hoped for and desired. Here, our present drags the future towards us, and the feeling we associate with it is what Hume describes as enthusiasm. This transportation is not – as Luther worried – away from earth, but away from time in the present. We cannot explain this feeling of transportation as ordinary, or through our ordinary experience of the world, and so ignorance does play a part in how it feels to be enthusiastic. But the feeling is, as yet, so positive, that it would never be wished away. Here Hume gets closer than any other at explaining why enthusiasm might persist, that persons might even enjoy the feeling. This, we will see, becomes a significant building block for Wieland and his fellow advocates of Enlightenment enthusiasm, for it looks to serve as the foundation for a useful (and defensible) form of enthusiasm that could – with some slight adjustments – be compatible with a fantasy of universal reason.

These discussions of religious and medical interpretations of enthusiasm give way to the moral parameters Wieland sought to define.[71] On the one hand, Wieland seems prepared to locate *Schwärmerei* as a kind of religious fanaticism. Yet he is also aware that such condemnations of religious experiences may not be apt, and that there are all kinds of religious experiences, some of them positive, which we should admit. Moreover, he seems prepared to label *Schwärmerei* as a kind of medical condition, referring to it alternatively as an "infestation," "inflammation," and a "fever." But he also sees these as experiences of the soul, not of the body, and thus seems to move away from the Locke-inspired discourse that enthusiasm, in whatever form, may be a corrupt overheating of the body. By positioning enthusiasm against *Schwärmerei*, describing the former as a nobility and virtue of being, Wieland relocates this discourse in the moral realm. At stake in distinguishing enthusiasm from *Schwärmerei* is the possibility that morality can be felt – enthusiasm is what we experience when we can actually feel that something is good – and also, that it can be used to counter the confusions of amorality present in *Schwärmerei*.[72]

Feeling dangers

How could this debate help us understand the political conceptions of enthusiasm and fanaticism? By Wieland's accounting, the costs of our inability to distinguish between enthusiasm from fanaticism are too great; we misunderstand the affective basis for functioning of "reason," as well as the justification for philosophy as a useful tool to encounter social and political problems. In our inability to say what we mean by enthusiasm, and further, our lack of capacity to clearly distinguish it from fanaticism, Wieland very much worried that we could not make sense of the forces that motivate change. Wieland's essay contest matters so much because it began a debate on how such change could be motivated, and how to be clear on the terms of such change.

Wieland hoped that enthusiasm could be preserved as a means for guiding pure reason. And yet, he also maintained the belief that reason could – in turn – guide society away from ignorance and towards Enlightenment. From his perspective, enthusiasm is what the philosopher feels, and offers to those who remain chained in ignorance. As Wieland wonders, "Who will drag these people towards such warmth?"[73] While this Platonic rhetoric is worrisome from a democratic perspective, it does highlight a more pressing anxiety: how can we motivate political change? This is a serious political question.

The political significance of enthusiasm first makes itself apparent in debates over the place of philosophy in public discourse, as well as the state of the university in social and political life. The public nature of thought – what it meant to think in and with a public – was itself one of the central tenants of the modern transformation of Enlightenment thinking. Such publicity remains today, even despite similar struggles, a central providence of contemporary democratic discourse. And thus making sense of how enthusiasm became a political affect – and not simply a religious or medical or moral one – is absolutely necessary.

Notes

1 On the history of this period in Iran, especially as it pertains to political enthusiasm and the promise of the revolution, see Ghamari-Tabrizi, Behrooz, *Foucault in Iran: Islamic Revolution after the Enlightenment* (Muslim International) (University of Minnesota Press, 2017). As Ghamari-Tabrizi reminds us, "The revolutionary movement in Iran offered a world-historical possibility to move away from a binary Islamist/secular politics, to imagine a form of unscripted political practices at the 'threshold of a novelty'" (p. xii). It is this "threshold of novelty" that I am most concerned with in this book.

2 Melinda Cooper, "The Law of the Household: Foucault, Neoliberalism and the Iranian Revolution," in *The Government of Life: Michel Foucault and Neoliberalism*, ed. Vanessa Lemm and Miguel Vatter (Fordham University Press, 2014), p. 29.

3 Michel Foucault, "What Are Iranians Dreaming About?" first published in *Le Nouvel Observateur* in October 1978, reprinted in Janet Afary and Kevin B. Anderson, *Foucault and the Iranian Revolution: Gender and the Seductions of Islamism* (University of Chicago Press, 2005), p. 207.

4 On the history of the revolution, and its many entanglements, see Ervand Abrahamian's *Iran Between Two Revolutions* (Princeton University Press, 1982), especially Abrahamian's account of Guerrilla organizations in opposition to the state (pp. 480–96), as well as the protests from June to December 1978 (pp. 510–25).

5 See, for example, Alberto Toscano, "Fanaticism, Revolt, and the Spiritualization of Politics," in *After the Postsecular and the Postmodern: New Essays in Continental Philosophy of Religion*, ed. Anthony Paul Smith and Daniel Whistler (Cambridge Scholars Publishing, 2010), esp. pp. 236–40; Christina Hendricks, "Foucault's Kantian Critique: Philosophy and the Present," *Philosophy and Social Criticism* 34, no. 4 (2008): 357–82; and Michiel Leezenberg, "Power and Political Spirituality: Michel Foucault on the Islamic Revolution in Iran," in *Michel Foucault and Theology: The Politics of Religious Experience*, ed. James Bernauer (Routledge, 2017), pp. 99–116. On Foucault's own writings on Iran, see Afary and Anderson, *Foucault and the Iranian Revolution*, appendix, esp. "What Are the Iranians Dreaming About?" from October 16, 1978, and "A Revolt with Bare Hands," from November 7, 1978. For a contemporary critique of Foucault, see Claudie and Jacques Broyelle, "What Are the Philosophers Dreaming About? Was Michel Foucault Mistaken about the Iranian Revolution?" reprinted in Afary and Anderson, *Foucault and the Iranian Revolution*, pp. 247–9.

6 See Leezenberg, "Power and Political Spirituality."

7 I am most influenced by Ghamari-Tabrizi's reading of these historical events in *Foucault in Iran*.

8 See Cooper, "The Law of the Household."

9 Immanuel Kant, "A Renewed Attempt to Answer the Question: 'Is the Human Race Constantly Improving?'" excerpted from *The Conflict of the Faculties*, reprinted in *Kant: Political Writings*, ed. H. S. Reiss (Cambridge University Press, 1970), p. 182.

10 Slavoj Žižek, *In Defense of Lost Causes* (Verso Press, 2017) p. 108.

11 A full translation of this proposed contest is provided in the Appendix at the end of this book. For comprehensive scholarly explorations of the concept of enthusiasm, see, for example, R. A. Knox, *Enthusiasm: A Chapter in the History of Religion* (Oxford University Press, 1950); Susie Tucker, *Enthusiasm: A Study of Semantic Change* (Cambridge University Press, 1972); and Michael Heyd, *"Be Sober*

and Reasonable": *The Critique of Enthusiasm in the Seventeenth and Early Eighteenth Centuries* (E. J. Brill, 1995). For the most recent historical revaluation of enthusiasm, especially for Enlightenment discourse, see Lawrence Klein and Anthony La Vopa, eds., *Enthusiasm and Enlightenment in Europe, 1650–1850* (Huntington Library Press, 1998). Concern for enthusiasm in political contexts has taken on specific urgency in the last decade. See, for example, Alberto Toscano's *Fanaticism: History of an Idea* (Verso, 2010).

12 Kristin Wömmel offers a slightly different etymology, claiming that the adjective *"entheos"* might best be read as "filled up by God," and thus defines enthusiasm as "full of spirit." This seems to confuse *Enthusiasmus* and *Begeisterung*. See her analysis in *Enthusiasmus: Untersuchung eines mehrdimensionalen Konstrukts im Umfeld musikalischer Bildung* (Springer, 2016), p. 17.

13 From J. A. Simpson and Edmund S. C. Weiner, eds., *The Oxford English Dictionary*, 2nd ed. (Oxford University Press, 1989).

14 On the Greek conception of ἐνθουσιασμός, see Walter Burkert's *Griechische Religion der archaischen und klassischen Epoche* (1977), translated into English as *Greek Religion: Archaic and Classical*, by John Raffan (Harvard University Press, 1985), see esp. Burkert's discussions of *"Enthusiasmos,"* "The Art of the Seer," and "Oracles," pp. 109–18. For more recent historical elaborations on Burkert's survey, see Pierre Bonnechere, "Divination," in *A Companion to Greek Religion*, ed. Daniel Ogden (Blackwell, 2010), pp. 145–60, esp. the section titled "Inspired Divination Through the Mediation of a Religious 'Magistrate,'" pp. 154–5.

15 Plato, *Phaedrus*, 244b, trans. Alexander Nehamas and Paul Woodruff (Hackett, 1997).

16 This is how Burkert describes it, in *Greek Religion*, p. 111.

17 For the most recent comprehensive general history of roman religion, see Valerie M. Warrior, *Roman Religion* (Cambridge University Press, 2006), esp. chap. 2 "Divination, Prayer, and Sacrifice," and chap. 5, "Religion and War." Though Warrior does not explicitly discuss fanaticism, she does provide an excellent accounting of the practices of the temple of Bellona.

18 From Simpson and Weiner, *Oxford English Dictionary*.

19 Toscano usefully explores the origins of this concept in his *Fanaticism*, see, for example, p. 112. While Toscano explores the framework of fanaticism in relationship to enthusiasm, my argument follows the mirror logic of tracing enthusiasm's multiple manifestations.

20 From chap. XXI of *The Divine Institutes*, bk I.

21 See Robert Turcan, *The Cults of the Roman Empire* (Blackwell, 1996), p. 41. Toscano has also focused on this narrative, but for alternative reasons. See Toscano, *Fanaticism*, chap. 2.

22 From his *Elegies*, bk 1, chap. 6, pp. 45–50. Translation available via Turcan, *Cults of the Roman Empire*, p. 41.

23 See Appendix, para. F.

24 For further discussions of these historical aspects of enthusiasm, see Knox, *Enthusiasm*; Tucker, *Enthusiasm*; and Heyd, *"Be Sober and Reasonable."* For a literary perspective on the place of enthusiasm, see John Mee, *Romanticism, Enthusiasm, and Regulation: Poetics and the Policing of Culture in the Romantic Period* (Oxford University Press, 2005).

25 This follows on the pattern set by Foucault, for example, in Michel Foucault, "What Is Enlightenment?" in *The Foucault Reader*, ed. Paul Rabinow (Pantheon Books, 1984), p. 33.

26 For a general elaboration on this point and its context, see Peter Gay, "The Geography of Hope," in *The Enlightenment: An Interpretation, The Science of Freedom*, rev. ed. (Norton, 1996), pp. 98–125.

27 The struggle between reason and affect is a familiar trope of Enlightenment discourse. The classic statement of this problematic for political theory is Albert Hirschman, *The Passions and the Interests: Political Arguments for Capitalism Before Its Triumph* (Princeton University Press, 1997). The most recent reviews of this problematic include Victoria Kahn, Neil Saccamano, and Daniela Coli, eds., *Politics and the Passions, 1500–1850* (Princeton University Press, 2006); as well as Rebecca Kingston, ed., *Bring the Passions Back In: The Emotions in Political Philosophy* (University of British Columbia Press, 2008). For the most provocative contemporary account of feeling and its current pathologies, see Libby Anker, *Orgies of Feeling: Melodrama and the Politics of Freedom* (Duke, 2014).

28 See Appendix, para. C.

29 To my mind, this discourse on enthusiasm directly parallels, and I would argue contributes to, Adorno and Horkheimer's concerns in the *Dialectic of Enlightenment: Philosophical Fragments* (Stanford University Press, 2002).

30 The medical quality of thought was a rhetoric employed throughout the eighteenth century, and as more than mere analogy. For a complete historical overview of this shift, see Heyd, *"Be Sober and Reasonable."* Also see Lionel Laborie, *Enlightening Enthusiasm: Prophecy and Religious Experience in Early Eighteenth-Century England* (Oxford University Press, 2015), esp. chap. 6, "Medicalising Enthusiasm."

31 I borrow the phrase "pathologies of reason" from Axel Honneth, "A Social Pathology of Reason: On the Intellectual Legacy of Critical Theory," in *Pathologies of Reason: On the Legacy of Critical Theory*, trans. James Ingram (Columbia, 2009), pp. 19–25.

32 See Appendix, para. F.

33 Excerpted from Jacob and Wilhelm Grimm's *Deutsche Wörterbuch*: "SCHWÄRMEREI, f. gebahren eines schwärmers – den kirchenglauben betreffend: das jr blinder dünckel … sich düncken lesst, die schrift strebe an viel orten wider diesen spruch, aber sie reimet sich viel mehr mit jm und strebt wider jre schwermerey. LUTHER 3, 405b; das jr schwermerey ein lauter lose geschwetz ist. 377a; das die lerer einer ketzerey oder schwermerey solten bekeret werden. 377b; widerteuffer und sacramentschender … brachten viel leut in jhre schwermerey. HENNENBERGER landt. 393; des Weigelianismi oder anderer neuen schwärmereien. SPENER pietismus (1710) 23; pietistische schwärmerei schien den grund zum ganzen nachfolgenden nebel gelegt zu haben. sie schärfte sein gewissen, und machte ihn gegen alle gegenstände von tugend und religion äuszerst empfindlich, und verwirrte seine begriffe. SCHILLER 1, 109; alle orden-stifter und ordens-brüder … der schwärmerey, der eitelkeit, des unsinns etc. zu schuldigen. CLAUDIUS 8 (1812), 228," http://germazope.uni-trier.de/Projects/DWB (accessed 20 July 2020).

34 Excerpted from Johann Christoph Adelung's *Grammatisch-kritisches Wörterbuch der Hochdeutschen Mundart* from 1811: "Der Schwärmer – [1717–18] des -s, plur. ut nom. sing. von dem vorigen Zeitworte. 1. Ein schwärmendes Ding, in welchem Verstande es besonders in der Feuerwerkskunst üblich ist, wo ein in Papier gefüllter kleiner Feuerwerkssatz, welcher, wenn er angezündet wird, vor dem Zerplatzen nicht nur ein schwärmendes Getöse macht, sondern auch ohne Ordnung hin und her schwärmet, ein Schwärmer genannt wird. Schwärmer werfen. In figürlichem Verstande heißt bey den Jägern ein Leithund, welcher sich leicht durch sinnliche Eindrücke von der Fährte abbringen läßt, ein Schwärmer. 2. Eine schwärmende Person, Fämin. die Schwärmerinn. 1) In der ersten figürlichen Bedeutung des Zeitwortes, eine Person, welche sich rauschenden Vergnügungen und Ausschweifungen überläßt. Ein Gassenschwärmer, Nachtschwärmer u. s. f. 2) In der dritten und vierten figürlichen Bedeutung, eine Person, welche undeutlich und in noch engerm Verstande, welche verworrene Vorstellungen zum Nachtheile deutlicher und klarer zum Bestimmungsgrunde ihrer Urtheile und Handlungen macht, wo es in allen Ständen, Geschäften und Wissenschaften Schwärmer und Schwärmerinnen gibt, welche Empfindungen und wohl gar Einbildungen für Wahrheit halten. S. das

folgende," http://lexika.digitale-sammlungen.de/adelung/online/angebot (accessed 18 July 2020).

35 On the slanderous nature of *Schwärmerei*, see Peter Fenves, "The Scale of Enthusiasm," *Huntington Library Quarterly* 60, nos. 1–2, Enthusiasm and Enlightenment in Europe, 1650–1850 (1997): 117–52; and Anthony La Vopa, "The Philosopher and the *Schwärmer*: On the Career of a German Epithet from Luther to Kant," *Huntington Library Quarterly* 60, nos. 1–2, Enthusiasm and Enlightenment in Europe, 1650–1850 (1997): 85–8.

36 See Adelung's *Grammatisch-kritisches Wörterbuch der Hochdeutschen Mundart* for an elaboration on this context.

37 On the problems of "doubling" for the imagination, see Kateb's discussion in "The Adequacy of the Canon," in *Patriotism and Other Mistakes* (Yale University Press, 2006), esp. pp. 399–401.

38 Fenves, "The Scale of Enthusiasm," pp. 120–1.

39 Adelung's definition for *Enthusiasmus* refers the reader to *Schwärmerei*, illustrating Wieland's point regarding this confusion. See Adelung's *Grammatisch-kritisches Wörterbuch der Hochdeutschen Mundart* entry for "*Enthusiasmus*" for details.

40 Appendix, para. D.

41 Appendix, para. F.

42 Appendix, para. K.

43 Here, it is worth recalling Amy Allen's worry on the exclusionary logics latent in Enlightenment rationality and its late inheritances, despite claims to universality. At some level, Wieland illustrates a fundamental blindness to the particularity of desire for a specific universality in reason. See, for example, Amy Allen, *The End of Progress: Decolonizing the Normative Foundations of Critical Theory* (Columbia University Press, 2016), pp. 28–34.

44 See La Vopa's recent discussion of Luther's redefinition of *Schwärmerei* in "The Philosopher and the *Schwärmer*," pp. 87–9. On Luther's political thought, see Cargill Thompson, *The Political Thought of Martin Luther* (Harvester Press, 1984). See also Sheldon Wolin's *Politics and Vision; Continuity and Innovation in Western Political Thought* (Princeton University Press, 2004), esp. chap. 5; and Quentin Skinner's account of the political context of the Reformation in *The Foundations of Modern Political Thought: The Age of Reformation*, vol. 2 (Cambridge University Press, 1988). For recent accountings of the religious significance of Luther's religious struggles, see Mark Edwards, "Luther's Polemical Controversies," in *The Cambridge Companion to Martin Luther*, ed. Donald K. McKim (Cambridge University Press, 2003), pp. 192–208; and Mark Edwards, "Luther

and the Storm of Faith," in *The Theological Origins of Modernity*, ed. Mark Gillespie (University of Chicago Press, 2008), pp. 101–28.

45 See La Vopa, "The Philosopher and the *Schwärmer*," p. 88.

46 For Luther's own accounting of these false prophets, see his *Against the Heavenly Prophets in the Matter of Images and Sacraments*, in vol. 1 of *The Selected Writings of Martin Luther* (Fortress Press, reprint 2007). See also Edwards's discussion of true and false prophets, in McKim, *Cambridge Companion to Martin Luther*, pp. 194–5.

47 See, for example, Dominique Colas's narration of these contests for power in early Protestantism in *Civil Society and Fanaticism: Conjoined Histories* (Stanford University Press, 1997), esp. chap. 4, "Swords Against Flail." See, for example, Colas's narration on pp. 99–118.

48 See Erik Erikson, *Young Man Luther: A Study in Psychoanalysis and History* (Norton, 1993), esp. chap. 2, "Fit in the Choir," p. 23.

49 Here I am merely restating La Vopa's thesis from "The Philosopher and the *Schwärmer*."

50 For a history of the Anabaptist movement, see Hans Jürgen-Goertz, *The Anabaptists* (Routledge, 1996), esp. his discussion of Luther and anticlericalism, pp. 36–43.

51 See Knox, *Enthusiasm*, pp. 126–35.

52 See Jürgen-Goertz, *The Anabaptists*, p. 46.

53 Knox, *Enthusiasm*, pp. 135–6.

54 See, for example, Jürgen-Goertz, *The Anabaptists*, pp. 118–31.

55 On the history of enthusiasm in the British context of religious dissenters, see Lawrence Klein, "Sociability, Solitude, and Enthusiasm," in *Huntington Library Quarterly* 60, nos. 1–2, Enthusiasm and Enlightenment in Europe, 1650–1850 (1997): 153–77; Jason Frank, "'Besides Our Selves': An Essay on Enthusiastic Politics and Civil Subjectivity," *Public Culture* 17, 3 (2005): 371–92; Isabel Rivers, *Reason, Grace, and Sentiment: A Study of the Language of Religion and Ethics in England, 1660–1780* (Cambridge University Press, 2008); and esp. John Pocock, "Enthusiasm: The Anti-Self of the Enlightenment," in *Huntington Library Quarterly* 60, nos. 1–2, Enthusiasm and Enlightenment in Europe, 1650–1850 (1997): 7–28, esp. pp. 10–18.

56 Pocock, "Enthusiasm," p. 16.

57 For the most recent historical portrait that documents precisely this shift in the secularization of concepts, see Stephen Gaukroger, *The Emergence of a Scientific Culture: Science and the Shaping of Modernity, 1210–1685* (Oxford University Press, 2006), esp. the section "The Natural Philosopher versus the Enthusiast," pp. 220–8. For the initiation of this debate, see Steven Shapin and Simon Schaffer,

Leviathan and the Air Pump: Hobbes, Boyle, and the Experimental Life (Princeton University Press, 1989). As discussed in the introduction, the classic statement of this problem is Weber's "secularization thesis," discussed (among other places) in *The Vocation Lectures* (Hackett, 2004).

58 On the medical critique of enthusiasm and its incorporation as an object of scientific discourse, see Heyd, *"Be Sober and Reasonable,"* esp. chap. 7, "The New Medical Discourse and the Theological Critique of Enthusiasm," pp. 191–210. It is worth noting here that Heyd argues the medicalization of enthusiasm begins the politicization of the concept. While it may be that such scientific discourse initiates the process, this is not historically apparent until, I would argue, Wieland's essay, and especially the reactions to it.

59 See Heyd, *"Be Sober and Reasonable"* for a review of these particular diagnoses.

60 Chap. 19 from John Locke's *An Essay Concerning Human Understanding* (1698) (the first German translations appeared between 1755 and 1757). For a discussion of Locke here, see Heyd, *"Be Sober and Reasonable,"* pp. 177–80. See also Mee, *Romanticism*, pp. 37–9; and Daniel Carey, *Locke, Shaftesbury, and Hutchison: Contesting Diversity in Enlightenment and Beyond* (Cambridge University Press, 2006), pp. 142–50. For an overview of the shifts in eighteenth-century discourse that Locke himself was immersed in, see B. W. Young, *Religion and Enlightenment in 18th-Century England: Theological Debate from Locke to Burke* (Oxford University Press, 1998).

61 This, anyway, in comparison to Wieland, who believes that if *Schwärmerei* were a medical condition then that would mean it was something to be corrected or cured, not something that should be considered "shameful."

62 *The Works of John Locke: A New Edition, Corrected, in Ten Volumes*, vol. 3 (Thomas Tegg, 1823), pp. 149–50.

63 Ibid., p. 150.

64 Ibid., p. 151.

65 Shaftesbury, *A Letter Concerning Enthusiasm* (1707) (with German translations appearing between 1776 and 1779). For discussions of Shaftesbury's conception of enthusiasm, see Frank, "Beside Our Selves"; Heyd, *"Be Sober and Reasonable"*; Rivers, *Reason, Grace and Sentiment*; and esp. Carey, *Locke, Shaftesbury, and Hutchison*, pp. 142–50.

66 Anthony Ashley Cooper Shaftesbury and Lawrence Eliot Klein, *Characteristics of Men, Manners, Opinions, Times* (Cambridge University Press, 1999), p. 10.

67 Ibid.

68 David Hume, "Of Superstition and Enthusiasm" (1741) (translated into German in the late 1760s). On the context of German reactions to Hume's thesis, see Lothar Kreimendahl, "Humes Kritik an Aberglaube und Schwärmerei im Kontext der Fragestellungen des englischen Deismus," in the special edition "Die Aufklärung und die Schwärmer," in *Aufklärung* 3:1 1988 (ed. Norbert Hinske). For a general discussion of Hume's thesis in the British context, see Mee, *Romanticism, Enthusiasm, and Regulation*, pp. 44–9. On Hume's defense of the use of passions to correct social phenomena, see Sharon Krause, *Civil Passions: Moral Sentiment and Democratic Deliberation* (Princeton University Press, 2008).

69 David Hume, *Essays Moral, Political, Literary*, ed. Eugene F. Miller, with an appendix of variant readings from the 1889 edition by T. H. Green and T. H. Grose, rev. ed. (Liberty Fund 1987), n.p. (emphasis added), https://oll.libertyfund.org/title/hume-essays-moral-political-literary-lf-ed#Hume_0059_255 (accessed 27 May 2021).

70 Ibid.

71 On Enlightenment and enthusiasm, see esp. Pocock, "Enthusiasm." Also important here (beyond what has been discussed already) is George Williamson, "Theophany and Revolution," in *The Longing for Myth in Germany: Religion and Aesthetic Culture from Romanticism to Nietzsche* (University of Chicago Press, 2004), pp. 19–71, esp. pp. 56–71.

72 Several of those not discussed here include Herder, Hamann, and Lessing. These are all addressed in significant detail by La Vopa in "The Philosopher and the *Schwärmer*." But, moreover, each is concerned with aspects of this debate that keep Wieland's question in the realm of the moral (and especially not the political). Though Herder does offer the important observation that "the human being is bound to the world with a thousand ties, restricted to himself, he finds himself in the narrowest prison. Whoever loosens him from himself, whoever creates a free, lively game for his energies, is his god, his awakener. And he plays on him as on an instrument; if the flute tones, if his inner strung sounds, he feels good; he lets it play. Hence the pleasure of the people to be put in enthusiasm; hence the drive and the joy of enthusiastic spirits to fill other with enthusiasm, to inspire them." Johann Gottfried Herder, *Philosopher und Schwärmerei, zwo Schwestern* (Herder's *Sämmtliche Werke*, vol. 9, ed. Bernhard Suphan, Berlin 1877, pp. 497–8), originally published 1776.

73 For an account of neo-Platonism as a kind of enthusiasm, see Pocock, "Enthusiasm."

2

On the borders of enthusiasm: beginning a very dangerous politics

Possession by a god, enthusiasm, is not the irrational, but the end of the solitary or inward thought, the beginning of a true experience of the new and of the noumenon – already Desire.
— Emmanuel Levinas, *Totality and Infinity: An Essay on Exteriority* (1961)

When does enthusiasm become political?

The historical narrative of enthusiasm leading up to Wieland's essay contest provides a window on to an intensely debated political ideal. Whether used as a religious derogation or described as a symptom of mental disease, enthusiasm appeared as a problematic phenomenon to be overcome, no matter the context. Much of Enlightenment discourse is saturated with the anxiety that lurking behind rational argumentation and its products, whether moral, religious, or scientific, is an uncontrollable affective irrationalism that risks the very validity of these progressions. But as dangerous as many feared enthusiasms might be, there were others who saw more possibility in enthusiasm than a mere problem to be solved.

Kant offers one of the most important and least studied answers to Wieland's question on why and how to distinguish between enthusiasm and fanaticism.[1] Enthusiasm is – as Kant puts it – the feeling that accompanies "the idea of the good," and in so doing, acts as "a straining of our forces by ideas that impart the mind a momentum whose effects are mightier and more permanent than are those of an impulse produced by the presentations of sense."[2] It is, he argues, the feeling that commingles inspiration and conviction, giving the sense that sometimes what one will do is also exactly what one should do.³ Read this way, enthusiasm is absolutely essential to how we experience politics and especially those political changes we might initiate.

As I describe in what follows, Kant gives us a useful, though complex, normative reading of enthusiasm. His reading is so useful because it makes sense of the promise enthusiasm embodies, helping us identify – and motivate – the feelings that accompany political change. Yet the groundwork on which Kant develops this normative frame is incredibly complex, both because of the historical context of his arguments, but also because of the incompleteness of some of his most crucial thoughts on this subject. While Kant spent much of his philosophical career struggling with enthusiasm, he seemed to shy away from offering a clear statement on the potential he found therein. It was as though the feelings themselves were too dangerous for his thinking, and yet also irresistible to him.

What Kant was absolutely clear on were where we most usually encounter the feeling of enthusiasm; we feel enthusiasm when we bear witness to great political change. This in itself need not be such a radical claim, but Kant goes further, making explicit the terms to think through how to cross the boundary between political actor and spectator, and the place of enthusiasm in constructing that pathway. Enthusiasm matters so much to politics then because it is the feeling of conviction that spurs political action. And it is this crucial claim, lurking in the dross, that I hope to excavate out of the mountain of Kant's thinking.

In this way, my reading of Kant can be understood as an elaboration of Jean-François Lyotard's account of enthusiasm as a "passage."⁴ Lyotard finds in Kant a speculative rationality at odds with the "old Kant" so often identified with the *Critique of Pure Reason* and the Nietzschean anxiety regarding the harsh rationality of the Enlightenment's cold disposition. This new, speculative Kant, Lyotard explains, thinks according to the "as if." In the midst of a revolution, the old Kant might view the politics at stake analytically and dispassionately, far removed from battlelines and political struggles. But the new Kant Lyotard points us to sees, in the hearts of spectators, a passage to a new politics. In the late eighteenth century, the French Revolution, at least as viewed from the bridges of Königsberg, did not look merely as a violent and destabilizing conflict. Instead, Kant might better be understood as viewing such a revolution "as if" it was actually an impetus for political change at home, and thus a chance to motivate a reconfiguration of the Prussian state.

Indeed, such thinking is much more radical than it might have initially appeared (even to Kant himself). No longer is Kant describing the enthusiast as a passive witness to the events of history; enthusiasm instead begins a new politics consequent to that spectatorship, building on and extending political actions in the world. Enthusiasm then is a contagious political spirit of progressive transformations. Neither political actors, nor their purported "greatness," but spectators become the source of authority, and one that spurs them to become new actors who will author new actions. Here, enthusiasm becomes political by shifting the very ground of how we experience new political authorities and their origins. And, while Kant himself would later disavow such thinking on enthusiasm, we – on our own authority – need not draw the same conclusions.

Paying close attention to the effect the form of Wieland's question has on Kant, and anyone who would work to distinguish between enthusiasm and fanaticism, I offer a counter-reading of the traditional view of Kantian enthusiasm, one that moves past the purified spectator immune to political engagement. As Kant exclaims, "The recent revolution ... arouses in the heart of all spectators ... desires which border on enthusiasm."[5] This admiration for a revolutionary political spirit has been read by other theorists of enthusiasm as Kant's politics of sympathy, where spectators rationalize an equality with political actors caught up in the revolution and the ideals those actors have committed to. I read this passage somewhat differently. I think we might better see the spectator as themselves intensely political, not just a distant witness to one political event, but as themselves a new actor invested with an insurgent force to transform their own political universe. This reading of enthusiasm makes sense of Kant's own anxiety regarding this "most dangerous" political idea. In short, by paying attention to both the form and the content of his argument, I read Kantian political enthusiasm as a performance, one that motivates revolutionary action.

Within orbits

Outside the French hamlet of Valmy, on the humid, foggy, and otherwise dismal morning of September 20, 1792, an ill-composed band of volunteer French soldiers prepared for battle against the superiorly armed and manned Prussian force.[6] The ground on which this battle took place was muddied from the previous days' rains. Enough so that cannon-shots would sink into the earth swallowed whole, and cavalry horses found unstable footing wherever they rode. This proved more problematic for the French troops, who that morning – as the fog was beginning to clear – found themselves surrounded in this mud on three sides by the advancing Prussians.

As the battle commenced, the French commander – François Christophe de Kellermann – attempted a strategic charge, only to find his horse impaired by the muddied terrain. Trapped in the open field, he proved an easy target for Prussian snipers, who quickly succeeded in killing the commander's horse, wounding Kellermann in the process. Both sides witnessed the fall of the French commanding officer with awe: The French, filled with a growing dismay; the Prussians, enthused by their own advantage.

But, just as medics were attempting to carry the dazed Kellermann off the field, he fought free of their guard and, grabbing an idle bayonet, charged alone by foot to face the advancing Prussian cavalry. As he did so, the battalions that stood behind him – perhaps impressed with their commander's nerve – began to chant "Vive la Nation!" This cry echoed throughout the valley, generating a monstrous soundscape, as more and more French troops joined their voices to the chorus.

Struck by the unity this phrase evoked, the French joined their commander's attack, while the Prussians – equally impressed with the power of this call – began a retreat. At the end of the day's battle, which had been decisively won by the far weaker French forces, a young Johann Wolfgang von Goethe, who happened to have witnessed the day's events, exclaimed to the defeated Prussians, "From this place and from this day forth commences a new era in the world's history, and you can all say that you were present at its birth."[7] The new era Goethe believed he was witnessing, we now know, was modern nationalism – the use of the concept of "the nation" to motivate political attachment and action; an imaginary community, that required enthusiasm for its discovery and creation.[8]

Goethe circled the battlefield during and after this momentous day, reflecting – through his orbit – on the moral and political significance of such a turn. That reflection, and his experience of spectatorship, removed as he was from the life and death battle itself, may be one of many contemporaneous models for what came to be one of the most famous and least studied answers to Wieland's question on the distinction between enthusiasm and fanaticism – Immanuel Kant's essay, "An Old Question Raised Again: Is Humanity Constantly Progressing?" There, Kant famously – if enigmatically – reflects, "This revolution ... has aroused in the minds of all spectators (who are themselves not a part of the game) a heartfelt desire for something, close to the border of enthusiasm, whose very statement is fraught with danger."[9] This claim has become a hallmark regarding the affective structure of modern revolution, and the place of enthusiasm in transformative politics. In this essay, Kant offers a philosophical defense of revolution, which is often read as distinguishing between the enthusiasm of political onlookers and the fanaticism (what Kant, following Wieland, called the *Schwärmerei*) of the revolutionaries.

Reason's raving

At first glance, turning to Kant as a resource for untangling the problems of political motivation might appear problematic.[10] Within debates on the public use of reason compared with public feeling, Kant's ideas are so often employed as tools to uphold the impartiality of public reason by his defenders, or used by critics as emblematic of the Enlightenment's failure to take seriously the place of emotion in the public sphere.[11] Both parties here see Kant as critical of public rhetoric, viewing it as an instigation of dangerous emotions that interfere with the "right" use of reason and the production of just political outcomes. Central to this reading have been two oft repeated passages; one from Kant's essay on the question "What is Enlightenment?": "Nothing is required for this (mass) Enlightenment, however, except freedom; and the freedom in question is the least harmful of all, namely, the freedom to use reason publicly in all matters";[12] the other from the *Critique of Judgment*:

> [R]eading the best speech of a roman public orator, or a contemporary parliamentary speaker or preacher, has always been mingled with the disagreeable feeling of disapproval of an insidious art, an art that knows how, in important matters, to move people like machines to a judgment that must lose all its weight with them when they meditate about it calmly.[13]

Defenders and critics alike found grounds for their claims in both of these passages. Defenders of Kant – or at least of his accounting of the public use of reason – saw the initiating of a defense of free persons, capable of making rational choices unmanipulated by rhetorical illusions. Critics argued Kant was misreading the subtleties of rhetoric and persuasion, and their value in both constituting allegiances and furthering practical political projects. As Bryan Garsten puts it,

> Regardless of where Kant received his notion that rhetoric sought to "move men like machines," he clearly worried not so much about its political effects as about its pernicious influence on habits of mind. Even when an orator aimed at praiseworthy ends, his involvement "spoiled" the maxims and dispositions of his listeners by discouraging them from thinking independently. Kant's argument was that rhetoric prevented individuals from thinking for themselves in the way that Enlightenment demanded.[14]

But *where* Kant received his notion of the danger requisite to "moving people like machines" is actually centrally revealing. Understanding the source of Kant's rejection of the orators, and his defense of public reason, taken in context, reveals a more subtle and helpful portrait of the kinds of political motivations that should be of use to contemporary democratic projects.

As historians have noted, transformations in the politics of Europe occasioned Kant to restructure the objects of and motivations for his critical project.[15] One critic notes:

> It is true, of course, that in the *Conflict of the Faculties*, Kant went beyond the systematic boundaries of this (e.g. critical) philosophy and raised the French Revolution to the level of "historical sign" for the possibility of a moral progress of humanity. But in the theory

itself (e.g. of historical progression) we find no trace of the constitutional assemblies of Philadelphia and Paris – at least not the reasonable trace of a great, dual historical event that we can now see in retrospect as an entirely new beginning.[16]

But this reading misunderstands Kant's project, seeing it as a continuation of outlining the moral parameters of practical reason, rather than, as I argue, an excavation of the concept of enthusiasm for political ends. Nowhere is this transformation more evident than in the shift in Kant's thinking on the concept of enthusiasm.

While much of Kant's early writings were directed at the problem of moral *Schwärmerei*,[17] after 1786, Kant begins to develop and defend a notion of enthusiasm that he thought central to the act of political judgment that is distinct from *Schwärmerei*.[18] Kant's reflections on enthusiasm eventually coalesce around his understanding of the role of history in a progressive political theory, grounded in reflections on contemporaneous historical transformations and their effects – present and future – for a new kind of politics. All of this was his attempt to answer what he thought of as a central question regarding human existence: Of what can we hope?[19]

The link between rhetoric and enthusiasm is central here. Turning persons "into machines" means dissolving individual will. Kant himself associated rhetoricians who manipulated crowds – dissolving personal wills in favor of the collective – with mystics, politicians, and religious leaders.[20] Relatedly, the kind of rhetoric Kant argued turned persons into machines was for him requisite to the concept of *Schwärmerei*. Getting clear on Kant's understanding of this term makes a contemporaneous translation difficult, even despite its common placement in eighteenth-century discourse.[21] At this point, *Schwärmerei* did seem to mean something like fanaticism. As Kant uses the term, it often, though not always, seems to refer to crowds of devoted religious followers, swooped up into a "swarm" by the impassioned preaching displayed. He is clear that, however we translate it, *Schwärmerei* diagnosed a state of being as well as an emotion. The *Schwärm* could be observed as developing in reaction to mystical displays, but the feelings of being in the swarm would also be described using the same word. As Peter Fenves puts it, "Members of a swarm are not only impossible to distinguish from one another but are also, for this reason, not even members of the swarm: instead of belonging to a stable collective according to which they would be recognized and named, each one is a temporary participant in an act of 'swarming.'"[22] The identity of the swarm is manifest in its activity – an activity that dissolves the individual of the ground of its identity. This was something Kant was very much concerned with.

The link between the "machine" and the *Schwärm* is that, in both, the conscious self is absolved of thought and the responsibility for thinking, meaning for Kant they are no longer human. This occurs through the extension of the imagination past the sensible – and the categories through which the sensible is made apparent – to the supersensible.[23] Thus, Kant describes *Schwärmerei* as "over-stepping the bounds of human reason";[24] "the delusion of wanting to see something beyond the bounds of sensibility, i.e., of dreaming according to principles, raving with reason"; "comparable to mania"; "a deep-seated and brooding passion"; "it is rule-less."[25] To be caught in a swarm was still a sickness, as Kant saw it. That one would be susceptible to fanatical inspiration – that is, that one could be susceptible to seeing beyond the senses – was a weakness that certain individuals suffered from and should not be taken as a universal condition. "Madness," as Kant put it, "is a passing accident that presumably strikes even the soundest understanding on occasion; mania (fanaticism) is a disease that deranges it."[26] And orators that prey on such weaknesses fuel delusions of the sick, rather than engaging the reasonable with sustained arguments; orations do not allow thinking.[27]

One such "*Schwärmer*" who exemplified Kant's early fears was Emanuel Swedenborg.[28] An eighteenth-century scientist and mystical theologian, Swedenborg's studies on the relationship between the soul and the brain led him to his own mystical "awakening" whereby he claimed to have been called by God to develop a new church on earth. Swedenborg claims that his awakening attuned him to the spirit world in a way never before possible. He was, apparently, able to describe with accurate detail the path of the great Stockholm fire, and the near destruction of his own house, while seated in a Gothenburg inn during the actual occurrence of the event. Kant viewed Swedenborg's awakening as dangerous, both to Swedenborg, but also to audiences who came to value his testimony.[29] As Kant, referring to Swedenborg, describes such "deceptions,"

> The deception of reason could to a large extent be prevented by subjecting the powers of the mind to control the will, and by exercising rather more restraint over an idle inquisitiveness. The deception of the sense, on the other hand, concerns the ultimate foundation of all our judgments, and if that foundation were defective, there is little that the rules of logic could do to remedy the situation![30]

By Kant's account, Swedenborg's fantastic revelations call into question the very basis of judgment, and his orations offer an opportunity for judgment itself to lose its balance.

Kant relies on a clear contrast here between oratory and rhetoric. The problem with an oratory that produces a swarm, as opposed to a rhetoric that induces enthusiasm, is that the possibility of judgment is relocated form audience to speaker. The "human machines" Kant describes are marked by the incapacity for making judgments; instead, they passively absorb the ideas that come to them from an outside source. Their autonomy is wrested from them by the very act of oratory itself. This distinction is made most clear by Kant's distinction between public and private use of reason. By his account, "the public use of one's reason [is] the use that anyone as a scholar makes of reason before the entire literate world."[31]

At first glance, this seems relatively unproblematic. There are, of course, limitations placed on how large the reading public is, and how well they can evaluate the information given – which would depend on class and social structures that Kant himself may not be willing to admit. But the claim that the information is in control of the audience and not the author himself – that it requires the audience's validation – and the complete audience's validation – is not far afield from contemporary evaluations of legitimate public information.

This account of public reason, however, becomes more complicated when compared with Kant's accounting of private reason. As Kant explains, "I call the private use of reason that which a person may make in a civic post or office that has been entrusted to him."[32] Such a rendering of the private use of reason is, I think, counterintuitive. If we read Kant closely here, he is claiming that orators, priests, politicians, and mystics alike are, when they speak,

delivering the private use of reason, and encouraging engagement via their private use, even if in a public sphere. The power
of engagement, and the means by which such knowledge is delivered, is mitigated by the roles in which each serve. As a mystic,
Swedenborg is bound by the constraints of his role to deliver a certain kind and style of knowledge. It is private in the sense that the
interpretation of the information is out of his and his audience's
control, and in control and alleviated by the system that defines
his role.

Kant is so careful to distinguish between rhetoric and oratory
then because he is worried about delineating a boundary between
private and public uses of reason. As he puts it, "rhetorical power
and excellence of speech (which together constitute rhetoric) belong
to fine art; but oratory (*ars oratoria*), the art of using people's
weaknesses for one's own aims (no matter how good these may
be in intention or even in fact), is unworthy of any respect whatsoever."[33] Rhetoric then depends on the strength of the audience
and maintains their ability to cast judgments. Oratory, by contrast,
hopes that judgments will be reserved. The emergence of the two is
indistinguishable from the strength of audiences and their security
within apolitical framework. He argues that, "both in Athens and
in Rome, it (oratory) came to its peak only at a time when the state
was hastened to its ruin, and any true patriotic way of thinking was
extinct."[34] Declining states create psychological fissures that allow
for internal weaknesses and the emergence of those who would prey
on them within the public sphere. Men as machines, as swarms, do
not emerge always; they arise at unique moments in history, when
traditional powers are declining.

The once famous case of Johann Heinrich Schulz, and Kant's
subsequent reaction to it, confirms the traditional problem of
Schwärmerei for Kant's understanding of the public use of reason.[35]
Schulz became the center of a public scandal on the problem of
preaching enthusiasm. In 1791 he was barred from preaching and
in May 1792 he was put on trial, charged with violating the religious edict of the Prussian state. For the state's part, the concern was
that Schulz was undermining political authority, preaching God's
word above the authority of the state. For Kant, the problem was
equally problematic for "reason." By his view, Schulz's preaching
allowed for the collapse of all authorities beside the *Schwärmer*'s

relationship to God. The state's prosecutor was very much concerned for the devolvement of state authority and its relationship to theological orthodoxy and religious instruction. Kant, by contrast, saw all teaching as undermined, insofar as reason itself dissolved in the face of Schultz's lessons.

Equally important here though are the forms of rhetoric that came to be associated with the powerful and the irrational, and the consequences of these different types of rhetoric. Kant believed that some rhetoric allowed for a "thinking through" of problems, while other oratory – especially religious rhetoric – did not. A rhetoric that allows us to think through public phenomena – a truly public rhetoric, in Kant's terms – could affect a positive kind of enthusiasm in the ideas generated. *Schwarmerei*, produced through mystical and the religiously fanatical presentations of divinely inspired revelations. Kant's distinction between rhetoric, and between public and private use of reason, do not immediately map onto this accounting of enthusiasm. But clearly Kant struggled with the dangers he saw as manifest in fanaticism and its generation in certain forms of speech. The question for Kant was how reason and affect were related through speech, and how to confront these more dangerous relations.

Political affect

How reason and affect relate to one another – how each aspect works to effect the other, so that we sometimes feel reasonable and at other points we might have a reasonable feeling – become a constant thread in Kant's later writings. And a recent turn in Kant scholarship has initiated a renewed interest in such philosophical knots, regarding Kant as a multidimensional thinker, beyond the critical rationalism he was so famous for.[36] Of special concern in this literature is the complex relationship of thinking to feeling that evinces itself in Kant's work. Understanding Kant's theory of emotions as a general categorization should help contextualize the shifting perspective Kant had on enthusiasm, shedding light on the relationship he saw between kinds of rhetoric and the requisite enthusiasm produced, as well as the effects such enthusiasm might have on reforming a political landscape.

According to Kant, the most general inference the human mind has with regards to the presence of an emotion is predicated on our experience of desire. For Kant, "Desire (*Begierden/appetito*) is the self-definition of the power of a subject to imagine something in the future as an effect of such imagination."[37] Over time, this predilection for the future becomes habitual. Thus, Kant explains, "Habitual sensuous desire is called inclination. Desiring without emphasis on the production of the object is wish."[38] Such habitual imaginings are indeed problematic, often creating conditions for individuals to convince themselves of the certainty and predictability (the conditionality) of the future.

That human subjectivity, by Kant's view, is conditioned by habit fits well with his broader view of rationality. But such habituality, when linked with desire, creates a pathway for unexplained preferences that cannot be conditioned by reason alone. These pathways are experienced as passions and prove problematically uncontrolled by their seeming "naturalness" with regards to repeated experiences of them. Kant explains that "the inclination which can hardly, or not at all, be controlled by reason is passion (*Leidenschaften/* affect)."[39] What Kant means by "control" pertains to the experience of the passion, as though the feeling comes unexpectedly and is unmitigated by what we would expect to feel or would want to feel. Inclination itself is not undetermined by reason, but certain inclinations arise beyond those determinations: "Inclination, which hinders the use of reason to compare, as a particular moment of choice, a specific inclination against the sum of all inclinations, is passion."[40] Thus, certain feelings (emotions) are mitigated and therefore controlled – at least a posteriori – by reason, while others (passions) remain unconditioned by our own subjectivity.

Persons' capacities to distinguish between feelings that are expected and can be "controlled" – in the manner Kant describes – and feelings that are unexpected depend on the predilection to moral interest. By way of explaining this predilection, Kant directs us to his notion of taste: "Taste makes, as it were, the transition from the charm of sense to habitual moral interest possible."[41] Taste is the ability to develop the moral feeling that is so important for how persons act in the world. But it cannot be conflated with morality, for in taste "judgment does not find itself subjected to a heteronomy from empirical laws, as it does elsewhere in empirical judging – concerning objects of such a pure liking it legislates to itself, just as reason does regarding the power of desire."[42] From this, we see latent in Kant's theory the notion that reflective judgments – those judgments that depend on known particulars that are unclassified within what one believes to be known universals – become so important to our epistemologies in that they allow us to locate reference both within and without ourselves, serving as a link between autonomous individuals and the plurality to which those individuals belong.[43]

Of utmost importance for understanding the connection between Kant's conception of taste is the notion of detachment.[44] For Kant, an individual's detachment from the world places one in the position of spectator.[45] The spectator is aware of events and experiences, but lacks concepts from which to measure them. What confronts the individual are not general categories, nor categories grounded in interest, but rather the "this" of a particular thing. There is nothing necessary about the particular – its "this-ness" is always contingent on the subjective experience of participating in the viewing of the object itself. Regarding the interest of the spectator, Kant claims, "Interest is what we call the liking we connect with the presentation of an object's existence. Hence such a liking always refers at once to our power of desire, either as the basis that determines it, or at any rate as necessarily connected with determining that bias."[46] Thus, interest is the subjective "taking-in" of the world – in observing the world, one is drawn to some aspects more than others. When we are capable of reflecting on our feeling of interest, we know we are experiencing emotion; when we are incapable of such reflection, we experience passion.

Much of what determines inclination for Kant comes from how we retrospectively categorize the pleasure of the feeling. Passion arises before the feeling and beyond the mitigation of reason. Emotion, by contrast, arises with the feeling of the experience, and – while this feeling is a surprise – that we can determine it as unexpected gives a foothold to mitigate the feeling through reason. Thus, Kant explains, "emotion is the feeling of a pleasure or displeasure at a particular moment, which does not give rise to reflection (namely the process of reason whether one should submit to it or reject it)."[47] Emotion gives opportunity for reflection, a posteriori: "Emotion is surprise through sensation, whereby the composure of mind is suspended," and then resumed. This is not the case for passion: "Passion, however violently it may present itself (as a frame of mind belonging to the faculty of desire), takes its time, and is deliberative in order to achieve its purpose. Emotion works like water that breaks through a dam; passion works like a river digging itself deeper and deeper into its bed."[48] Kant describes both emotion and passion in terms of a subject's temporal experience of these feelings. But emotion, which originates and dissolves within a recognizable moment of time, creates conditions for rethinking experiences related to the emotion. Passion, by contrast, develops as a consequence of habit and our experiences contained within those habits, thus becoming unrecognizable to reason as that feeling which has determination.

This distinction of the temporal experience of emotion compared with passion is, for Kant, central to the experience of freedom associated with reason. Emotion, by its appearance and disappearance in time, is an experience that reminds persons of the efficacy and impotency of reason. Subjective consciousness can, in the experience of emotion, be forced by such strangeness to recognize the limits of reason to determine one's own experiences of the world. And this remembrance is itself a monument to our experience of the feeling of freedom. Passion, by contrast, allows no such feeling, as passion continues to linger, preventing any remembrance of reason or cause. As Kant describes it, "Emotion produces a momentary loss of freedom and self-control. Passion surrenders both, and finds pleasure and satisfaction in a servile disposition."[49] Again, Kant returns to control and our experience of control as a predicate to freedom. But this is not to suggest that he intends to eliminate or mitigate these experiences. Rather, "To have an emotion so much under control that one can cold-bloodedly deliberate whether or not one ought to be angry (for example) appears to be something paradoxical. Passion, on the other hand, no man wishes for himself. Who wants to have himself put in chains when he can be free?"[50] To have an emotion is undeterminable, but how we engage with habits – that is, how critically we engage with them – can determine the possibility of the development and securing of a ground for passion. Without such critical engagement, habits that lead to passions may and are likely to occur, thus destabilizing reason and creating conditions for un-freedom.

Such un-freedom is precisely the problem that we saw in Kant's criticism of rhetoric as oratory. The *Schwärm* produced by oratory acts as a passion, arising out of unknown sources, directed to objects out of one's control. But Kant is not so dogmatic as to reject all public feeling:

> Emotion taken by itself alone is always imprudent; it makes itself incapable of pursuing its own purpose, and it is therefore unwise to allow it to arise intentionally. However, in projecting the morally good, reason can produce the enlivening of our will (in sermons, political speeches to the people, and speeches just to oneself) by combining its ideas with illustrations (examples) which have been attributed to the ideas; consequently it is enlivening, not as effect, but as the cause of an emotion with respect to the good, wherein reason still holds the reins, creating an enthusiasm of good intentions, which, however, must be attributed to the faculty of desire and not to the emotion as a stronger sensuous feeling (e.g. *Schwärmerei* as passion).[51]

Kant elicits the point that some emotions interact with reason, neither functioning in solitude, by which motivations emerge.[52] This emergence of dependence on the emotive and the rational is requisite to the condition of the idea of the good. And, though I must consider what counts as the good, and make judgments that allow me to acquiesce to the idea of the good, the feeling I have that can be associated with the good confirms it as that which I have come to consider as its product. Kant calls the feeling of the good enthusiasm:

> If the idea of the good is accompanied by affect (as its effect), this affect is called enthusiasm. This mental state seems to be sublime, so much so that it is commonly alleged that nothing great can be accomplished without it. But in fact, any affect is blind, either in the selection of its purpose, or if that were to have been given by reason, in the manner of achieving it. For an affect is an agitation of the mind that makes it unable to engage in free deliberation about principles with the aim of determining itself according to them. Hence there is no way it can deserve to be liked by reason. Yet enthusiasm is sublime aesthetically, because it is a straining of our forces by ideas that impart to the mind a momentum whose effects are mightier and more permanent than are those of an impulse produced by presentations of sense.[53]

While enthusiasm can be directed towards any object, it is blind as to what the meaning of those objects are. Such objects appear attractive (e.g., morally good), because we are motivated towards them. Kant, at least in these passages in his *Critique of Judgment*, seems especially concerned with delineating that there is no normative content in the feeling of enthusiasm itself. A position he will not always hold. But, connected to his discussion of *Schwärmerei*, it does at least appear that there is the normative condition that pure reason can still function to identify the conceptual object by which enthusiasm is felt, while enthusiasm may be blind, reason is not, and the two work together to help guide individuals to what counts for them as morally good.

In his early attempts to engage the subject, enthusiasm and *Schwärmerei* may appear similar, but I argue that Kant actually struggles to distinguish the one emotion, which by judgment can still function, from the other passion where rationality become unsuitable, in part because the individual can no longer locate themselves in the equation of what is being motivated and instead is consumed by the feeling for the object by which one is being motivated towards. This is why, for Kant, *Schwärmerei* becomes an "overstepping the bounds of human reason,"[54] as it no longer is clear where the "I" that experiences reason is located. Such a "delusion of wanting to SEE something beyond all bounds of sensibility, i.e., of dreaming according to principles (raving with reason),"[55] means that the individual is no longer secure in what the bounds of reason are, and why reason can and cannot be directed towards certain concepts or objects – noumenal, phenomenal, or otherwise.

Kant draws this distinction out in his accounting of the practice of judgments, and how we respond to the experience of those judgments over and in time. As is well known, Kant's critique of judgments depends on the diction between determinative and reflective judgment. Determinative judgments subsume the objects of such judgments under an already known and determined category – experienced as universal. Reflective judgments, by contrast, are the product of having been confronted with undeterminable events – at least within given categories – that must then have categories constructed for them that could, within reason, be acquiesced too by all those who it could be imagined would also confront such experiences in a similar way. Determinative judgments are, by this distinction, stabilizing; they confirm the world as that which was already known; reflective judgments, by contrast, are constructive, admitting new experiences that could not have been imagined before their experience. The problem with rhetoric is how it interacts with these two categories of judgments and our making of them. Rhetoric, as oratory, that attempts at arising the swarm, mollifies reflective judgments, making audiences believe that what has been said was already known and believed as necessary, that is, and as ontologically prior to the event of hearing the speech. Rhetoric that is not oratory harbors no such hope form its audience, and instead at least tacitly assumes that the audience may engage – and perhaps should engage – in reflective judgments regarding the ideas presented.

A prelude to politics

Attention to the shifts in Kant's thinking on enthusiasm are crucial, for they highlight just how slippery a concept this feeling proves to be. Kant engages in the performance of enthusiasm in two distinct places in his published works. The first, in the *Critique of Judgment*, where enthusiasm is juxtaposed with *Schwärmerei* as two means of establishing the grounds for feeling in evoking judgments. The second appears in *The Conflict of the Faculties*, in the essay "An Old Question Raised Again: Is the Human Race Constantly Progressing." Such texts can appear relatively far apart, as their subjects – forms of human judgment and the structure of the German University – can appear relatively disparate. Yet both discussions share an important textual similarity; each utilizes the same example of Moses's ascension from Mt. Sinai and his presentation of the beginnings of Hebrew Law.

The Moses story in question is the story of receiving and then enacting the Hebrew Law through the Ten Commandments. When Moses comes down from Sinai, he famously finds some of the Hebrew tribesmen worshiping a false idol – a calf resembling the ancient Egyptian god *Apis*. Presented with this conflict, Moses responds by initiating a potential political division. He asks those present if any will join him: "Whoever is for the Lord, to me!"[56]

This is a remarkable political moment: Moses has returned with the new law, but a law that no one yet understands or knows, only to see his people caught in a reactionary retrogradation that is itself also a violation of the new law. In the absence of Moses, Egyptian custom became the dominant theological authority again. The Hebrew people, having freed themselves from slavery, now have returned willingly to the religion that authorized such enslavement in the first place.

With Moses's return and the presenting of the new law, a fundamental conflict persists between the authority of enslavement and the logic of the revolutionary law. Moses's invitation to join him actually preforms a revolution, inviting the people to determine for themselves the authoritative law that is still as yet unknown. Only when the Levites actually take him up on his offer do we see the beginning of the violence of that enactment, for now there are those who have performed a true commitment to the new law – so faithful are they that they perform its sacrament before knowing it. This, in direct contrast to those who refuse its admission, even as others choose to entertain the promise of this new authority. The narrative continues, "The Levites gathered around him. And he said to them, 'Thus said the lord God of Israel, put every man his sword on his thigh, and cross over and back from gate to gate in the camp, and each man kill his brother and each man his fellow and each man his kin.' "[57] This evoking of the civil war has played a central part in Western political thinking, especially regarding the question of foundations, and whether violence is essential to those moments or if nonviolent revolution can muster the same effects. As Kant explains it:

> Perhaps the most sublime passage in the Jewish law is the command-ment: Thou shall not make unto thee any graven image, or any like-ness of anything that is in heaven or on Earth, or under the Earth, etc. This commandment alone can explain the enthusiasm that the Jewish people in its civilized era felt for its religion when it compared itself with other peoples, or can explain the pride that Islam inspires.[58]

This passage has within it a concentration of Kant's theory of pol-itical enthusiasm. It forces a fissure between two partial positions. In the case of Moses's presentation of the law, the fissure is between those who commit themselves to the past – in this case the religion and ideology of Egypt, and those who will commit to an unknown future. That temporality is divided between past and future, and makes the crisis of the present more palpable and enduring.

How sovereign this force of enthusiasm really is becomes a serious question here, both for how we understand the idea of law, and how we understand the role of enthusiasm in the generation of a moral law. As Kant continues,

> The same holds also for our presentation of the moral law, and for the predisposing within us for morality. It is indeed a mistake to worry that depriving this presentation of whatever could commend it to the senses will result in this carrying with it no more than a cold and lifeless approval without any moving force or emotion. It is exactly the other way around. For once the senses no longer see anything before them, while yet the unmistakable and indelible idea of morality remains, one would sooner need to temper the momentum of an unbounded imagination so as to keep it from rising to the level of enthusiasm, than to seek to support these ideas with images and childish devices for fear that they would otherwise be powerless.[59]

When Moses says this is the moment when you must decide, he is asking for a choice that itself will be sovereign, declaring the foundation of the experience of law as a moral cause; that is, Moses asks all the Hebrew people whether they will accede to this law, and thereby find presence in the future; or reject this law, and find presence in the past. He also asks whether they will consider the golden calf as a false god, even retrospectively. In this way he asks whether anyone will perform the law. Those who answer yes, exhibit political enthusiasm.

But, as moving as this enthusiasm appears to be, Kant also finds concern, for we should worry when enthusiasm becomes a weapon of the state. Kant explains, "That is why governments have gladly permitted religion to be amply rushed with such accessories: they were trying to relive every subject of the trouble, yet also of the ability, to expand the soul's forces beyond the barriers that one can choose to set for him so as to reduce him to mere passivity and so make him more pliable."[60] Kant finds a basis for contemporaneous political problems in this moment. Past authoritarian regimes – both in France, but also in Prussia – have evolved with a political logic that stands in opposition to freedom. The past has failed to uphold the moral law, and it is because of this that a new instantiation of law arrives.[61] This demands a rebellion. By identification with the law, and thus a partiality, those who have sided with the law must rebel and work against the identification of the group.

This evocation of Jewish rhetoric finds basis in several historicized particulars. The first has to do with the rhetoric of the French Revolution itself. The moment of Moses at Mt. Sinai was a sustained rhetorical symbol employed as a moment of contrition from past to future throughout the revolution.[62] Hauke Brunkhorst makes the compelling case that much of this rhetoric was an evocation of Rousseau's political ideals. But there seem to also be vibrant relations between the French rhetoric, Rousseau, and Kant.[63] Rousseau's evocation here, at least, seems to reinstate directly Kant's understanding of the political enthusiasm of the spectacle:

> It is an amazing and truly unique spectacle to see an expatriate people, without either location or land for nearly two thousand years; a people that has been modified, oppressed, and mingled with foreigners for even longer; … and yet preserving its customs, its laws, its morals, its patriotic love, and its initial social union when all its links appear broken. The Jews give us this amazing spectacle.[64]

Here Rousseau notes the palpable qualities of a revolutionary moment in history where acquiescence to a moral law, or in this case the new laws, attenuates an endurance in the future beyond all conflicts. It is an enthusiasm above the power of leaders, war, conquest, and assimilation that allows the law to persist. Kant's evocation of the moment at Mt. Sinai as a moment of enthusiasm builds from this Rousseauian position. The spectacle of Sinai, like the spectacle in France, points to the power of enthusiasm within politics, as a stretching point from which to build allegiances.

The second structural point of reference with regards to Kant's evocation of the Jews comes from contemporaneous theoretical debates within Prussian Enlightenment thought, the much-noted pantheisms debate. Following on Mendelssohn's position regarding the use of the Old Testament as a philosophical, rather than religious historical text, Kant aligns himself with Mendelssohn, and his position regarding Spinoza's debates that dominated the intellectual landscape in Prussia during the 1780s. This turns out to be both philosophical and a political position, at least as far as Kant was concerned. In the first part of the conflict of the actualities, in the essay entitled "The Philosophy Faculty versus the Theology Faculty," Kant lays out the basis for competing authority claims regarding moral arguments, and the necessary relationship each body of claims are made within and their relationship to governments action. As theology is linked toward governmental positions, the story goes, critical education becomes less possible if the structuring of the university privileges the theology faculty. If, by contrast, the philosophy faculty was raised to the dominant position in the hierarchy, it would allow free and more requisite development of thought, eventually collapsing hierarchy altogether. This, Kant explicates, through a comparison between the bible as philosophy and the Bible as a theological text, and his exploration of such phenomena in the third critique, as well as the essay "An Old Question Reconsidered," fit within this framework and are further explorations of Mendelssohn's thesis.

Each of these evocations, the rhetoric of the revolution, as well as the pantheism debate, provide clear context for the direction Kant intends his notion of political enthusiasm to be directed. Kant seemed to believe enthusiasm a necessary functioning in the political practice of constitution and revolution. But, unlike the pantheists, including Jacobi and Hamann, among others, Kant would not concede to the nihilistic frame that truth-claims and historical consciousness depended on retrograded logic. To make a philosophy of the future, as Kant intended to do, was to uphold freedom as the answer to the fundamental question: "What can be hoped for?" Political enthusiasm was the feeling that came when one had answered "freedom," as spectators of the revolution who perceived the moral cause would have to have done.

The path of revolution

How does such thinking translate when it appears in a political context (especially the context of revolution)?[65] Attention to revolution as revealed makes sense of the necessity of spectators' enthusiasm for the event-ness of revolution as meaningful and purposive.[66]

Given the above observations, revolution seems to depend on witnesses that recognize the event-as-rupture, beginning a new history. Yet how are we to understand the mechanics of recognizing revolution? Kant seems to argue that public consciousness of a political event cannot seemingly engender reorientation if such happenings are regarded as the norm.[67] It seems that the usual account of revolution as a speeding up of history reveals the need to account for who's history is speeding up, and how that acceleration occurs.[68] Here we should consider how identity may matter as much as speed in the experience of the disruption of history.

Evidence for reading of revolution as dependent on spectators who are themselves distinct from the event of revolution as it unfolds presents itself in the metaphoric content of political "revolution."[69] The metaphor of revolution draws force from its original scientific usage as a term employed to denote the movement of celestial bodies. Copernicus's *De Revolutionist Orbium Coelestium* (1543) gave the term definition.[70] His thesis regarding the heliocentric pattern of the rotation of bodies explained the regularity of those bodies' return to the same place along predictable circular pathways – their revolutions around the sun. What had been standard in previous models was the problematic of celestial retrograding, wherein forward-moving bodies appeared all of a sudden to pause and/or move backward along otherwise regular pathways. The appeal of Copernicus's hypothesis was in providing a simplified model of celestial bodies, moving the center of their evaluation and measurement from the point of view of the stationary earth to the view from the sun. This allowed for more regularity in the explanation of those otherwise inexplicable events. What remained unexplained in the geocentric model of heavenly spheres, and which Copernicus's heliocentric model famously solved, was the problem of appearances.

This Copernican "revolution" was not simply an explanation for what the universe was, both in appearance and reality, but it also acted to dislodge those theological arguments that had relied on the geocentric narrative; the replacement of the divine with human understanding. What Copernicus allowed was an explanation of celestial patterns despite appearances, that yet made sense of these appearances. Human understanding of reality now depended more on itself than anything for an accounting of the world. The relocation of the center of the universe in the heliocentric model not only cosmographically displaced the theological center, it replaced it with a model of the human imagination, and one in full display of its power.

Significant here for the borrowing implicit in the modern political metaphor of revolution is the division of appearances from the understanding. No longer is it the case, after Copernicus, that the world can be said to appear as it really is. In providing a celestial model despite appearances, Copernicus uncovered a view that depended on the location of the spectator. What made this model so significant was his account of what the spectator was observing, and not what was objectively occurring in the universe from a divine view, for now the earth too was a celestial body in motion. As Koselleck puts it, "In the same way stars run their circular course independent of Earthly men, while at the same time influencing or even determining their lives ... revolutions do take place above the heads of their participants, but those concerned remain imprisoned in their laws."[71]

Copernicus's notion of revolution explained the cyclical return of celestial bodies. How does this translate into the metaphor of revolution employed to explain political phenomena? From the point of view of revolutionaries, it is the account of a new order, despite previous appearances, that proves significant. Revolutions, at least form the view of revolutionary actors, reveal that whatever logic may have existed in the previous order was somehow out of step. When recognized as legitimate, revolutions help to make sense of an order in the world. Change of government is a break – overthrowing of an established order by those who had been subject to it. What matters for the completion of a successful revolution is the new form of order revealed in the break – in the event-ness of the break. Things turned upside down means confusion and disorder. Revolution, as part of a pattern that can be determined, is anything but disordered. Just as Copernicus revealed a model that explained an ordered pattern despite appearances, so too do all modern political revolutions uncover an order that had been masked by an *ancien régime*. Following on the Copernican logic implicit in the metaphor, revolution is order revealed.

The mechanism on which that revelation occurs depends on spectators' capacity to abstract themselves from the trajectory of that ordering. The idea of return, implicit in the *re-* of revolution, is the revelation of an order, of its "coming again." The path on which the events occur is now no longer hidden – spectators, who were separated from it, are no longer. In this way, the idea of political

revolution is fundamentally metaphorical. In order for that metaphor to reveal itself, there must be someone who is not part of the
revolution who can still yet bear witness to it. Only such a witness
can reveal if the images of revolution come from the past or from
the future.[72]

What is enthusiasm that it operates to distinguish the spectator
from the revolutionary actor, and yet gives definition to the revolution as such? As we have started to see, Kant's own accounting
of enthusiasm becomes valuable in that context as a resource to
explain moral progress, and relatedly how the project of a philosophical education helps in human progress against unjust governments. Kant advocates here for a restructuring of the university and
its role as critic of the state. In this context, Kant saw enthusiasm
as the posing of the question of opening – an affective sign that
all systems of order have the capacity to be (re)opened. This was
a dangerous claim, both politically and philosophically. Kant was
asserting that it might be possible, through the enthusiasm of spectators, to define the moral progress of humanity. Implied here was
that not all states and governments would necessarily find themselves in line with such progress.

Here we might remind ourselves of how Kant understood signs,
and the measure of the immeasurable. Foucault is especially useful, when he explains, "Kant says that this Enlightenment has
a *Wahlspruch*: now a *Wahlspruch* is a heraldic device, that is, a
distinctive feature by which one can be recognized, and also a
motto, an instruction that one gives to oneself and proposes to
others."[73] Kant is looking for a *Wahlspruch*: "What then is this
instruction? *Aude sapere*: 'dare to know' 'have courage, the auda-
city, to know.' "[74] Courage here becomes an object – that which one
must have, must be possessed by, in order to know. The activity
Kant sees in Enlightenment – not the knowing that comes from it,
but the entry into the Enlightenment – is the daring. And here we
might suggest that lurking beneath this daring is not the affect of
courage, but of enthusiasm. That enthusiasm allows us to dare.

For Kant, such enthusiasm proves to be the link between witness and revolutionary, revealing the unfolding of time through
the actions of one to another. If one feels oneself to be a spectator, in Kant's sense of that word, then one has already found
oneself in a unique experience. It is the particularity of the event

that inspires Kant. The "surprise" Kant associates with emotions (*Affekten*) is only possible in the experience of the particularity of an event, allowing individuals access to a conception of the good, via *enthusiasm*, that transcend familiar experiences.

For Kant, the revolution is itself a sign of a future history that he aligns with normative predictions regarding the transformation of the age. As he argues it,

> The Revolution which we have seen taking place in our own times in a nation of gifted people may succeed, or it may fail. It may be so filled with misery and atrocities that no right-thinking man would ever decide to make the same experiment again at such a price, even if he could hope to carry it out successfully at the second attempt. But I maintain that this revolution has aroused in the hearts and desires of all spectators who are not themselves caught up in it a sympathy which borders almost on enthusiasm, although the very utterance of this sympathy was fraught with danger.[75]

Of utmost importance here for understanding the distinction, and yet dependence, between the revolutionaries and the moral interest of the spectator-enthusiasts is Kant's notion of detachment.[76] The spectator is aware of events and experiences, but – importantly – lacks originary concepts from which to measure them. Alienation establishes the position of spectator. That is, the events present themselves to the spectator as alien. What confronts the individual-as-spectator are not general categories, nor categories grounded in interest, but rather the "this" of a particular happening. This is what makes the spectator necessary for the experience of an "event" as such, and not simply common daily routine. If one feels oneself to be a spectator, in Kant's sense of that word, then one has already found oneself in a unique experience. It is *the particularity* of the event that inspires Kant.

This is not to say the experience of enthusiasm is somehow unmitigated. Rather, its mitigation is precipitated by our conception and experience of the moral. As Kant explains, "True enthusiasm is always directed exclusively towards the ideal, particularly towards that which is purely moral (such as the concept of right), and it cannot be coupled with selfish interests."[77] Kant sees reason and enthusiasm interacting through the mediation of the moral good, unencumbered by the totalizing and stultifying effects of self-interest. The spectator experiences enthusiasm at that moment which, above all others, makes clear the conception of the good, both as a feeling of that which is good, and by that which can be reasoned as good. The interrelation between feeling and thought confirms the experience of enthusiasm, but as that which is always already partial (the spectator experiences the world differently from the actor).

Kant models this account of political spectators on Copernicus's hypothesis.[78] As Kant asserts in this same essay on enthusiasm, "The planets, as seen from the Earth, sometimes move backward, sometimes forward, and at other times remain motionless. But seen from the sun – the point of view of reason – they continually follow their regular paths as in the Copernican hypothesis."[79] For Kant, enthusiasm is the feeling of order revealed through reason – a feeling that is as vibrant in the experience of the reality of the Copernican hypothesis as it is in political revolution. Kant labeled his own rethinking of the limits of reason – what we can know for certain of the world is limited to how the world appears to us as spectators of it, a second Copernican revolution.[80] Yet spectators must not be limited to mere appearances: "Of course, man can see, but not foresee with certitude for the divine eye there is no distinction in this matter; because, in the final analysis, man requires coherency according to natural laws, but with respect to his future free actions he must dispense with this guidance or direction."[81] Enthusiasts – as political spectators – witness change, and can, from a distance so to speak, also see the future that revolutionaries uncover.

The enthusiast is capable of distinguishing what is witnessed – theirs is a sense of externality. Thus, Kant articulates a clear distinction between the political ramifications of enthusiasm and revolutionary spirit. For many onlookers, in Prussia and elsewhere, the Jacobin activities were seen as clearly abhorrent, and came to stand as symbolic of the evils of the revolution itself. For Kant, such evaluations were too single-minded – missing the greater significance the revolution held – not just for the French, but for Europeans and beyond. Kant drew a clear distinction between these swarms of Frenchmen and their motivations for political revolution, on the one hand, from those of the onlookers who witnessed the revolution as a world-historical event, on the other. While the violent Jacobin activists could be easily described as *Schwärmer*, true witnesses of the revolution might best be described as feeling enthusiasm. As he puts it, "the attitude of the onlookers as it reveals itself in public while the drama of great political change is taking place ... openly express universal yet disinterested sympathy for one set of protagonists against their adversaries, even at the risk that their partiality could be of great disadvantage to themselves."[82] This conditionality of the *Schwärmer* leads Kant to articulate the experience of political enthusiasm. For Kant enthusiasm for the revolution – not the violence, but the ideals that motivate such action – stand as a sign of human progress. By this account, spectators play a role in the constitution of events as events, and their reactions are central to the definition of that experience. The spectator-enthusiasts Kant describes are invested in the normative grounds that initiate their enthusiasm. This is not to say that they see the violence of the revolution as morally justifiable. But it is to say that they find themselves inspired by the outcomes towards which others have engaged, and the future history revealed therein. As Foucault explains, "Thus Enlightenment must be considered both as a process in which men participate collectively and as an act of courage to be accomplished personally."[83]

Kant takes on a more complex notion of the distinction between *Schwärmerei* and enthusiasm, than the traditional *Aufklarung* position. Kant articulates a clear distinction between the political ramifications of enthusiasm and *Schwärmerei*. According to his view, the Jacobins in France can readily be viewed as political *Schwärmerei*. Caught up in the fervor of the times, these crowds were like a swarm, adhering this way and that to the sway of public opinion as dictated by elites.[84] And, it should be noted, while no definite date can be given for Kant's reflections on the revolution, we do know that his ideas predate October 1794 by "some time" – and given no direct reference to the Terror, can reasonably be thought to have been penned sometime before news of those events reached Germany in 1793. Interestingly, by the time of publication, Kant makes no effort to mitigate his view, despite public knowledge of the increasingly violent events in France.[85] Kant makes a clear distinction between these swarms of Frenchmen and their motivations for political revolution from those of the onlookers who witness the revolution as a world-historical event. As he puts it, "the attitude of the onlookers as it reveals itself in public while the drama of great political change is taking place ... openly express universal yet disinterested sympathy for one set of protagonists against their adversaries, even at the risk that their partiality could be of great disadvantage to themselves."[86] By this account, spectators play a role in the constitution of events as events, and their reactions are important to the experience of the events, just as *Schwärmerei* in part depends on the anti-*Schwärmerei* for diagnosis, here too, on historical grounds, political *Schwärmerei* require acknowledgment in order to have articulation of their condition.

This leads Kant to articulate the experience of political enthusiasm. Here I say "experience" because it is unclear whether Kant himself is attempting to articulate a category of expression, or if he is indeed expressing his own feeling and the reason for that feeling regarding the motivations and legitimacy of the revolution as such. In either case, Kant is quite clear that the revolution has within it sign of a future history that he aligns with normative predictions of the transformation of the age, it is as much a revolution for Kant as for the French. The experience of enthusiasm, especially in political contexts, depends on both a partiality and a dialogistic with alternative enthusiasms (e.g., *Schwärmerei*). But to what end? Why does Kant develop this threshold between these twin concepts? The *Schwärmer* have already charged ahead, without access to the rhetoric that would allow a "thinking through"; the enthusiast as spectator witnesses the charge, but can, from a distance, also see the ideal object that has motivated such a swarm. This witnessing provokes the feeling of enthusiasm. And, in political contexts, the outcome is a partiality that finds itself wanting the universal.

What are the results of that wanting? Here we see a clear shifting of ground, and what begins as a standing still becomes a motion towards action. I want to use this moment as a break, and one that Kant himself is initiating. Rather than reading the essay on enthusiasm and revolution as a benign statement of testimony, I suggest that we take Kant seriously that this is an essay "fraught with danger." If we turn to the text as a performance, and a performance of political enthusiasm, we see some profound differences. Instead of the control and calculation that Kant seemed so committed to through much of his earlier reflections on emotion and rationality, this enthusiasm essay becomes Kant's opportunity to perform a revolutionary opening. Reading Kant as performing enthusiasm, rather than describing it, should be our entry into what is so potent, and so dangerous, regarding his thinking, and open us to the true significance of the feeling of political enthusiasm.

Exhausted enthusiasm

What makes Kant's model so significant, at least according to this new reading, is that spectators become actors. This is the hope of essay "An Old Question Raised Again: Is the Human Race Progressing?" The very question invites action, and the rhetoric throughout the text creates a threshold for us as readers to cross. We move from being readers who see the revolution as a concept that may happen, to those who stand at the "border of enthusiasm," to those who might risk crossing it, and finally those who must.

The revolutionary psychology depends on the hope that the revolution is never complete – and in this way may want to always see other revolutionary movements as joinings. For what revolutions establish is that a normative break with society's own constitutive values and a politics that maintains those values is possible. What receives less focus in contemporary discourse is how to establish a government from such a break – how to begin the impossible project of concreteness. Modern democratic politics has endured this paradox – indeed in may be constitutive of what democratic polity is. But it should not be though constitutive of what revolution is, lest democratic societies come to see other revolutions only ever as already their own.

Taking seriously Kant's struggle with the concept, we find, in his "enthusiasm" essay, an opportunity to read a much more radical notion of political engagement, one that collapses enthusiasm and *Schwärmerei*. This collapse makes sense of the revolutionary potency of enthusiasm – the distinction of the false binary between spectators and actors, revealed through the metaphoric content in modern political conceptions of revolution. Here we see clear tensions implicit in the role of spectators of revolutions, and that these spectators must necessarily condition revolutions according to already-existing normative structures. The political project of revolutions is to uncover historical normative orders. This is always a risk, fraught with danger. Yet only through such uncovering can we explain the perception of new legitimate normative orders, and thus to speak of history as innervating for those who live within it. The metaphoric content implicit in political revolution reveals the centrality of enthusiasm to its definition.

Notes

1 For the most recent work on Kant's reading of this concept, see, for example, Robert Doran, *The Theory of the Sublime from Longinus to Kant* (Cambridge University Press, 2015); Robert Clewis, *The Kantian Sublime and the Revelation of Freedom* (Cambridge University Press, 2009); and Jeffrey Lomonaco, "Kant's Unselfish Partisans as Democratic Citizens," *Public Culture* 17, no. 3 (2005): 393–416.

2 Immanuel Kant, *Critique of Judgment (Kritik der Urteilskraft)*, trans. Werner S. Pluhar (Hackett, 1987), from Ak. 5:272 (p. 132 in the English ed.).

3 As noted in the previous chapter, enthusiasm is derived from the Greek ἐνθουσιασμός – originally meaning something like being possessed by a god.

4 Jean-Francois Lyotard, *Enthusiasm: The Kantian Critique of History* (Stanford University Press, 2009).

5 Immanuel Kant, "A Renewed Attempt to Answer the Question: 'Is the Human Race Constantly Improving?'" excerpted from *The Conflict of the Faculties*, reprinted in *Kant: Political Writings*, ed. H. S. Reiss (Cambridge University Press, 1970), p. 182.

6 For a discussion of the battle at Valmy as symbolic of the genesis of nationalist ideology, see Rogers Brubaker, *Nationalism Reframed: Nationhood and the National Question in the New Europe* (Cambridge University Press, 1996), pp. 1–4, esp. fn 1. For an historical accounting of the battle at Valmy and its significance for the French Revolution generally, see François Furet and Denis Richet, *La Révolution Française* (Hachette, 1965), p. 185.

7 Johann Wolfgang von Goethe recounts the battle at Valmy in his *Campaign in France in the Year 1792*, trans. Robert Farie (Oxford University Press, 1849), pp. 77–85.

8 Regarding the concept of the nation and its development, see E. J. Hobsbawm, *Nations and Nationalism Since 1780* (Cambridge University Press, 1990); Rogers Brubaker, *Citizenship and Nationhood in France and Germany* (Harvard University Press, 1992); David Miller, *On Nationality* (Oxford University Press, 1995); and Maurizio Virolo, *For Love of Country: An Essay on Patriotism and Nationalism* (Clarendon Press, 1995). For a recent diagnosis of the

relationship between the concept of "the people" and "the nation," see Margaret Canovan, *The People* (Polity Press, 2005). It is of central importance to theorists of nationalism that the patriotism evinced in the battle at Valmy occasions an alignment between militaristic duty and political attachment. For a critique of this alignment, and the sustained enmity in instances of political attachment generally, see Margaret Canovan, "Patriotism Is Not Enough," *British Journal of Political Science* 30 (2000): 437. For the central positions regarding the moral dangers involved in patriotism, see George Kateb, "Is Patriotism a Mistake?" *Social Research* 67, no. 4 (Winter 2000): 904–24; and Alasdair MacIntyre, *Is Patriotism a Virtue?* (University Press of Kansas), esp. p. 15.

9 Immanuel Kant, "An Old Question Raised Again: Is the Human Race Constantly Progressing?" in *The Conflict of the Faculties* (*Der Streit Der Fakultäten*), trans. Mary J. Gregor (University of Nebraska Press, [1979] 1992), p. 152. English Translation is my own. For another translation, see Kant, "A Renewed Attempt to Answer the Question: 'Is the Human Race Constantly Improving?'" p. 182.

10 Though, it should be noted, there is a growing literature that is attempting to reread Kant as a valuable resource for relating emotions and political motivations. For an overview of this recovery, see Pauline Kleingeld, "Kantian Patriotism," *Philosophy and Public Affairs* 29, no. 4 (2000): 313–41. Also important are Philip Fisher, *The Vehement Passions* (Princeton University Press, 2002); Howard Caygill, "Kant and the Relegation of Passions," in *Politics and the Passions, 1500–1850*, ed. Victoria Kahn, Neil Saccamano, and Daniela Coli, (Princeton University Press, 2006), pp. 217–30; and Robert Solomon, *A Passion for Justice: Emotions and the Origins of the Social Contract* (Rowman & Littlefield, 1995).

11 For the two traditional views in this debate, see John Rawls, "Themes in Kant's Moral Philosophy" (1983), and Habermas, "Morality and Ethical Life: Does Hegel's Critique of Kant Apply to Discourse Ethics?" (1983), both reprinted in *Kant and Political Philosophy: The Contemporary Legacy*, ed. Ronald Beiner and William J. Booth (Yale University Press, 1993). For an overview of Habermas's and Rawls's inheritance (and perhaps misappropriation of Kant's thought), see Thomas McCarthy, "Kantian Constructivism and Reconstructivism: Rawls and Habermas in Dialogue," *Ethics* 105 (October 1994): 44–63; and Rainer Forst, *Kontexte der Gerechtigkeit: Politische Philosophie jenseits von Liberalismus und Kommunitarismus* (Suhrkamp, 1994). For a critical account of Habermas's misunderstanding of Kant, see Tracy B. Strong and Frank Andreas Sposito, "Habermas's Significant Other,"

in *The Cambridge Companion to Habermas*, ed. Stephen K. White
(Cambridge University Press, 1995), pp. 277–82. Recent critical
appraisals of Kant on rhetoric include Simone Chambers, "Rhetoric
and the Public Sphere," *Political Theory* 37, no. 3 (2009): 323–
50 at p. 325; and Bryan Garsten, *Saving Persuasion: A Defense of
Rhetoric and Judgement* (Harvard University Press, 2006), p. 86.

12 From Kant's "Beantwortung der Fage: Was ist Aufklärung?" first
published in *Berlinischen Monatsschrift* (December 1783), p. 37.

13 From Kant, *Critique of Judgment*, fn 63 Ak 5:328 (p. 198).

14 Garsten, *Saving Persuasion*, p. 88.

15 This reference comes from Habermas's reflections on what he sees as
a perplexing shift in Foucault's thinking on Kant, as discussed in his
"Foucault's Lecture on Kant," published in *Thesis Eleven* 14, no. 4
(1986), trans. Sigrid Brauner and Robert Brown. Here Habermas com-
plains that Kant makes the mistake of entangling his critical project.

16 Jürgen Habermas, *Between Facts and Norms: Contributions to a
Discourse Theory of Law and Democracy*, trans. William Rehg
(Polity Press, 1997), p. 768.

17 For a discussion of translation issues regarding the concept of enthusiasm, see Peter Fenves, *A Peculiar Fate: Metaphysics and World
History in Kant* (Cornell University Press, 1991), pp. 241–3; also
see Peter Fenves, *Raising the Tone of Philosophy: Late Essays by
Immanuel Kant, Transformative Critique by Jacques Derrida* (Johns
Hopkins University Press, 1993). For discussions of Kant's understanding of moral *Schwärmerei*, see Henry Allison, *Kant's Theory
of Freedom* (Cambridge University Press, 1990), p. 155. Regarding
Habermas's misunderstanding of Kant and the relationship between
value skepticism and enthusiasm, see Strong and Sposito, "Habermas's
Significant Other."

18 For a discussion of the complexity of these philosophical shifts in
Kant's thought, see Richard Velkley, *Freedom and the End of
Reason: On the Moral Foundation of Kant's Critical Philosophy*
(University of Chicago Press, 1989).

19 As Kant explains it, "Metaphysics answers the first question, morals the
second, religion the third, and anthropology the fourth. Fundamentally,
however, we could reckon all of this as anthropology, because the first
three questions relate to the last one." From the *Lectures on Logic*,
trans. J. Michael Young, ed. Allen W. Wood (Cambridge University
Press, 2004), p. 538 (p. 25 in *The Jäsche Logic*).

20 Kant's worry of a rhetoric that turns persons into machines presages
the use of a similar rhetoric employed for mobilization in the wake
of the Weimar Republic – see Jeffrey Herf's discussion in *Reactionary*

Modernism: Technology, Culture, and Politics in Weimar and the Third Reich (Cambridge University Press, 1984), esp. his accounting of the rhetoric of *"stahlernde Romantik,"* pp. 195–7.

21 Again, for a discussion of translation issues regarding the concept of enthusiasm, see Fenves, *A Peculiar Fate*, pp. 241–3; and Fenves, *Raising the Tone of Philosophy*.

22 Peter Fenves, "The Scale of Enthusiasm," *Huntington Library Quarterly* 60, nos. 1–2, Enthusiasm and Enlightenment in Europe, 1650–1850 (1997): 120.

23 For further discussions on this point, see Jane Kneller, "The Failure of Kant's Imagination," in *What Is Enlightenment? Eighteenth-Century Answers and Twentieth-Century Questions*, ed. James Schmidt (University of California Press, 1996), pp. 456–60; see also Jane Kneller, *Kant and the Power of Imagination* (Cambridge University Press, 2007), esp. chap. 5; and G. F. Munzel, *Kant's Conception of Moral Character: The Critical Link of Morality, Anthropology, and Reflective Judgment* (University of Chicago Press, 1999).

24 Immanuel Kant, *Critique of Practical Reason*, trans. Mary Gregor (Cambridge University Press, 1997), Ak. 5:85–6 (p. 73).

25 Kant, *Critique of Judgment*, Ak. 5:275 (pp. 135–6).

26 Ibid. For some sources that read "enthusiasm" as a disease (and would have influenced Kant in this regard), see, for example, John Locke's *An Essay Concerning Human Understanding* (1698) in *The Works of John Locke: A New Edition, Corrected, in Ten Volumes*, vol. 3 (Thomas Tegg, 1823), pp. 149–50. See also Michael Heyd, *"Be Sober and Reasonable": The Critique of Enthusiasm in the Seventeenth and Early Eighteenth Centuries* (E. J. Brill, 1995), esp. ch. 7, "The New Medical Discourse and the Theological Critique of Enthusiasm," pp. 191–210. As I illustrate in the previous chapter, for all the disagreement among Kant and the popular philosophers, there was much in common regarding their condemnation of *Schwärmerei*. For a similar accounting, see Anthony La Vopa, "The Philosopher and the *Schwärmer*: On the Career of a German Epithet from Luther to Kant," *Huntington Library Quarterly* 60, nos. 1–2, Enthusiasm and Enlightenment in Europe, 1650–1850 (1997): 86.

27 See Susan Shell, *The Embodiment of Reason: Kant on Spirit, Generation, and Community* (University of Chicago Press, 1996), pp. 106–32. On the relationship between philosophy and mysticism in eighteenth-century Germany, La Vopa notes, "Schwärmerei became the handy foil in philosophy's efforts to establish itself as the public use of reason." See La Vopa, "The Philosopher and the *Schwärmer*," p. 86.

28 For Kant's critical accounting of Swedenborg, see "Dreams of a
   Spirit-Seer Elucidated by Dreams of Metaphysics," in *Theoretical
   Philosophy, 1755–1770*, trans. and ed. David Walford and Ralf
   Meerbote (Cambridge University Press, 2003). For a critical discussion of Kant's early failure to adequately engage with Swedenborg's
   ideas, see Hartmut Böhme and Gernot Böhme, "The Battle of Reason
   with the Imagination," trans. Jane Kneller, in *What Is Enlightenment?
   Eighteenth-Century Answers and Twentieth-Century Questions*, ed.
   James Schmidt (University of California Press, 1996), pp. 444–9.
29 As Walford notes, Kant, in a letter to Charlotte von Knobloch (August
   10, 1763), seems initially rather taken with Swedenborg's accounts of
   the spirit world. As Kant saw it, the event of Swedenborg's predictions
   regarding the Stockholm fire "seems to me to have the greatest eviden-
   tial force; it really does deprive every doubt (of Swedenborg's powers) of any justification' (Ak 10:46/*Theoretical Philosophy*, p. 453).
   Why Kant shifted his view from positive to pejorative has not been
   accounted for, though Kant's growing preoccupation with judgment
   may point the way to his logic that, in the end, Swedenborg – even if
   correct in his assessment of the spirit world – presents his visions in a
   way that undermined the very act of judgment.
30 From Kant's "Dreams of a Spirit-Seer" (Ak 2:361) p. 347, excerpted
   from a section entitled "Ecstatic Journey of an Enthusiast (*Schwärmer*)
   through the Spirit-World."
31 Immanuel Kant, "An Answer to the Question: 'What Is
   Enlightenment?'" in *The Conflict of the Faculties*, reprinted in
   Kant: Political Writings, ed. H. S. Reiss (Cambridge University
   Press, 1970), p. 42.
32 Ibid.
33 Kant, *Critique of Judgement*, p. 328 fn 63 (p. 198 in English ed.).
34 Ibid.
35 See Immanuel Kant, "Review of Schulz's Attempt at an Introduction
   to a Doctrine of Morals for All Human Beings Regardless of Different
   Religions," in *Practical Philosophy*, trans. and ed. Mary Gregor and
   Allen Wood (Cambridge University Press, 1999), Ak 8: 10–14. For a
   detailed discussion of Schulz's import to these debates in Prussia, see
   Michael J. Sauter, "Preaching, a Ponytail, and an Enthusiast: Rethinking
   the Public Sphere's Subversiveness in Eighteenth-Century Prussia,"
   Central European History 37, no. 4 (2004): 544–67, esp. pp. 550–60.
36 On Kant as a radical thinker, see Tracy Strong, *Politics without
   Vision* (Chicago University Press, 2012). For a general review of the
   "emotional turn" in Kantian philosophy, see Kelly D. Sorensen, "Kant's
   Taxonomy of the Emotions," *Kantian Review* 6 (2002): 109–28.
   See also Nancy Sherman, *Making a Necessity of Virtue: Aristotle and*

Kant on Virtue (Cambridge University Press, 1997); Paul Guyer, *Kant and the Experience of Freedom* (Cambridge University Press, 1993); and Allen Wood, *Kant's Ethical Thought* (Cambridge University Press, 1999). In political theory, the "emotional" rethinking of Kant was very much inspired by Hannah Arendt, *Lectures on Kant's Political Philosophy*, ed. Ronald Beiner (Chicago University Press, 1982). For relevant accounts in political theory, see Linda Zerilli, "We Feel Our Freedom: Imagination and Judgment in the Thought of Hannah Arendt," *Political Theory* 33, no. 2 (2005): 158–88; Laura Hengehold, *The Body Problematic: Political Imagination in Kant and Foucault* (Penn State University Press, 2007); and Anthony J. Cascardi, "Communication and Transformation: Aesthetics and Politics in Kant and Arendt," in *Hannah Arendt and the Meaning of Politics*, ed. Craig J. Calhoun and John McGowan (University of Minnesota Press, 1997), pp. 99–131.

37 Immanuel Kant, *Anthropology from a Pragmatic Point of View* (Anthropologie in pragmatischer Hinsicht, 1798; 7: 119–333), ed. Oswald Külpe (354–6). Königlichen Preußischen (later Deutschen) Akademie der Wissenschaften (ed.), 1900–, Kants gesammelte Schriften, Georg Reimer (later Walter De Gruyter). I've made use of the following to accompany my translations: Immanuel Kant, *Anthropology from a Pragmatic Point of View*, trans. Victor Lyle Dowdell (Southern Illinois University Press, 1978), p. 155.

38 Kant, *Anthropology from a Pragmatic Point of View*, p. 155.

39 Ibid.

40 Ibid., p. 172.

41 Kant, *Critique of Judgment*, p. 229.

42 Ibid.

43 Kant claims, "Because the subject has this ability within him, while out-side him there is also the possibility that nature will harmonize with it, judgment finds itself referring to something that is both in the subject himself and outside him." Kant, *Critique of Judgment*, p. 229.

44 See Guyer's account of the "dialectic of disinterestedness," in *Kant and the Experience of Freedom*, p. 48.

45 This should not be confused with Smith's account of the "impar-tial spectator." Where Smith is concerned with assessing the *moral value* of another's actions from a detached and impartial position, Kant is concerned with the individual's aesthetic experience of an event for themselves (and the assessment of how others might have experienced such an event). It is the particularity of the event that inspires Kant. For an excellent recent account of Smith's "impartial spectator" from his *The Theory of Moral Sentiments* (reprinted in Great Books in Philosophy series, Prometheus Books, 2000); also see

Charles Griswold, *Adam Smith and the Virtues of Enlightenment* (Cambridge University Press, 1999). For accounts of Smith's influence on Kant, see Manfred Kuehn, *Scottish Common Sense in Germany, 1760–1800: A Contribution to the History of Critical Philosophy* (McGill-Queen's University Press, 2001).

46 Kant, *Critique of Judgment*, p. 45.
47 Kant, *Anthropology from a Pragmatic Point of View*, p. 155.
48 Ibid., p. 156.
49 Ibid., p. 174.
50 Ibid., p. 157.
51 Ibid., p. 158.
52 See Sorensen, "Kant's Taxonomy of the Emotions."
53 Kant, *Critique of Judgment*, p. 132.
54 Ibid., pp. 85–6.
55 Ibid., p. 135.
56 Exodus, 32:27.
57 Exodus, 32:27.
58 Kant, *Critique of Judgment*, Ak 5:274 (p. 135).
59 Ibid.
60 Ibid.
61 Problem of biblical authority, cf. 23, section 291, Exodus 32; on scripture as rational symbol, see section 294, R 73, Moses Mendelssohn.
62 For an accounting of Moses in the rhetoric of the French Revolution, see Michel Vovelle, *Die Französiche Revolution: Sozial Bewegung und Umbruch der Mentalitäten* (Fischer, 1985) pp. 130–1. See also Hauke Brunkhorst, *Solidarity: From Civic Friendship to a Global Legal Community* (MIT Press, 2005), pp. 61–4.
63 For an accounting of Kant's relationship to Rousseau, see Velkley, *Freedom and the End of Reason*; and Richard Velkey, ed., *The Unity of Reason: Essays on Kant's Philosophy by Dieter Henrich* (Harvard University Press, 1994).
64 Jean-Jacques Rousseau, "Political Fragments," in *Social Contract: Discourse on the Virtue Most Necessary for a Hero – Political Fragments and Geneva Manuscript*, trans. Judith R. Bush, Roger D. Masters, and Christopher Kelly, vol. 4, *The Collected Writings of Rousseau* (University Press of New England, [1913] 1994), pp. 33–4.
65 An earlier version of this argument appears in Andrew Poe, "Enthusiasm and the Metaphor of Revolution," *Law, Culture and the Humanities* 10, no. 3 (2014): 324–35.
66 I base this on a reading of Kant's essay "A Renewed Attempt to Answer the Question: 'Is the Human Race Constantly Improving?'"

67 Arendt argues, "It certainly is not conspiracy that causes revolutions ... The loss of authority in the powers-that-be, which indeed proceeds all revolutions, is actually a secret to no one, since its manifestations are open and tangible, though not necessarily spectacular." Hannah Arendt, *On Revolution* (Viking Press, 1963), p. 260. By her account, revolutions always depend on their publicity, even from the beginning.

68 See Reinhardt Koselleck, "Representation, Event, and Structure," in *Futures Past: On the Semantics of Historical Time* (Columbia University Press, 2004), pp. 105–15.

69 In, "Historical Criteria of the Modern Concept of Revolution," Koselleck starts has genealogy of the concept of revolution with attention to this metaphoric content (pp. 45–6). My reading is a continuation of his. See Reinhardt Koselleck, "Historical Criteria of the Modern Concept of Revolution," in *Futures Past: On the Semantics of Historical Time* (Columbia University Press, 2004), pp. 39–55.

70 For a detailed account of the context of Copernicus's project and the language of revolution in scientific discourse, see Thomas S. Kuhn, *The Copernican Revolution: Planetary Astronomy in the Development of Western Thought* (Harvard University Press, 1957); and, more recently, Robert Westman, *The Copernican Question: Prognostication, Skepticism and Celestial Order* (University of California Press, 2011).

71 Koselleck, "Historical Criteria of the Modern Concept of Revolution," p. 46.

72 Kant uses such Copernican language to engage the problem of evaluating moral progress within a revolution. See Kant, "A Renewed Attempt to Answer the Question: 'Is the Human Race Constantly Improving?'" As he explains, "There are three possible forms which our prophecy (signs from a future history) might take. The human race is either continually regressing and deteriorating, continually progressing and improving, or at a permanent standstill, in relation to other created beings, at its present level of moral attainment (which is the same as continually revolving in a circle around a fixed point)" (p. 178).

73 Michel Foucault, "What Is Enlightenment?" in *The Foucault Reader*, ed. Paul Rabinow (Pantheon Books, 1984), p. 35.

74 Kant, "An Answer to the Question: 'What Is Enlightenment?'" p. 54.

75 Kant, *Conflict of the Faculties*, p. 182.

76 See Guyer's account of the "dialectic of disinterestedness," in *Kant and the Experience of Freedom*, p. 48.

77 Kant, *Conflict of the Faculties*, p. 183.
78 Arendt was well aware of this metaphorical origin, and was worried regarding its misuse. See, for example, Arendt, "The Meaning of Revolution," in *On Revolution*, p. 42.
79 Kant, *Conflict of the Faculties*, p. 180.
80 See Henry Allison, *Kant's Transcendental Idealism* (Yale University Press, 2004), pp. 35–8. See also N. R. Hanson, "Copernicus' Role in Kant's Revolution," *Journal of the History of Ideas* 20, no. 2 (1959): 274–81. For Kant's own thinking on celestial bodies, see Immanuel Kant, *Allgemeine Naturgeschichte und Theorie des Himmels* (Johann Friedrich Petersen, 1755).
81 Kant, *Allgemeine Naturgeschichte und Theorie des Himmels*, p. 151.
82 Kant, "An Old Question Raised Again: Is the Human Race Constantly Progressing?" p. 152.
83 Foucault, "What Is Enlightenment?" p. 35.
84 Kant, *Conflict of the Faculties*, p. 143.
85 See Mary Gregor's introductory essay to Kant's *Conflict of the Faculties*; also, for what has become the traditional reading on Kant regarding these matters, see Lewis W. Beck, "Kant and the Right of Revolution," *Journal of the History of Ideas* 32 (1971): 411–22.
86 Kant, *Conflict of the Faculties*, p. 182.

3

Our unknown zeal: or what goes wrong when we seek political relief

Suddenly it grows dark, the wind is howling loud,
And heaven, sky, and land appear a frightful jumble.
Toward the stars flies up the ship, then plunges down again,
Sails on washed by waves, with naught but ruin all around,
Here lightning, there thunder, the whole ether storming,
Swell towering up on swell, and cloud on cloud,
The ship is shattered, and I ... nothing happened to me,
Because I only watched the storm from shore.
                                    – Johann Joachim Ewald, "Der Sturm" (1755)

Terra firma is not the position of the spectator but rather that of
the man rescued from shipwreck; its firmness is experienced wholly
out of the sense of the unlikelihood that such a thing should be
attainable at all.
                                    – Hans Blumenberg, *Shipwreck with Spectator: Paradigm*
                                    of a Metaphor for Existence (1979)

Views of enthusiasm

Enthusiasm, no matter its form or historical moment, seems to
transform those who are subject to it. From religious meetings to
mental disorders, enthusiasms relay experiences that introduce the
subject to themselves anew. Almost despite context, enthusiasm
looks to be a sort of "transportation" of subjects, traversing the
condition of alienation and isolation, and arriving at exhalation
and transcendence. Enthusiasts appear rescued, whether by God or
one of its many substitutes. Or at least, so the story usually goes.

Kant's reading of enthusiasm allows us to make sense of this
affective force, and its relocation in politics. Of course, Kant was

not unaware of all the serious dangers enthusiasm posed to political life. For him, the biggest danger was that the enthusiast may, at first glance, appear irrationally committed to a political cause, willing to do anything and everything for its success. Or at least, this is what critics of enthusiasm might see in the enthusiast's fervor.

I am especially worried that perceiving enthusiasm as always the negative double of some healthy and pure rational politics creates a system of hierarchies that mistakes the enthusiastic for something it is not. This distorted reflection of enthusiasm becomes an ideological and politicized manifestation of domination, carving pathways by which power can structure its own negated and alienated self. This casting out of the degraded twin has become the victor's view of enthusiasm. Perhaps there is another view?

Here I ask that we turn to an underlying logic of capture on which political power sometimes relies. Exploring how power works to capture passions may help us make sense of how "political" enthusiasm truly operates in our experience of it. As a ground for this exploration, I turn to the thoughts of Hannah Arendt, and her effort to defend a form of enthusiasm as necessary for public discourse.

Crucial to this reading has been Arendt's *Lectures on Kant's Political Philosophy* and her inheritance of what she takes as his theory of spectatorship.[1] In her now famous lectures, Arendt seems to uncover a theorization of politics unlike any other in Kant's thinking. For her, Kant's ideas on history reveal a new politics in the form of political judgment, and specifically the judgment of spectators on events of world historical significance. As Arendt explains,

> Kant said explicitly that he was not concerned with the deeds and misdeeds of men that make empires rise and fall, make small what was formerly great and great what was formerly small. The importance of the occurrence (*Begebenheit*) is for him exclusively in the eye of the beholder, in the opinion of the onlookers who proclaim their attitude in public. Their reaction to the event proves the "moral character" of mankind.[2]

Here Arendt reflects directly on the famous passage of Kant's where he claims – so she reads – that it is the witnesses' enthusiasm that determines the historical significance of action and events. Here, the judgment of the spectator, revealed in the enthusiasm that manifests itself in their experience of their judgment, becomes the basis for Kant's political thought, at least as Arendt understands it.[3]

The instantiation of the event is as the spectator perceives it. The motion that comes from the event being perceived is what Arendt names as action. As she reflects on it, "to act, in its most general sense, means to take an initiative, to begin (as the Greek word *archein*, 'to begin,' 'to lead,' and eventually 'to rule,' indicates), to set something into motion (which is the original meaning of the Latin *agere).* Because they are *initium*, newcomers and beginners by virtue of birth, men take initiative, are prompted into action."[4] Action here is conceived as constitution, a beginning that, in the way it begins, entails the possibility of the continuation of new beginnings. Such a beginning could not be conceived of prior to its manifestation. And we feel the significance of this beginning because of our enthusiasm. Indeed, here lies the eventfulness of the act – our enthusiasm allows us to see that the act was unexpected. Arendt continues,

> It is in the nature of beginning that something new is started which cannot be expected from whatever may have happened before. This character of startling unexpectedness is inherent in all beginnings and in all origins. Thus, the origin of life from inorganic matter is an infinite improbability of inorganic processes, as is the coming into being of the Earth viewed from the standpoint of processes in the universe, or the evolution of human out of animal life.[5]

Actions are beginnings, but only beginnings as origins, modeled on the origin of life itself. We need the spectator, and the spectator's feeling of enthusiasm, to navigate this landscape, and to confirm new beginnings. An unstated, but central thesis, underlying Arendt's thinking here is that we can identify natality with our enthusiasms. Indeed, it is to this end that Arendt's thinking may be so absolutely crucial to how we conceive of the political significance of enthusiasm.

It is perhaps worth reminding ourselves here that Arendt is usually associated with a positive reading of Kant's politics and his notion of revolutionary enthusiasm. And, while I am certainly sympathetic to Arendt's ultimate aims, I worry that she herself inherits a binary notion of enthusiasm, one that turns political enthusiasm into an apolitical affect, trapping enthusiasm in a logic that subverts it to a utopian vision of public action. Read this way, her argument contains a dangerous seed that works to undermine the very claims I think make her view of enthusiasm so sympathetic. Paying attention to this contrasting logic, this Arendtian reading of enthusiasm may inadvertently help facilitate the collapse of political enthusiasm in contemporary political discourse, lending serious intellectual resources to its depoliticization. The consequence of such a trapping is that Arendt ends up reduplicating a malformed view of enthusiasm that undermines her very project of political action and natality. Perhaps we should then push against this binary logic underlying Arendt's thinking on enthusiasm, and the culmination of that logic in a kind of depoliticization. By delineating varieties of the binaries of enthusiasm, we might form a new ground for the rethinking of enthusiasm.

In the course of this chapter, I offer an exploration of the delicate limits of political enthusiasm and its apolitical collapse. I begin by outlining Arendt's thinking on revolution and enthusiasm. I continue with an account of spectatorship, including Arendt's own attempts to rethink political "vision" and her use of visual metaphors. This bridge is crucial, for how Arendt understands enthusiasm as the affect of spectatorship has become a centerpiece of her political thought, as well as a dominant conception of political enthusiasm in modern political discourse. And, while spectatorship may be one vessel by which enthusiasm appears to enter the political imagination, I show that this is a malformation of enthusiasm, hampered by relief, as Arendt's accounting of the affect of relief highlights her thinking on the potency and impotency of spectatorship. I then conclude with a critique of possession that troubles her claims on enthusiasm, opening up the possibility of a more performative reading of Kant than she seems to allow.

Standpoints

In the contemporary world, so much of politics depends on their public presentation, and thus the standpoint of the spectator who bears witness to the political event. The action of the event is an action that creates, and part of what it creates is the standpoint from which one could bear witness to the unexpected in it.

Arendt continues: "The fact that man is capable of action means that the unexpected can be expected from him, that he is able to perform what is infinitely improbable. And this again is possible only because each man is unique, so that with each birth something uniquely new comes into the world. With respect to this somebody who is unique it can be truly said that nobody was there before."[6] The standpoint that allows one to bear witness to action also allows one to see a somebody, a doer of great deeds, where before there was an anonymous person.[7] The eventfulness of action depends, it later seems, on an enthusiasm that the onlooker feels, both for the action and for the great actor who is capable of such eventfulness (and part of that enthusiasm is a link between the actor and the spectator).

Here we face a problem of disposition. The only standpoint from which one could possibly conceive of such origins is not a posteriori, but only ever from within. The dialectic that exists between the doer of the action – that somebody – and those onlookers who might feel the greatness of the action, seems a somewhat suspicious desire. Here, despite her many efforts, Arendt appears very close to a fascist imaginary, one that celebrates the greatness from the position of ordinariness. We might wonder how that desire to be "somebody" operates in this dialectic between the doer and the audience. Is there a supplanting of self and other in witnessing great deeds? Does one who acts do so with foreknowledge of such greatness? At first glance, this would seem an impossibility, especially given everything Arendt insists about beginnings. And yet, we might start to worry that, in the desire to be somebody rather than nobody, too much is at stake. In the doing of deeds, the desire to be somebody has the consequence of a logic of utility, carried in from behind the action, and setting the terms of its reception. How contagious is the desire to be somebody? How deep does this logic run in how we view our own actions, as well as the actions of others?

All events, which is to say all acts that would count as true actions for Arendt, are only ever such if they live up to the standard of new beginnings. The novelty of the action defines it as event; enthusiasm is the feeling that allows us to trace this novelty. Thus, Arendt exclaims, "the new therefore always appears in the guise of a miracle."[8] If we think of the miracle as the event without human cause, and in that way a happening that becomes an object of wonder, we can begin to envision the newness that Arendt associates with action. In the miracle of the event, we find the source of what Arendt later, drawing from Kant, names as the enthusiasm of the onlookers (for it is for them that the action is miraculous). The onlookers are so crucial to this framing because of their standpoint, for how we understand standpoint, it seems, explains how we understand action (this all too central phenomenon in Arendt's own political theory). Indeed, as Arendt later argues,

> Is the general standpoint merely the standpoint of the spectator? (How serious Kant was about the enlargement of his own mentality is indicated by the fact that he introduced and taught a course in physical geography at the university. He was also an eager reader of all sorts of travel reports, and he – who never left Königsberg – knew his way around in both London and Italy; he said he had no time to travel precisely because he wanted to know so much about so many countries.) In Kant's own mind it was certainly the standpoint of the world citizen. But does this easy phrase of idealists, "citizen of the world," make sense? To be a citizen means among other things to have responsibilities, obligations, and rights, all of which make sense only if they are territorially limited. Kant's world citizen was actually a *Weltbetrachter*, a world-spectator.[9]

At issue here, by Arendt's reading, is how we understand the scope of the spectator's view, and especially those spectators who retain the standpoint that allows them to conceive of new historical beginnings. Following on from her reading of Kant, it appears as though the spectator becomes the *Weltbetrachter*, those with a view of the world (and here, in this moment, the general viewpoint becomes synonymous with an enthusiastic worldview).

Spectatorship thus becomes linked to action through enthusiasm. Nowhere is this link more crucial than in the idea of revolution. For it turns out that how we understand the significance of revolution, and the affective ground by which revolution comes to be justified, requires a sympathy manifest in enthusiasm. As Arendt exclaims,

> Kant's actual theory in political affairs was the theory of perpetual progress and a federal union of the nations in order to give the *idea* of mankind a political reality. Whoever worked in this direction was welcome. But these ideas, with whose help he reflected on human affairs in general, are very different from the "wishful participation

bordering on enthusiasm" that caught the spectators of the French Revolution and "the exaltation [of] the un-involved public" looking on in sympathy "without the least intention of assisting." In his opinion, it was precisely this sympathy that made the revolution a "phenomenon ... not to be forgotten" – or, in other words, that made it a public event of world-historical significance. Hence: What constituted the appropriate public realm for this particular event were not the actors but the acclaiming spectators.[10]

Arendt famously argues that political spectators are necessary for the constitution of public spaces, providing the terms by which action can be understood as novel re-authorings of political realities. From her early work in *The Human Condition,* to her later reflections in her *Lectures on Kant's Political Philosophy*, Arendt revealed a deep attention to spectatorship. Lurking beneath this theory rests a confusion regarding the place of enthusiasm in the political action, relying on a binary between spectators and actors that counters the potency of her thinking on action which she develops earlier in her *Vita Activa*. While Arendt clearly struggles against the pathology of the passivity of relief in *The Human Condition*, she inadvertently advocates for relief as the central affect of spectatorship. In attempting to liberate spectatorship, Arendt inadvertently binds it to the affect of relief.

By turning to enthusiasm as the affect that authorizes public appearances, we see more clearly the politicality Arendt meant to capture with her theory of spectatorship (and also the limit of spectatorship as mere viewing). While Arendt presents us with the pathology of relief, she herself has a theory of passive action caught by a logic of "waiting" (the spectator lies in wait to cast "judgment"). Here, we should worry, for Arendt seems – at the very moment when it is desired – to give up on the politics of enthusiasm, even as she claims it. The separation of enthusiasm and fanaticism may result in the depoliticization of both concepts, resulting in ideological thinking that pretends to be political.[11]

Flash forward: another revolution

Rather than lingering on ancient modes of revolution, I will cut to a more contemporary frame, highlighting the significance of Arendt's thinking for recent theorizing on ideology and revolution.

Take for example the so-called Arab Revolution – across the Maghreb, from Tunisia to Egypt and Libya, and beyond. This revolution has elicited both happiness and fear from those who have witnessed it. As Seyla Benhabib recently exclaimed: "The Arab revolutionaries are struggling for democratic freedoms and joining the contemporary world after decades of lies, isolation, and deception ... transformative hopes have been kindled; the [old] political and economic orders have been shown to be fragile and susceptible to change."[12] Hopes kindled – this seems to be the mantle of revolution today. Such nonviolent struggles for democratic freedoms stand against corrupt and tyrannical regimes. Yet such declarations also reveal an important problematic: Benhabib's pronouncement of "joining" points to an already-existing normative order. This "joining" characterizes revolution as a conservative project, preserving a normative structure already in place for those enthusiastic spectators who bear witness. If all that is happening in the Arab world is a "joining," then that revolution – and the many other "democratic revolutions" since 1989 – may simply be the continuation of a history of *the* Western revolution of liberty. Here spectators may be hoping too much for validation of their own revolutionary projects.

Benhabib's observations prompt the question of what precisely "revolution" as a progressive phenomenon might be.[13] Are all instances we name as "revolutions" always part of a previously formed and ongoing total revolution?[14] If we think this is right, then we may be admitting an insidious democratic pathology; a desire for *our* own self-confirmation in the foreign struggle of another – a kind of political voyeurism.[15] If we think not, and there is good reason to answer this way, then there should be some defense of revolution we can offer as progressive. By this I mean simply that if revolution were progressive, it would not depend on an already-existing normative order (liberal democracy); rather, it would reveal a progression from one historical reality to another, admitting the possibility of radical breaks in history.

Much historical evidence of political affect points to ways in which revolution is best viewed as progressive, beginning a new history, and not as "joining" an already existing order. This difference is implicit, though often ignored, in Copernicus's metaphoric language of revolution inherited in the modern use of the political concept.[16] Copernicus offered an account of the heavens as pathways for planetary revolutions. Such a model depends on an understanding of the location of the witness, uncovering the earth and humanity as outside the center of the universe. In Copernicus's model, the witness is as central to the idea of revolution as the thing in revolution itself.

Similar logics, translated in this metaphor, reside in political revolution. There too, revolutions require spectators to annunciate their parameters. Yet what differs from the Copernican model is the presence of political interests for both spectators and revolutionaries. For revolutionaries, their actions reveal their understanding of a new history that they already imagine themselves within; for those spectators who legitimate them, revolutions re-form history to include such new expressions.[17] This doubleness is only possible when spectators are distinct from revolutionaries.[18] As Arendt explains it, the enthusiasm of the spectator stands as a sign of progress, revealed in the revolution as historical event, rather than as routinized norm.[19]

But how can we read such signs? And what follows from that reading? My turn to the metaphor of revolution is meant to highlight aspects of revolution absent in the rhetoric of "joining," most especially this expression of enthusiasm. This is significant insofar as theorists who speak of revolution as joining rely on conceptions of enthusiasm to legitimate their models, even as their thinking moves against it.

Much recent theorizing on the question of revolution – including Benhabib's own remarks on the Arab Spring – begin with Arendt's notion of revolution as a moment of natality.[20] What revolution allows is the chance to begin, and this novelty is only possible when those who will begin are free from external, unrepresentative, and private constraints. As Arendt asserts, "That men are equipped for the logically paradoxical task of new beginning and hence beginnings – that the very capacity for beginning is rooted in natality, in the fact that human beings appear in the word by virtue of birth."[21] This fundamental notion of political actors as "beginners" connects with the very modern notion of novelty – of seeking out that which is genuinely new – and rests at the center of Arendt's rethinking of revolution.

Revolution, by Arendt's view, is the beginning of new foundations, and it is the security of those foundations that seem so significant to her as a modern political problem. If it was a mere desire for novelty that conditioned revolution, the stability of the revolution as such – as some new upheaval – would lose its normative force. As Arendt explains it, "The experience of foundation, combined with the convention that a new story is about to unfold in history, will name men 'conservative' rather than 'revolutionary,' eager to preserve what has been done and to assure its stability rather than open for new things, new developments, new ideas."[22] At some point novelty must have taken hold of those who had it as an idea to begin *the* revolution. And yet once it was within their grasp to conserve that idea, it also seems right to suggest that they are no longer "revolutionaries." The moment of revolution is very short here – all too short.

Arendt moves quickly between the categorization of the events of revolution and those (once-revolutionaries) who propel them. While such revolutionaries may be unstable as a category of persons, shifting between radical progressivism and conservatism, their instability need not inhibit the functioning of the revolution. Indeed, it is significant from Arendt's view that revolutions always have the potential to transfer the revolutionary spirit that operates within it onto new actors, thus unfolding the revolution as a public (and politicizing) idea. This movement between revolution and revolutionary, and the shifting ground on which one locates answers to the question "For whom?" A revolution is actually an upheaval, contains a powerful political force, one that we can identify through the feeling of enthusiasm. The idea of revolution maintains its fundamental powers through its threat to already existing institutions; that is, not as an act of pure conservation – despite Arendt's insistence – but as a progressive force that uncovers something not yet known to the nonrevolutionary world. We identify this change with political enthusiasm.

What matters so much to the definition of revolution, both for the initiator of the revolutionary event, but also for the spectator of it, is that it is experienced as *an event*.[23] Arendt is fully aware of the place of the spectator in this definition. Reflecting on Kant's theory of judgment, Arendt explains, "The importance of the occurrence (*Begebenheit*) is ... exclusively in the eye of the beholder, in the opinion of the onlookers who proclaim their attitude in public."[24] What Arendt leaves too little explained is how precisely the actors and spectators depend on each other for this important *event-ness* of revolution. She implies that revolutionaries themselves see their project as a "beginning" – an opening up of a new politics. But if revolution requires spectators for categorization as "event," as Arendt describes it, then it would seem this new politics has already begun. Unless revolutionaries are themselves divided, seeing their project as both beginning and having already begun, it would seem that Arendt's logic here is inversed. That is, it might appear, from the revolutionaries' perspective, that revolution is an apolitical phenomenon, having already been decided. If revolution is really a "beginning," and thus – for Arendt – a political phenomenon, it would seem to be so not for revolutionaries, but rather for spectators, taken by surprise in the event-ness. Spectators here seem essential for understanding the political nature of revolution. Arendt seems to imply that revolutionaries can only regard their project as having already begun, and require spectators to rethink it as a beginning, and thus as a politics.

That revolution is only ever possible through judgments offered by an audience of spectators leaves open a space for understanding revolution as "joining." If the terms and rhetoric with which spectators understand events fall within the purview of their own revolutionary inheritance, there may be incentives to regard the revolution as one's own. Yet in this way, spectators would only ever see revolutionary actions within their own history, and precisely not as events or disruptions. Crucial here is that revolutions – where spectators see actions as already within their own histories – are then precisely not events; revolution as joining mistakes one's own interests as primary and stable. What first appeared as revolution is not destabilizing, but rather self-validating. In this pathology, spectators are the true revolutionaries, despite their own stability.

Remember, from Kant's perspective, revolution was precisely the sort of event for which no right could be authorized.[25] No state could authorize forceful rebellion, even under the imagined paradox of a failed or failing state. As Kant claimed, "Force, which does not presuppose a judgment having the validity of law, is against the law; consequently the people cannot rebel except in cases which cannot at all come forward in a civil union."[26] These famous passages are often read as Kant's rejection of revolution as a valuable normative concept on which to maintain a politics. As Lewis Beck puts it, "In place of revolution, Kant favors evolution."[27] But Beck's view already depends on our reading revolution as something that can or should have right as its foundation. Kant looks to be an anti-revolutionary thinker in these passages because he does not defend the right of the revolutionaries to rebel against a state, no matter the justice of that state. The only way to confront injustice, by this view, is by the incremental reform of the state itself.

Yet Kant seems more focused here on the state's relationship to the revolution and its legality, and less to what constitutes a revolution as such. Indeed, what Kant may very well be arguing is that precisely in order for a revolution to be *a revolution* (and not some pretense to it) it must be such as to threaten the very viability of state structure – already extralegal, and beyond the very political limits of the state. If there is any place for conservation here, it is in that which has not yet been achieved.

Defining revolution as always beyond the state, Kant points us to the need for some additional authority that constitutes the legitimacy of revolutionary action. For Kant, it is the potentiality of a shared future between spectators and actors, rather than a shared revolution, which serves as a basis for such authority, and in fact motivates the performativity of enthusiasm within revolution. Both actors and spectators stand intimately connected, in search of ideational and normative definition. While this project begins in revolutionary action, it can only continue to actualize – and thus receive definition – in the enthusiasm of the spectators.[28]

Though Kant offers us some important tools for transforming epistemologies (from the knowledge structure and opinions formed through the use of moral judgments to those produced from political judgments), he remained less explicit on the necessity of these transformations to the maintenance of a well-functioning democracy.[29] Though Arendt was very much aware of the dangers of democratic rule,[30] her unique portrait of what democracy could be – and the kind of freedom that emerges form that political arrangement – are worth serious reflection, especially within the context of assessing the dangers of commingling moral and political judgment.[31] For Arendt, judgment proves to be such a crucial faculty for democratic politics because it gives ground to the opinions of citizens who, more often than not, evince political action as spectators of world events.[32] Arendt hoped to develop a concept of judgment that citizens could employ to situate themselves within the political arena, independent of rules and mandates that might be asserted from external authorities, and instead grounded on each individual's own capacities as thinking, feeling, autonomous beings. Following from Arendt's reconceptualization of the experience of political life, I argue that a more complete portrait of the value of political judgment in a theory of democratic citizenship begins to emerge.

By Arendt's account, *political* judgment is the faculty that enables us to think for our community in dialogue with ourselves (distinct from the dialogue we engage in between our *selves*).[33] In making such judgments, we represent the thoughts of others and incorporate them into a dialogue with our own thoughts on events – particularly on those events where moral categories escape us. It is not simply thinking (in which I engage the plurality with myself), but another faculty that aids in my engaging this second plurality (the plurality with others); "representative" thought engages my imagined plurality of others. For Arendt, political judgment is "the faculty of thinking the particular; but to think means to generalize, hence it is the faculty of mysteriously combining the particular and the general."[34] Moral judgment cannot navigate from the particular in this way. The other "I" in this dialogue (the second "I" that Arendt calls "conscience") has with it moral standards that it takes as universals that are known. Moral judgment then, must unite known universals with unknown particulars. In contrast, political judgment finds known particulars and tries to find unknown (and impossible) universals. Arendt adds, "[judgment] is relatively easy if the general is given – a rule, a principle, a law – so that the judgment merely subsumes the particular under it. The difficulty becomes great if only the particular be given for which the general law has to be formed."[35] Judgment is then only a political activity when individuals turn *not* to universal objective norms in order to evaluate events, but instead look towards the political community and the intersubjective space that marks that community as the location of these unknown universals. In making political judgments where no universal is given, moral statements can play no part. That is, we derive no acceptable results from such judgments, from which we can base our actions in the world. This is Arendt's reformulation of Kant's theory of reflective judgment; in making reflective judgments of the world, we have no rule to think with; instead, we develop a rule for ourselves.

What, then, is the relationship between political judgment and thinking? Though thinking may be a moral activity, it is itself not the same as judging. For Arendt, "Thinking deals with invisibles, with representations of things that are absent; [political] judging always concerns particulars and things close at hand. But the two are interrelated in a way similar to the way consciousness and conscience are interconnected."[36] Accordingly, thinking and moral judgment are important for distinguishing how an individual is in the world – it is, indeed, how an individual decides to be in the world. The conscious "I" engages with its moral self, and moral judgments are the consequence of this engagement. A related process occurs when the act of thinking is turned towards the political world, and political judgments emerge from this process. But, again, they cannot be the same faculty, as the acts themselves are unique:

> If thinking, the two-in-one of the soundless dialogue, actualizes the difference within our identity as given in consciousness and thereby results in conscience as its by-product, then judging, the by-product of the liberating effect of thinking, realizes thinking, makes it manifest in the world of appearances, where I am never alone and always too busy to be able to think.[37]

Judging (as political judging) draws us into the political world where we are a unique self from the self of thinking. Thus, thinking both engages morality and adds to political judgment; *thinking* is the link between moral judgment and political judgment.

But because of this, thinking also highlights why both types of judgment must remain distinct as categories. Moral judgment pertains to my relationship to myself. Political judgment, in contrast, pertains to my relationship with my community – understood here as a represented plurality. For Arendt, there is a distinction between moral judgment and political judgment: we must be able at one point to be participants in the plurality we maintain with ourselves (in moral judgment), and at another moment in the plurality we maintain with others (in political judgment). That is, for democratic politics to function well, we should be able to rule and be ruled by ourselves, and also be able to rule and be ruled by others. The maintenance of this first type of plurality requires moral judgment; the second type of plurality depends on political judgment.

Importantly here, commingling these two types of judgment would force the loss of both experiences of plurality that Arendt's theory seems to desire.

A fantasy without relief

On October 4, 1957, humanity became alienated from itself ... or at least so Hannah Arendt has argued the point. The Soviet launching of Sputnik-1 (Спутник-1) was, according to Arendt, an event "second in importance to no other."[38] As she narrates it:

> In 1957, an Earth-born object made by man was launched into the universe, where for some weeks it circled the Earth according to the same laws of gravitation that swing and keep in motion the celestial bodies – the sun, the moon, and the stars. To be sure, the man-made satellite was no moon or star, no heavenly body which could follow its circling path for a time span that to us mortals, bound by Earthly time, lasts from eternity to eternity. Yet, for a time it managed to stay in the skies; it dwelt and moved in the proximity of the heavenly bodies as though it had been admitted tentatively to their sublime company.[39]

The significance of this launching is not immediately obvious from her accounting, for it is not based on technological progression, or the aesthetic sublimity of such an accomplishment. What matters according to Arendt, was the affective response this event provoked, and what is revealed in that response. She continues:

> This event, second in importance to no other, not even to the splitting of the atom, would have been greeted with unmitigated joy if it had not been for the uncomfortable military and political circumstances attending it. But, curiously enough, this joy was not triumphal; it was not pride or awe at the tremendousness of human power and mastery which riled the hearts of men, who now, when they looked up from the Earth toward the skies, could behold there a thing of their own making. The immediate reaction, expressed on the spur of the moment, was relief about the first "step toward escape from men's imprisonment to the Earth."[40]

The reaction felt by so many persons in response to this achievement was not joy or happiness or accomplishment or awe, but – oddly – relief. Arendt's accounting of relief has a certain anxiety to it – a judgment about those who should or could feel one way (joyful, full of awe, or wonder, or some other positive affective response), but do not. Instead of joy, Arendt speculates that the dominant feeling which came to characterize this transformative moment is exactly that we would associate with the removal of pain and thus a negation of a negative affect.

Why is this a problem? What is the danger Arendt hopes to highlight for us, that she would begin her accounting of political action and the complexities of the "human condition" with such an enigmatic narrative? The danger here lies in the experience of novel events. Arendt is so concerned at this moment – and hopes that we will share in her concern – because of what is revealed in feeling relief. We might consider feeling relief, phenomenologically, as the experience of release. Arendt's rhetoric throughout her prologue reflects this anxiety. Rather than spectators conceptualizing events as transformative, captured by new modes of thinking and being in the world, Arendt presents us with spectators who can only conceptualize events according to preexisting troupes. To feel relief at a moment where we might feel joy confuses the eventfulness of this new beginning. It is as though spectators had viewed humanity's momentous entry into space not as a beginning but as a continuation, being released from a previous incarceration (in this case, our imprisonment on earth). Even worse, this escape from prison will continue to haunt us, forming the affective ground on which we understand humanity's entry into the universe beyond the earth.

That haunting is part of the problem from Arendt's view, for it establishes a temporal frame of eventfulness that is always already a priori. To always encounter events determinatively means a fundamental limiting on our conception of freedom. In fact, the very name "sputnik" might coincidentally signal this determinative and imprisoned logic, as the root of the Russian is literally "satellite," but figuratively "guardian"; the feeling of relief that humanity has launched a guardian into space, reveals a certain lurking pathology that Arendt subtly calls our attention to. For a theorist of action that seems so bound up in beginnings, we should worry about an a priori framing that always already forestalls such novelty in the historical moments she critiques.

My concern here is not so much to criticize Arendt for her inexactness, nor to make light of Arendt's thinking, but rather to uncover the complexity and incongruity of this anxiety. If political theorists point to anxiety as the site of political pathologies, those desires we have that, in how we desire them or the practices we set out to desire them, result in their opposite, we might be as careful in how we annunciate those anxieties as how we respond to them.[41]

In an era of economic insecurity, political terror, and state repression, the desire to feel simple relief is perhaps greater now than it has ever been before. Yet the affect of relief is a pathological one, and worth being cautious, both for its causes and its consequences.[42] Arendt, however, seems subtly well aware of this danger and throughout her theorizing makes numerous attempts to call contemporaries to this problem. And yet how we might respond politically to relief is not left clear.

The problem of relief is, Arendt implies, caught up in our political – or apolitical – experience of necessity. What Arendt seems most worried about is the free acceptance of the feeling of necessity when it is itself unnecessary, feeling relief, when one could feel joy – thinking determinately, when one could think reflectively. This desire to take on necessity when it is unnecessary is itself pathological from her perspective. As she herself argues the point, "with the rise of society, that is, the rise of the 'household' (*oikia*) or of economic activities to the public realm, housekeeping and all matters pertaining formerly to the private sphere of the family have become a 'collective' concern. In the modern world, the two realms indeed constantly flow into each other like waves in the never-resting stream of the life process itself."[43] The consequence of that flow – and the magnification of the realm of the household is the spreading of the sphere of necessity.

And it is precisely on these grounds, where Judith Butler, among others, has drawn concern. Arendt's reliance on ancient Greek conceptions of necessity, and the exclusion of women, children, the poor, and the foreign, among others, from the public sphere of freedom seems a deep chauvinism that destabilizes her thinking. As Butler explains, Arendt "quite emphatically distinguishes the private sphere as one of dependency and inaction from the public sphere as one of independent action," asking "How are we to think about the passage from the private to the public, and do any of us leave the sphere of dependency 'behind' even as we appear as self-standing actors within established public spheres?"[44] Butler's concern is for the logics of dependence that Arendt seems bound to. What consequences does such dependence pose for our imagination, and specifically for how we think about political spaces and their appearances?

One profound consequence of this contagious depoliticizing necessity in Arendt's thinking is it seems to make any rebellion of the powerless against the powerful impossible. Again, as Butler explains,

> When the poor come streaming into the streets, they act from necessity, from hunger and need, and they seek to "achieve such liberation [from life's necessities] ... by means of violence." As a result [Arendt] tells us, "Necessity invaded the political realm." The political movement that is motivated by hunger is understood to be motivated by necessity and not freedom, and the form of liberation it seeks is not freedom, but an impossible and violent effort to be freed from the necessities of life.[45]

Any such liberation the powerless might strive for, any such action that might originate from a fugitive and paradoxical moment of overruling, seems apolitical – at least as Butler reads Arendt. Butler continues, "It would seem to follow that social movements of the poor are not seeking to relieve the poor of poverty, but of necessity, and that, as [Arendt] clearly states, the violence between men for whom the necessities of life are already taken care of is 'less terrifying' than the violence undertaken by the poor."[46]

And yet there is a paradox here between Arendt's hope for a political action that is free from necessity and Butler's defense of the politicality of the powerless. The conflict that exists between these arguments rests on an abstract register that neither author remains in. Instead, as each moves into phenomenological accounts of political action in and through public spaces, their account of the appearance of political action become remarkably similar. This is because lurking beneath their concerns, as well as their portrait of political action, are shared notions of the affective logics that each relies on to make sense of when assemblies form and become political. The moment when a body assemblies and demonstrates political force is exhibited through the affect of enthusiasm.

Precarious spaces

The danger we face in Arendt's notion of relief is that it seems to carve out a psychic space that protects precarity. On the one hand, those who feel relief at the escape from the earth, and forces outside human agency, may be subjecting themselves to the echo of their own imprisonment on earth. And yet, on the other hand, in denying such reactions, Arendt forecloses the possibility of political transformations that might relieve the power imbalances and hierarchies established through the occupation of this planet by the human species. It is as though we, by Arendt's view, are only free insofar as we choose to reside within the frame that is given to us to be human already, and not to new frames that might allow for a rethinking of the human, as well as human dominance/a re-setting of human and nonhuman equalities. This holding-on-to-the-earth-as-"prison" logic may passively maintain political inequalities that perpetuate logics of domination.

Central to Arendt's thinking on necessity and the body is the experience of pain. As she explains:

> Absence of pain is no more than the bodily condition for experiencing the world; only if the body is not irritated and, through irritation, thrown back upon itself, can our bodily senses function normally, receive what is given to them. Absence of pain is usually "felt" only in the short intermediate stage between pain and non-pain, and the sensation which corresponds to the sensualists' concept of happiness is release from pain rather than its absence.[47]

Here we see the central claim that relief and happiness are caught up in stabilizing existing power. Not being able to recognize that division is the central pathology of the contemporary expanse of the social that Arendt is so well known and criticized for.

Relief, then, becomes the foundation of the social. By Arendt's accounting, once upon a time politics and freedom was possible because boundaries were possible. Only with a clear boundary between what was necessary (what one had to do) and freedom (what a person could choose to do) is politics itself a distinct sphere of activity. To be political once meant to be outside the home, so the boundary between the two mattered for the construction of the public space. Now, this is not so easily distinguished. As Arendt explains, "In our understanding, the dividing line (between the public and private realms) is entirely blurred, because we see the body of peoples and political communities in the image of a family whose everyday affairs have to be taken care of by a gigantic, nationwide administration of housekeeping."[48] The line that once stood between these distinct spheres (and their determinations in necessity and freedom), has now become blurred.

What is this "blur"? How does it occur and what results from its appearance? The "blur" obscures our vision of these two worlds, and especially what divides them. The consequences of this obscuring are not that we "lose sight" of them completely – not that they stop existing – but rather that the line between them becomes harder to determine. Arendt worries this has manifold results, including the confusion of what is public and what is private, both in our judgments and in the judgments of others. But the blur also becomes an obscuring of political vision – for no longer is it clear from where We can make free judgments, and that all are in agreement about the position from where one makes such judgments. Moreover, the blur becomes productive of a unique space all its own – the social.[49]

The confusion of the blur is what Arendt names as the social, where the nation state becomes the site of a "gigantic housekeeping," mixing politics and home. Arendt worries that this admixture results in a fundamental confusion. For *societas* is not simply a "coming together" for any specific purpose as such, but in fact was originally a joining with others to either a) rule or b) commit a crime. Indeed, this contradictory framework of the "social" world obscures quite a lot. If we follow Arendt here, we might rightly worry that we are mistakenly forming communities which cannot distinguish between being lawful and being criminal.[50] To be free once meant to be free from the inequality of the household, entering a zone free from necessity where one could make the choice to rule. With the blurring of public and private through the social, such clarity is no longer possible. In society, we no longer recognize if we are free or enslaved, lawful or criminal. And, in such confusion, relief appears as an emblematic affect.

Relief, in moving those who feel it from a temporal present to the horizon of the past event that haunts us in the feeling of release, looks to mimic revenge. It drives an action that is not new, but linked directly to the past, through the agency of another. The counter to relief, and the affective world relief seems to trap us in, looks more like forgiveness. Arendt is especially clear that part of living together, as a plurality on earth, entails the capacity to act in entirely unexpected ways. To "live with" and not "live for/against" means, according to Arendt, a capacity for political action that, precisely at the moment where our friends and enemies would expect one action/affect/word/deed, we engage in the opposite. There is no better model for such action than forgiveness. As Arendt explains,

> Forgiveness is the exact opposite of vengeance, which acts in the form of re-acting against an original trespassing, whereby far from putting an end to the consequences of the first misdeed, everybody remains bound to the process, permitting the chain reaction contained in every action to take its unhindered course. In contrast to revenge, which is the natural, automatic reaction to transgression and which because of the irreversibility of the action process can be expected and even calculated, the act of forgiving can never be predicted; it is the only reaction that acts in an unexpected way and thus retains, though being a reaction, something of the original character of action. Forgiving, in other words, is the only reaction which does not merely re-act but acts anew and unexpectedly, unconditioned by the act which provoked it and therefore freeing from its consequences both the one who forgives and the one who is forgiven.[51]

Forgiveness, is precisely a new beginning, both for those who act it, and for those who receive it, placing both in union with each other. It is the pure freedom of the unexpected.

And yet, even in the miraculous moment of forgiveness, we might be concerned. For we face a danger that the potency of the unexpected novel action is itself only novel because it breaks with the past (and thus is still linked with it). To forgive is to take the past and choose to view it from another perspective – to be a spectator who is not trapped by the logic it would seem to hold. And yet, the past still reverberates (despite Arendt's hope that it would not). Necessity operates here in two counter modes: What we would expect to happen (what necessity would determine), stands counter to the freedom to choose otherwise; but exactly in our expectation, necessity lingers as the force of what makes the unexpected so powerful for Arendt's model of action.

These echoes of necessity run throughout Arendt's theory of political action, with outcomes that may strike us as troubling.

As Butler themself reminds us, "Referring to 'the poor who come streaming out into the street,' [Arendt] writes that something irresistible motivates them, and this 'irresistibility, which we found so intimately connected with the original meaning of revolution, was embodied.' And yet she immediately links this 'element of irresistibility' with 'the necessity which we ascribe to natural processes.' "[52] The danger for Arendt is the prediction – the calculation – that necessity portends. The counter, for Arendt, is the unexpected action – like forgiveness (as it is unexpected by everyone). Here the logic of the unexpected action seems grounded in inaction/the negative. Consider the examples Arendt deploys, reading forgiveness as, the "necessary corrective for the inevitable damages resulting from action may be seen in the Roman principle to spare the vanquished (*parcere subiectis*) – a wisdom entirely unknown to the Greeks – or in the right to commute the death sentence, probably also of Roman origin, which is the prerogative of nearly all Western heads of state."[53] Action reveals itself here in inaction. The active is only active as negation of the expected action.

But what of action that begins in necessity and breaks with it? What of positive action? Here Butler, better than Arendt, gives us a reading of the sort of action that would fit the model professed by Arendt, but without the negative limits her examples seem constrained by. By Butler's account, assembly is precisely this sort of counteraction. As Butler explains,

> Acting in concert can be an embodied form of calling into question the inchoate and powerful dimensions of reigning notions of the political. The embodied character of this questioning works in at least two ways: on the one hand, contestations are enacted by assemblies, strikes, vigils, and the occupation of public spaces; on the other hand, those bodies are the object of many of the demonstrations that take precarity as their galvanizing condition.[54]

Here action is neither forgiveness, nor revenge, but the simple self-standing and self-possession of collective assembly. Such an example is crucial, for it draws Arendt's notion of the unexpected against itself, escaping the reifying political powers that her examples seem to depend on (the victor who spares her opponent/the king who offers a stay of execution/the sovereign who confirms the very basis of sovereignty through a logic of forgiveness). Butler moves action into a world where the counter-sovereign/the powerless have the capacity to behave unexpectedly. If Arendt and her defenders can respond to this critique, there must be more to her theory of spectatorship and its link to action than we have examined thus far.

The lost star

Arendt's theorizing of vision reaches a limit that she herself hopes to move past, into a less well-articulated, but perhaps more interesting thesis of the embodied and disoriented self of the imagination. What is so important for Arendt's thinking through her reflection on the *Vita Activa*, and *On Revolution*, and even her *Lectures on Kant's Political Philosophy* – indeed, what seems to bind much of her theorizing generally – is the proper use of the free political imagination. As she explains, "Imagination alone enables us to see things in their proper perspective, to be strong enough to put that which is too close at a certain distance so that we can see and understand it without bias and prejudice, to be generous enough to bridge abysses of remoteness until we can see and understand everything that is too far away from us as though it were our own affair."[55] The question of propriety is a complicated one, even for Arendt, and especially so within moments of disaster. And yet it will be these moments that prove so crucial to her theorizing regarding the necessity of political imagination.

By Arendt's accounting, the experience of disaster is marked by a fundamental disorientation. No matter the form (war, famine, earthquake, or shipwreck), or the terms (social, economic, personal, political), disaster is an eventual disruption of our ordinary ways of thinking and being. We find some evidence for this in the etymology of the term; "dis-aster" is quite literally a "lost star," implying – through metaphor – the lost capacity to navigate open waters. Here disaster appears as the event that marks loss and disorientation, the event where we had to learn to begin to orient ourselves again to the world and our lives within it.

How has this thinking been inherited? One reading of Arendt that tries to move her away from the pathologies of spectatorship is Tracy Strong's *Politics Without Vision: Thinking without a Banister in the Twentieth Century*. Strong points beyond disaster as a mere event, to the condition of such disorientation. It is, Strong argues, no longer the case that politics is the response to the temporary inability to navigate. Rather we – those generations who have survived the twentieth century – who have found ourselves in a condition where the very terms of navigation are permanently upended. In his wonderful rethinking of what political theory should now be, Strong asks his readers to reflect critically on our own historical situatedness, and especially the historical conditionality of political theory today. When historically humanity has waged such wars against itself, and evinced profound dominations as we have seen globally in the twentieth century, it has become impossible to imagine a return to the terms of navigation and the ordered perspective of knowing where we are. Strong's claim is not that we simply have lost our way, or lost that which ordered our way – Nature or Reason or God or some other metaphysically orientating force on which we might find authoritative ground for our judgments – but that we may never find ourselves in that condition of authoritative ground again. We can no longer define ourselves by our own safety, and the security of our orientation. Instead, we must begin to accustom ourselves to disorientation.

Such disorientation raises new questions of political life. In the midst of disorientation, how will we pilot ourselves? How will we guide ourselves – rule ourselves – without any vision? The title of Strong's book is of course a reversal of Sheldon Wolin's *Politics and Vision*, which set "vision" as a practice of theorizing of politics with new legitimation. In the middle of the twentieth century, when the academic discipline of political science was just beginning to find ground in the behaviorist revolution, Wolin waged an insurgent campaign against the ideological centrality of methodology. As he argues the point, "Because facts are more multi-faceted than a rigid conception of empirical theory would allow, they are more likely to yield to the observer whose mental capacities enable him to appreciate a known fact in an unconventional way ... Vision, as I have tried to emphasize, depends for its richness on the resources from which it can draw."[56]

For Wolin, "vision" was not the factual reporting of what was, or could be, seen by all, but rather what might be seen, but could not be. His was a struggle against the epistemological presumptions that contemporary political science relied upon, specifically the use of standards and theories to determine the world for those theories (the testing of hypotheses), as opposed to the inquiry of and reflection of the political world as one finds it. Written in 1960, Wolin's initial edition of *Politics and Vision* was meant to illicit hope for such inquiry and its place in a sustained reflection on politics. Wolin sought to distinguish between vision as mere perception and vision as our aesthetic imagination. Vision as perception entails a division between a spectator and actor or an event. Here the vision is that which allows the spectator to perceive the political reality that presents itself in the world – Wolin uses the example of the speaker who addresses a political rally. Here vision is subjective, and – so Wolin worried – also deceptive, grounded in a fundamental division between what is and what one perceives. This can best be contrasted with vision as an aesthetic or even a theological practice, where vision is meant as that which can be or is imagined, and thus not linked reactively to any singular event in the world. Wolin's hope was for, and seemingly constituted by, this second sort of vision. Political theory, according to Wolin, was the inquiry into that vision and of that vision. A means to look upon the political world one found oneself in, and to consent the tensions and dangers and pathologies that one faced in that world.

But, as Strong points out, Wolin could not maintain that hope. In the second, expanded edition of *Politics and Vision*, Wolin's own view of his own polity and his normative commitments (from "liberalism to democracy") had changed. As Wolin reports, "the experience of combatting totalitarian regimes had sunk more deeply into the practices and values of American political elites than observers have acknowledged, and that, if anything, this influence has intensified today."[57] Wolin goes on to reflect on the logics of totalization and totalizing power that have evinced themselves in the contempt of American polity, and the costs of these transformations. The task, from Wolin's perceptive, is "to nurture the civic conscience of society." That is, political power, and elite domination, have reached such a pathological zenith, that the demos itself has lost its own conscience, and until the instability of that condition so rectified, the American superpower will move closer and closer to fulfilling its own totalitarian fantasies.

Here, we start to see the limits of vision. Echoing George Kateb, Strong reflects, "Is the canon of political theory adequate to the task of enabling readers in our time to take in and comprehend the awful events of the twentieth century?"[58] As Kateb continues, "The awful events of the twentieth century seem, if only in their scale, to break out of the conceptual net found in the sequence of canonical texts written up to 1900 or so." Kateb's claim that political theory finds purpose in helping us in "facing the worst" parallels Arendt's claim in *The Human Condition*:

> What I propose in the following is a reconsideration of the human condition from the vantage point of our newest experience and our most recent fears. This, obviously, is a matter of thought, and thoughtlessness – the heedless recklessness or hopeless confusion or complacent repetition of "truths," which have become trivial and empty – seems to me among the outstanding characteristics of our time. What I propose, therefore, is very simple: it is nothing more than to think what we are doing.[59]

The notion of vision is, on the one hand, linked to imagination, and the possibility of seeing a new sort of politics, one that fulfills the demands that might appear in the failures of the current political climate. Here vision is seeing *what else*, and *what could*. And yet, on the other hand, vision can also mean a link to an object. Drawing the viewer into a particular frame. Here vision might itself too depend of course on the object of its own attachment (like Hegel's account of consciousness, driven by desire).

The platonic *eidoi* from Book 7 of Plato's *Republic* seems a paramount formulation of this logic of seeing. The philosopher who begins in a condition of slavery, chained in standing position, unable to move one's head, only able to see. Breaking free from such entanglements, the freed slave wanders into the light, where the world is seen anew for the first time, beyond the shadows. And yet the link is still with objects, and thus with a material world that is destructible. Plato's allegory famously narrates that beyond the things of the word are the ideas themselves inverse to the shadow world; this world is as light itself. Here we see the guided poetics of vision in its most profound metaphor. Just as the objects of the world illicit our imaginations, so too does light act as a means of understanding the very essence of the world. The limit here, of course, is that such seeing to the world was what organically became the terms of enslavement, and there may be just as much enticement to enslave oneself again, even to the logic of Enlightenment.

What Arendt and others observe as a counter to such notions of vision is the possibility of an epistemic frame, set by the imagination and propelled through the metaphor of "thinking without banisters." Arendt would use this phrase in numerous instances through the later portion of her thinking. Sometimes referring to banisters or handrails or path marks, the metaphor is one of navigating, whether on a staircase without banisters or a ship without handrails or a forest trail without path marks, without security. What matters most is that movement – free movement, without security, a wandering – becomes the dominant metaphor for a new politics – a politics without vision. Unlike the Platonic mode of a politics that finds its basis in breaking free from enslavement, and the relief of that freedom, the politics without vision, that is caught in thinking without banisters, finds itself admitting the surmounting disaster. We might reflect that the very disappearance of the banisters are themselves a "sign" of unusually disorientating times.

We see this especially in what might be thought of as a "second" allegory of the cave, offered up in Kant's famous "An Answer to the Question: 'What Is Enlightenment?'" There we begin to see a focus on walking and movement as part of the logic of courage. For Kant, it is not the idea of sight that is the source of Enlightenment, but rather the courage to stand and to move, even in the midst of what one does not know or see. If we can read Arendt following Kant's lead in this way, no longer can we even pretend to have the luxury of watching politics from the safety of shore.

Haunting visions

How can we correlate Arendt's thinking on a politics "without vision" to her theory of spectatorship? The trap of vision we see Arendt and others pointing to is importantly an epistemology – "thinking without banisters." The danger of this politics, as Butler and others have observed, is the relation between thinking and judging, on the one hand, and acting, on the other. While we may see more clearly why Arendt finds so much anxiety in the feeling of relief (because it pathologically desires both to escape and not escape that which constrains it), what still remains unclear is how spectatorship could move past such confines. How can Arendt begin to theorize a mode of action that breaks with previous conditions of thought (as "thinking without banisters" demands), and at the same time, allows for the sort of spectatorship that resists necessity and has the courage to judge in the face of catastrophe?

So as to develop this mode of spectatorship, Arendt turned to Kant, and specifically his notion of the "general standpoint," as a means of thinking in the face of disaster. (Spectatorship here begins to slip into thinking/imagining, and not viewing.) As Arendt explains, what she is seeking in this notion of spectatorship and judgment is what Kant defined as *Selbstdenken*, "to think for one-self" or literally "thinking for self," a mode of critical rationality that, quoting Kant, gets read as "the maxim of a never-passive reason" (for to give in to passive reason is what Kant names as prejudice).[60] This "think-for-self" is most active when it moves among imagined perspectives, accelerating deeper and deeper in to the plurality of those perspectives. As Arendt explains,

> The greater the reach – the larger the realm in which the enlightened individual is able to move from standpoint to standpoint – the more "general" will be his thinking. This generality, however, is not the generality of the concept – for example, the concept "house," under which one can then subsume various kinds of individual buildings. It is, on the contrary, closely connected with particulars, with the particular conditions of the standpoints one has to go through in order to arrive at one's own "general standpoint."[61]

The "general standpoint" is one of "impartiality"; it is a viewpoint from which to look upon, to watch, to form judgments, to reflect on human affairs. Crucial here is the movement from standpoint to standpoint, wherein the "general" starts to take shape. Arendt's rhetoric here mirrors her metaphoric imagery of the demands of thinking in the face of disaster. The claim to think "without a banister (handrail)" conjures the narrative of moving through the ocean on a ship, without the security of understanding how safe those movements are. Here, in the "general standpoint," we find a journey through particular "standpoints," without clarity on the safety of those individual views, or the thinking that reflects the totality of standpoints through the "general" view that encompasses them all.

Such movements from standpoint to standpoint is reminiscent of Kant's notion of Enlightenment as motion (rather than sight).

But the politics of such motion are made more evident by Arendt. For her, such motion from standpoint to standpoint, beyond the security of knowing what will and should come next, requires a compulsion to trespass. As she explains it,

> Trespassing is an everyday occurrence which is in the very nature of action's constant establishment of new relationships within a web of relations, and it needs forgiving, dismissing, in order to make it possible for life to go on by constantly releasing men from what they have done unknowingly. Only through this constant mutual release from what they do can men remain free agents, only by constant willingness to change their minds and start again can they be trusted with so great a power as that to begin something new.[62]

The political vitality of a community depends on such trespassing's – relations that form new positions and take on new meanings within the web of human existence. But notice here that trespassing gets framed in the mode of necessity ("in order to make it possible for life to go on"), and forgiveness, as we discussed before, takes on the mode of action. Is the spectator in motion between standpoints, trespassing viewpoints on the way to the "general standpoint," or is the spectator stationary, waiting for the actor to form the general standpoint by which forgiveness becomes the constitutive mode of action?

For all the fluidity that exists in this model, Arendt's thinking also seems to demand an absolute ordering. The "general standpoint" reads like a conclusion of standpoints, and one that operates under representative logics, working to gather all standpoints (even those that remain unknown to it) within its orbit. This gathering reads like a haunting, though this also seems to contradict the logics of natality that are so often linked with Arendt's theory of action.

One crucial moment where these two modes come to head appears in Arendt's own discussion of the public in her *Vita Activa*. If we expect action to begin in such a way that it begins for all, and that the general standpoint will be total in its representative logic, how far can we carry such thinking? A moment of conflict seems to appear for Arendt between the living and the dead. As she explains it,

> The public realm, as the common world, gathers us together and yet prevents our falling over each other, so to speak. What makes mass society so difficult to bear is not the number of people involved, or at

least not primarily, but the fact that the world between them has lost its power to gather them together, to relate and to separate them. The weirdness of this situation resembles a spiritualistic séance where a number of people gathered around a table might suddenly, through some magic trick, see the table vanish from their midst, so that two persons sitting opposite each other were no longer separated but also would be entirely unrelated to each other by anything tangible.[63]

Arendt presents us here with the unusual problem of our psychic experience of mass society. It is not the case, she suggests, that we face some internal difficulty because of the sheer "number of people" – this is not a Malthusian problem of population that would define "mass" as the identity of so many people that we somehow lose our sense of individuation and therefore togetherness (as some classical population studies might suggest). Rather, the problem we find in bearing mass society – which I take to mean something along the lines of existing and enduring within the facticity of that society, is related to something more subtle – and haunting – that the world we live in that we call mass society loses the very power to allow us to relate together. This public power, as Arendt describes it, is a trinity of overlapping forces, working to simultaneously gather, relate, and separate.[64] These agricultural referents point to the naturalizing rhetoric Arendt hopes to deploy to make sense of the problem of mass society and the power of the public. Important here is the condition of loss – that the problem of mass society is that a certain "public" power has been lost, and that we live in this absence, noticing – if we pay any attention at all – that there should be a force that can hold us collectively together, even as it holds us apart.

So as to illustrate this phenomenon, Arendt in *The Human Condition*, offers up the unusual analogy of a seance gone wrong (revealed through the strange disappearing of the seance table itself). Seance itself has its etymological origins in the Latin *sedēre* – to sit: Once read as the meeting of a purposeful body assembled for a collective discussion, seance only later came to mean "sitting together" to investigate sacred, spiritual, or ghostly apparitions. It is an intentional sitting, a coming to rest, and doing so in order to speak to those who might no longer be able to be spoken to. This "communication" with the spirits/the dead is what makes the seance a unique form of activity – not communication with the living, but with the living and the dead – trespassing all ordinary (maybe even natural) boundaries.

A seance is meant to be a making of appearance.[65] The dead should appear – made present by the sitting of others around the table. And in their sitting and speaking and communicating the dead are called to and given the chance to call back. This chance – this invitation – is the objective of the seance. In calling to the dead, the seance is a chance for appearance of those who are without bodies, but with spirit. The weirdness Arendt describes is not the appearance of dead, but rather the disappearance of the table. At exactly the moment when we might expect the dead spirit to appear, when all our senses and hopes and desires are cued in on such an appearing – when we sit in anticipation of such spiritual possession – at that moment, the table disappears. To what end?

One reading would suggest Arendt wants to make clear that for those who take the seance seriously, this disappearing would seem to be an absolute shock. If a seance is the making of spirits appear, the disappearing of the body of the object where that appearance was meant to take place is the inversion of what was expected. But that inversion has a novelty to it – the unexpected, spontaneous rupture is, in a way, a preface to Arendt's notion of action described later in *The Human Condition*.

Yet another reading points to the logic of expectation that is already at play in the happening of the seance. In a room, gathered around a table, those people who partake in the seance, those living who hope to commune with the dead, are so focused on this impossibility – so consumed with the overcoming of reality to trespass reason – that their attention, in a way, allows for this magic trick. It becomes the terms for this disappearing.

Here the conflict of the "general standpoint" as Arendt defends it, starts to present itself in stark contrast. On the one hand, action should be that which is public and available to all. Forgiveness is action because it is the unexpected alteration of reality for those who offer it and to those whom it is offered to. Pure action cannot be limited to one side or the other. As Arendt explains, "Everything that appears in public can be seen and heard by everybody and has the widest possible publicity." And specifically, "Appearance – something that is being seen and heard by others as well as by ourselves – constitutes reality."[66] The standpoints that begin as unknowns to the spectator who moves through them still remain as particulars, even as the general standpoint begins to form. The plurality of viewpoints is significant to the fabric of the web Arendt hopes political society can become. And yet, on the other hand, the general standpoint may not be available to those who stand in conflict with it from the particular standpoints form which it is constructed.

Arendt hopes that the enthusiasm she links to the general standpoint – an enthusiasm that becomes constitutive of political reality through the spectator's general viewpoint – will be potent enough to persuade others of this public reality. As Arendt asserts,

> The presence of others who see what we see and hear what we hear assures us of the reality of the world and ourselves, and while the intimacy of a fully developed private life, such as had never been known before the rise of the modern age and the concomitant decline of the public realm, will always greatly intensify and enrich the whole scale of subjective emotions and private feelings, this intensification will always come to pass at the expense of the assurance of the reality of the world of men.[67]

And yet exactly the psychic frameworks required to construct public realities are those which require a fluidity of private standpoints, without clarity of the transition between the two. It is this motion – the motion that Arendt attempts to inherit from Kant's notion of Enlightenment – that remains lingering in her theorizing. Who would accept the "general standpoint" of the spectator?

Bodies appearing

Arendt's theorizing on the spectator has become a significant interpretation of the place of enthusiasm in the political imagination. And yet the binary logics that underlie her theorizing leave enthusiasm too fragile and unstable. While she is clear that enthusiasm is distinct from empathy, and that it originates and occupies the "general standpoint" of the spectator who judges events in their total meaning, what remains unclear is how such spectatorship – and the "general standpoint" in particular – work to motivate and shape a theory of action. If enthusiasm is the constitutive affect of political engagement, how precisely it operates, and what forms its limits, are left too vague in her theory. The binary that began in Wieland's question of whether or how we might distinguish between enthusiasm and fanaticism perpetuates itself in Arendt's thinking, productive of the split between spectator and actor, thinking and action, relief and enthusiasm.

Even as Arendt argues against a political point *beyond*, she collapses into her own critique. Trapped in exteriority, Arendt works to formally create conditions where distinction and binary continue. Enthusiasm, in this way, becomes unenthusiastic – we are trapping it, rather than releasing it. The anxiety that operates here seems to be one of ventilation – what we might name as the liberal notion of release. How she moves us out of it still gets caught in the binary she hopes to escape, keeping things contained and closed. It is as though, in her thinking on action as the beginning that begins new frames for acting, Arendt has forgotten the groundless ground on which such beginnings appear. How to begin to resist the impulse of relief in action is still a pressing question.

Perhaps we might begin to traverse a different pathway. Part of the limit of Arendt's thinking seems to be the temporal frame that beginnings set on how she understands actions. What would happen to our thinking on action if we subtracted such conditions, or at least retuned them? Following Foucault, we should perhaps ask, how can we endure the present? What action might be needed if we can? What action might be needed if we cannot?

Notes

1 Ronald Beiner, "Interpretative Essay: Hannah Arendt on Judging," in *Lectures on Kant's Political Philosophy*, ed. Ronald Beiner (University of Chicago Press, 1989), pp. 89–156; Ronald Beiner and Jennifer Nedelsky, eds., *Judgment, Imagination, and Politics: Themes from Kant and Arendt* (Rowman & Littlefield, 2001); Seyla Benhabib, *Situating the Self* (Routledge, 1996); Seyla Benhabib, *The Reluctant Modernism of Hannah Arendt* (Sage, 1996); Seyla Benhabib, "Judgment and the Moral Foundations of Politics in Hannah Arendt's Thought," in *Judgment, Imagination, and Politics: Themes from Kant and Arendt*, ed. Ronald Beiner and Jennifer Nedelsky (Rowman & Littlefield, 2001), pp. 183–204; Elisabeth Ellis, *Kant's Politics: Provisional Theory for an Uncertain World* (Yale University Press, 2005); Dana Villa, "Beyond Good and Evil: Arendt, Nietzsche, and the Aesthetics of Political Action," *Political Theory* 20, no. 2 (1992): 274–308; Linda Zerilli, " 'We Feel Our Freedom': Imagination

and Judgment in the Thought of Hannah Arendt," *Political Theory* 33, no. 2 (2005): 155–88; and Stanley Cavell, *The Claim of Reason: Wittgenstein, Skepticism, Morality, and Tragedy* (Oxford University Press, 1979), esp. chap. 1 on critique and judgment.

2 Hannah Arendt, *Lectures on Kant's Political Philosophy* (University of Chicago Press, 1992), p. 46.

3 This reading has received much attention in recent debates on political judgment. For a recent review of these debates, see, for example, Zerilli, "We Feel Our Freedom."

4 Hannah Arendt, *The Human Condition* (University of Chicago Press, [1958] 1998), p. 177.

5 Ibid., pp. 177–8.

6 Ibid., p. 178.

7 See Patchen Markell, "Anonymous Glory," *European Journal of Political Theory* 16, no. 1 (2017): 77–99.

8 Arendt, *The Human Condition*, p. 178.

9 Arendt, *Lectures on Kant's Political Philosophy*, p. 44.

10 Ibid., p. 61.

11 See Karl Mannheim, *Ideology and Utopia: An Introduction to the Sociology of Knowledge* (Martino Fine, 2015). For some analysis of enthusiasm and ideology, see Daniel Guerriere, "The Truth, the Nontruth, and the Untruth Proper to Religion," in *Phenomenology of the Truth Proper to Religion* (SUNY University Press, 1990), pp. 75–101.

12 Seyla Benhabib, "Freedom and Democracy: The Power and the Paradox of Revolutions," *Reset: Dialogs on Civilizations*, October 13, 2011, www.resetdoc.org/story/00000021780 (accessed June 7, 2021).

13 My interest here is in modern conceptions of revolution. Ancient models of revolution proscribed decline and ascension from one form of government to another according to a specific cyclical pattern. What fundamentally distinguishes this notion of revolution from more modern conceptions is the place of historical normativity in the concept.

14 Reinhart Koselleck suggests that all revolutions might be "World Revolutions" (p. 52), and this could be right. The difference between "world" and "total" is significant; revolution of the "world" could simply mean others recognizing that a revolution has happened, while "total" revolution would mean the same revolution for all. See Reinhart Koselleck, "Historical Criteria of the Modern Concept of Revolution" in *Futures Past: On the Semantics of Historical Time* (Columbia University Press, 2004), pp. 39–54.

15 Bonnie Honig explores a similar pathology in her *Democracy and the Foreigner* (Princeton University Press, 2003), where she uncovers the desire for renewal that operates in liberal policies of immigration.

16 My rendering here elaborates Koselleck's account in "Historical Criteria of the Modern Concept of Revolution," though Arendt is herself well versed in this metaphoric content, as she discusses in *On Revolution* (Viking, 1963), p. 42, for example.

17 Here I am influenced by Rebecca Comay's argument on the "fantasy" of revolution in her recent *Mourning Sickness: Hegel and the French Revolution* (Stanford University Press, 2011). We differ in that my theorizing of revolution is indebted to Kant (Comay's is to Hegel). Other work on Kant's conception of history and the role of enthusiasm in revolution include Yirmiahu Yovel, *Kant and the Philosophy of History* (Princeton University Press, 1980); and, more recently, Robert Clewis, *The Kantian Sublime and the Revelation of Freedom* (Cambridge University Press, 2009), esp. pp. 169–83.

18 This is perhaps revealed in differing experiences of the speed of history, for being part of the event would seem to necessitate a distinct experience of time from those who merely witness its happening. See Reinhart Koselleck's accounting of speed, history, and revolution, in "Representation, Event, and Structure," also from *Futures Past* (pp. 105–15). There he argues, "(W)here formerly long-term processes became abbreviated through altering or even accelerating speed, the spaces of experience were rejuvenated by the continual requirement to adapt" (p. 113).

19 Again, for historical overviews of the changing conception of enthusiasm in German thought that help situate Kant's arguments, see George Williamson, "The Restoration Revolt Against Enthusiasm," in *Seventeenth-Century Contexts* (Faber & Faber, 1960), pp. 202–39; Peter Fenves, "The Scale of Enthusiasm," *Huntington Library Quarterly* 60, nos. 1–2, Enthusiasm and Enlightenment in Europe, 1650–1850 (1997): 117–52; and Anthony La Vopa, "The Philosopher and the *Schwärmer*: On the Career of a German Epithet from Luther to Kant," *Huntington Library Quarterly* 60, nos. 1–2, Enthusiasm and Enlightenment in Europe, 1650–1850 (1997): 85–115. For some attempts to consider the place of enthusiasm in contemporary democratic theory debates, see Jason Frank, " 'Besides Our Selves': An Essay on Enthusiastic Politics and Civil Subjectivity," *Public Culture* 17, no. 3 (2005), esp. p. 372; Jeffrey Lomonaco, "Kant's Unselfish Partisans as Democratic Citizens," *Public Culture* 17, no. 3 (2005): 393–499; and Bonnie Honig, "Between Decision and Deliberation: Political Paradox in Democratic Theory," *American Political Science Review* 101, no. 1 (February 2007): 1–17.

20 For an overview on this point, see Zerilli, "We Feel our Freedom." For Arendt's account of natality, with its emphasis on the "openness" of the new beginning set-forth in revolution, see Arendt, *On Revolution*.

21 Arendt, *On Revolution*, p. 211.
22 Ibid., p. 41. Arendt's notion of conservatism seems right, but the account of time that underlies this account is perplexing.
23 For further elaboration on this point, see, for example, William Connolly, *A World of Becoming* (Duke University Press, 2010).
24 Arendt's most detailed accounting of spectators comes in her lectures on Kant. See Arendt, *Lectures on Kant's Political Philosophy*, p. 46.
25 See part 1 of Kant's *Metaphysics of Morals*, "Metaphysical First Principles of the Doctrine of Right," where he argues, "There is, therefore, no right of sedition (*seditio*), much less a right of rebellion (*rebellion*) ... The reason a people has a duty to put up with even what is held to be unbearable abuse of supreme authority is that its resistance to the highest legislation can never be regarded as other than contrary to law, and indeed as abolishing the entire legal constitution. For a people to be authorized to resist (authorized for revolution), there would have to be a public law permitting it to resist ... This is self-contradictory" (pp. 96–7 (Ak 6:320)). For further discussion on this point, see Christine Korsgaard, "Taking the Law into Our Own Hands: Kant on the Right to Revolution," in *Reclaiming the History of Ethics: Essays for John Rawls*, ed. Andrews Reath, Barbara Herman, and Christine Korsgaard (Cambridge University Press, 1997), pp. 297–328. Two classical defenses of Kant's views on revolution are Lewis W. Beck, "Kant and the Right of Revolution," *Journal of the History of Ideas* 32 (1971): 411–22; and H. S. Reiss, "Kant and the Right of Rebellion," *Journal of the History of Ideas* 17 (1956): 190–1.
26 From Kant's *Reflexion*, 8051, Ak. XIX, 594–5; cf. Beck, "Kant and the Right of Revolution," p. 412; also cf. Reiss, "Kant and the Right of Rebellion."
27 Beck, "Kant and the Right of Revolution," p. 414.
28 Benhabib ("Freedom and Democracy," fn 1) confirms as much, situating her claims regarding the national taking of public space as an Arendtian inheritance, one where the premise is that through the end of the violence of corruption comes a new order of liberty (not happiness). And as the positive ends of revolution are Arendtian, the dangerous means are Burkean in tone – where "any violent intervention in the providential evolution of history is likely to produce itself an unleashing of violence and counter-violence that revolutionaries themselves cannot control." This balance between hope and despair – or to use Benhabib's language "joy and apprehension" – comes from what she describes as the standpoint of philosophers – "what Kant called the enthusiasm of philosophers in the face of revolution,

expressing both joy and apprehension." It is this standpoint that I want to call into question, and use as a ground, both to renter the face of reception, and open it up as a possibility – that, at least conceptually, in political revolutions may be possible, not as a joining, but as uncovering.

29 It is unclear whether Kant himself believed that these transformations in epistemologies would produce the "kingdom of ends" – for a discussion of this point, see Korsgaard, "Taking the Law into Our Own Hands"; Steven M. Delue, "Kant's Politics as an Expression of the Need for His Aesthetics," *Political Theory* 13, no. 3 (1985): 409–29; and most importantly Arendt, *Lectures on Kant's Political Philosophy*. What I hope is clear, however, is that there is an unresolved tension in Kant's theory between individuals' respect for others as individuals and respect for the moral law, that Kant found difficult to overcome – see Delue, "Kant's Politics"; Beiner, "Interpretive Essay"; and Beiner and Nedelsky, *Judgment, Imagination and Politics*, p. xxiii, n32, for elaborations on this point. It is on this precise point that Arendt's claims regarding Kant's *Critique of Judgment* as a second politics have been regarded with such suspicion – see, for instance, Patrick Riley, *Kant's Political Philosophy* (Rowman & Littlefield, 1983); or George Kateb, "The Judgment of Hannah Arendt," in *Judgment, Imagination, and Politics: Themes from Kant and Arendt*, ed. Ronald Beiner and Jennifer Nedelsky (Rowman & Littlefield, 2001), pp. 121–38. Though there is some evidence for this suspicion, I also believe the discussion in the first section of this chapter illustrates some important theoretical resources to support Arendt's reading.

30 See Patchen Markell, "The Rule of the People: Arendt, *Arche*, and Democracy," *American Political Science Review* 100, no. 1 (2006): 1–14, esp. p. 11, for the most recent assessment of Arendt's democratic theory.

31 For a related argument regarding the dangers of commingling morality and politics for Arendt, see Villa, "Beyond Good and Evil."

32 Arendt, *Lectures on Kant's Political Philosophy*, p. 53; and Arendt, *The Human Condition*, p. 52.

33 As Villa also observes ("Beyond Good and Evil," p. 274), this is not a consensus-based model for political judgment. Just as Kant described in his account of reflective judgment, the "I" represents what "I" imagine others' opinions to be and does not seek agreement in so doing. See Immanuel Kant, *Critique of Judgment (Kritik der Urteilskraft)*, trans. Werner S. Pluhar (Hackett, 1987), p. 59.

34 Arendt, *Lectures on Kant's Political Philosophy*, p. 76.

35 Ibid.
36 Hannah Arendt, *The Life of the Mind* (Harvest/Harcourt, [1971] 1978), p. 193.
37 Ibid.
38 Arendt, *The Human Condition*, p. 1. For some historical context on Arendt's thinking on space and alienation, see Kelly Oliver's recent *Earth and World: Philosophy After the Apollo Missions* (Columbia University Press, 2015), esp. chap. 3.
39 Arendt, *The Human Condition*, p. 1.
40 Ibid.
41 For a related discussion on pathology, see, for example, Claude Fischer, "On Urban Alienations and Anomie: Powerlessness and Social Isolation," *American Sociological Review* 38, no. 3 (1973): 311–26.
42 "Heine sometimes thought that he, the poet and lord of dreams who lived in a permanent Sabbath state (he thought), could do something like the work of the Sabbath and ennoble a people made ignoble by circumstances. Arendt had little patience for such aspirations. Indeed, the entire 'hidden tradition,' to which she gives shape in her essay by tracking the efforts of even admirable conscious pariahs, is one conjugated only by individuals and limited thereby. No action in concert occurs here and no alteration results in the conditions of worldliness. Arendt wants to credit the insight and courage of those who chose the path of the pariah rather than the parvenu. Their acts were not without consequence. But, she recognizes, they operated in limiting situations and their example can be no model for us now. They had no political significance. They cared for the world but could not act effectively upon it." Bonnie Honig, "The Laws of the Sabbath (Poetry): Arendt, Heine, and the Politics of Debt," *UCI Law Review* 5, no. 2 (2015): 480.
43 Arendt, *The Human Condition*, p. 33.
44 Judith Butler, *Notes Toward a Performative Theory of Assembly* (Harvard University Press, 2015), p. 44.
45 Ibid., p. 46.
46 Ibid.
47 Arendt, *The Human Condition*, p. 113.
48 Ibid., p. 28.
49 My thinking here, to a certain extent, parallels Hanna Pitkin's in her *The Attack of the Blob: Hannah Arendt's Concept of the Social* (University of Chicago Press, 1998), though I see the blur as a distinct metaphoric reality from the blob.
50 Arendt, *The Human Condition*, p. 31.

51 Ibid., pp. 240–1.
52 See Butler, *Assembly*, p. 46. On "irresistibility" in Arendt, see Pitkin, *Attack of the Blob*, p. 11.
53 Arendt, *The Human Condition*, p. 239.
54 Butler, *Assembly*, p. 9.
55 Hannah Arendt, "Understanding and Politics," in *Essays in Understanding: 1930–1954* (Harcourt, 1994), p. 323.
56 Shelden S. Wolin, *Politics and Vision: Continuity and Innovation in Western Political Thought* (Princeton University Press, 1960), p. 1073.
57 Shelden S. Wolin, *Politics and Vision: Continuity and Innovation in Western Political Thought*, 2nd expanded ed. (Princeton University Press, [1960] 2016), p. xvi.
58 George Kateb, "The Adequacy of the Canon," in *Patriotism and Other Mistakes* (Yale University Press, 2006), p. 384.
59 Arendt, *The Human Condition*, p. 5.
60 Arendt, *Lectures on Kant's Political Philosophy*, p. 44.
61 Ibid., p. 44.
62 Arendt, *The Human Condition*, p. 239.
63 Ibid., pp. 52–3. On tables and seances, see, for example, Isobel Armstrong, "Bodily Things and Thingly Bodies: Circumventing the Subject–Object Binary," in *Bodies and Things in 19th-Century Literature and Culture* (Springer, 2016), pp. 17–41. For a psychological analysis of such phenomena, see Carl Jung's reflections in "On Occultism," where he argues: "Experiments in divination are known from the grey dawn of history. Thus, Ammianus Marcellinus reports from AD 371 that a certain Patricius and Hilarius, living in the reign (364–78) of the Emperor Valens, had discovered by the 'abominable arts of soothsaying' who would succeed to the throne. For this purpose, they used a metal bowl, with the alphabet engraved round the rim. Over it, amid fearful oaths, they suspended a ring on a thread. This began to swing, and spelt out the name Theodorus. When their magic was divulged, they were arrested and put to death." Jung cites Justinus Kerner's "The Somnambulant Tables: A History and Explanation of these Phenomena," from 1853, as well as Thury's "Les tables parlantes au point de vue de la physique generale," from 1855. See Carl Jung, *Collected Works of C. G. Jung: The First Complete English Edition of the works of C.G. Jung* (Routledge, 2015), p. 8145. Arendt may very well have Marx's own reference to tables and his argument on fetishism. See Armstrong, "Bodily Things and Thingly Bodies," p. 22.

64 Arendt's conception of critique is as a separation. As she notes, the origins of critique are "from *krinein*: Means separate, and then discern and judge. By separating we discern and judge. Seeming contradiction to synthesis: by making the synthesis between sky and blue, we separate blueness from sky. This also the origin of all abstract thought." Excerpted from Arendt's notes from her 1964 course at the University of California at Berkeley. From Courses, University of California, Berkeley, "Political Theory of Kant," 1955, 1949–75, Hannah Arendt Papers, Manuscript Division, Library of Congress, Washington, DC.

65 Useful here is Banu Bargu's reflections on the table as a site of common. See "The Politics of Commensality," in *The Anarchist Turn*, ed. Jacob Blumenfeld, Chiara Bottici, and Simon Critchley (Pluto Press, 2013), pp. 35–58.

66 Arendt, *The Human Condition*, p. 50.

67 Ibid.

4

Strike! Enthusiasm in several political acts

I lay before you a plan of freedom – adopt it, and you rid the world of inequality, misery, and crime. A martyr in your cause, I am become the prophet of your salvation. A plan of happiness is pointed out and dedicated to you. With it I devote to you my life and body, my soul and blood.

> – William Benbow, "Grand National Holiday, and Congress of the Productive Classes" (1832)

Inspired

Enthusiasm, an affect once associated with abstraction and testimony to divine inspiration, has its origins in religious experience.[1] In the long history of this Western phenomenon, it was generally thought that the only real measure of humanity's access to divinity could be confirmed by the expression of something named "enthusiasm." Over time a series of religious reformations coupled with modern social and political Enlightenments, transformed enthusiasm from a religious affect into a political danger. And, by the end of the eighteenth century, enthusiasm seemed to have become a centerpiece of revolutionary, rather than religious, life.[2]

Because of this complicated admixture of religious and revolutionary potencies, we should not be surprised that Marx – the quintessential theorist of the modern revolution – struggled to orient himself to the concept of enthusiasm.[3] If capital's power manifests itself in abstractions that re-disguise materiality, enthusiasm might appear as a significant resource for capitalism, generating new pathways for novelty.[4] But Marx's language on enthusiasm shifts, specifically from *Enthusiasmus* to *Begeisterung*, tracing

Marx's changing thinking on the communist revolution, as well as the religious imaginary. Following this shift, we see an opening for a new modality of enthusiasm that can be deployed against capitalism and towards collective agency, in the form of a revolutionary occupation.

Marx's struggle with religion, and its notable absence in his theory of a communist future, is well known.[5] Contextually, Marx is often read as one who means to assault the passivity of religion, in contrast to the necessary activity of the Enlightenment of communism.[6] Indeed, the religious experience he so often describes looks to be emblematic of a logic of abstraction. As he famously exclaims, "Religion is the general theory of the world – its encyclopedic compendium, logic in popular form, spiritualistic *point-d'honeur*, its enthusiasm (*Enthusiasmus*), its moral sanction, its solemn complement, its general consolation and justification."[7]

What would Marx mean here by referring to religion as the enthusiasm of the world? His own vocabulary in this passage seems particularly abstract. In its totality of form and spirit, Marx presents religion with a force that is undeniable. As he continues, "Religious misery is at once the expression of true suffering and also the protest against true misery. Religion is the sigh of the desperate creature, the heart of a heartless world, the ghost of a spiritless condition. It is the opium of the people."[8] Here, in this famous passage, Marx illustrates the potency of religion's force. There is a double, liminal quality to religion; religion appears to be both something and nothing – both pain and the protest against pain, heart and heartlessness, spirit and spiritlessness. Significantly, this double quality becomes a vehicle for bourgeois forces. Capital – so easily dressed in religious disguise – deploys such forces to exploit, with the consequence of deep-seated alienation. In naming enthusiasm (*Enthusiasmus*) as central to this double quality of religion, Marx highlights for us his thinking on this phenomenon. He sees enthusiasm as something of a passage between the presence and absence of reality – a sort of threshold between illusion and true reality.

Marx's early language on enthusiasm demonstrates that this phenomenon might be caught between abstracted and material realities. This is especially clear in his pairing of the concepts of enthusiasm (*Enthusiasmus*) *and* interest (*Interesse*). Reflecting on the dangerous bourgeois logics he sees as apparent in earlier modalities of revolution, Marx explains,

> If the [French] revolution was a failure, it was not because the masses were "enthusiastic" and "interested" in the revolution, but because the most numerous part – the part distinct from the bourgeoisie – was not really interested in the principle of revolution, did not have a peculiarly revolutionary principle – only an "idea" – and so only an object of momentary enthusiasm and apparent uprising.[9]

Marx's use of the idiom enthusiasm (*Enthusiasmus*) seems to borrow from the Greek *etymology* – to be inspired, possessed by a god. Interest, by contrast, conveys the importance of something – that which is of interest is that something which would make a difference (from the Latin *interresse* – to be between, "inter" and "esse," to be of difference). Joining enthusiasm and interest together, Marx highlights a notion of enthusiasm as that affect which "makes a difference" or at least that feeling that "a difference" is being made. This is consistent with several instances of Marx's use of enthusiasm (*Enthusiasmus*) in his thought, prior to 1848. As Marx summarizes, "No class of civil society can play this [transformative] role without arousing a moment of enthusiasm (*Enthusiasmus*) in itself and in the masses ... a moment in which it is truly the social head and the social heart."[10] The moment of enthusiasm matters; though Marx seems, at least in his early work, unclear as to why.

In Marx's early uses of the term "enthusiasm" he seems to simply recapitulate the religious affect, even in political contexts. But such an expression of enthusiasm risks the agency of those who experience it. I propose that, at least within his terminology, we see an anxiety regarding the utilization of enthusiasm. If enthusiasm is an affect that shows us difference, what is the moment of difference, and who is making it? Attention to Marx's changing language on enthusiasm highlights a resolution to this problematic. Indeed, in his later writing, we see a rethinking of enthusiasm, such that it might become possible to counteract the illusionary qualities latent in the previous "religious" conception.

As his work progresses, Marx begins to deploy a new vocabulary for enthusiasm. This shift in his language and his thinking is most obvious in the *Communist Manifesto*, where the language of the "specter" (*Gespenst*) highlights a move in vocabularies away from revolution as confrontation, and towards a language of haunting through occupation.[11] The work of the *Manifesto* highlights another form of political power – a "public" power – that lies in collectivity itself. This collectivity is best conceived as a specter, haunting the living, coopting the ghostly power of capital from itself. This specter becomes the "true democracy" to be fulfilled, where free development of each and all is possible. As Marx explains,

> The bourgeoisie, when it comes to rule, has destroyed all the feudal, patricidal, idyllic conditions. It has mercilessly torn the multicolored and variegated feudal ties that bound humanity to any natural order and left no other link between man and man than pure, naked interest. It has drowned the holy shudders of pious fanaticism (*Schwärmerei*), of chivalrous enthusiasm (*Begeisterung*), of petty-bourgeois sadness in the icy waters of selfish calculation.[12]

At this crucial moment in the *Manifesto*, when Marx is explicating the logic of "overturning" essential to the bourgeois activity of revolution, we see an important edit. The bourgeoisie have eradicated zealotry (*Schwärmerei*) and chivalrous enthusiasm (*Begeisterung*) in the icy waters of calculation. At first gloss, the emphasis here appears to be on calculation. But a close reading must also account for the specificity of Marx's language, and what is present and absent: why *Schwärmerei* and *Begeisterung*, and not *Enthusiasmus*? Why this shift in vocabulary?[13]

The shift we find illustrated here highlights for us a change in Marx's own thinking. *Enthusiasmus* may be left out precisely because it was the centerpiece of the bourgeois revolutions. Marx's use of this new synonym for enthusiasm – *Begeisterung* (which we might read etymologically as *mit Geist erfüllen* – filled with spirit/ghost) – is crucial, for it allows him to move away from the language of religion and divinity and towards the language of haunting. Here, enthusiasm is transformed, precisely at the moment where the word disappears. Enthusiasm-as-*Begeisterung* becomes with spirit, with ghosts, enlivened with inspirations; a clear shift away from thinking on enthusiasm as "god within." The *Manifesto* makes possible that shift by its claim to embody the specter that haunts (*Gespenst/Geist*). Here, Marx introduces us to embodied ghosts, beyond the bourgeois lifeworld and the means of production. This goes to the center of the bourgeois anxiety of production – all that is solid melts away. This shift from "being with god" to "being with spirits" offers a new affective vocabulary that helps to make manifest the activity of occupation (the haunting of capitalist systems of power). Taking over and occupying the networks of bourgeois power, and accelerating those networks – networks of communication, networks of transport, networks of power – enthusiasm as haunting (*Begeisterung*) becomes the means of countering the illusions manifest in bourgeois enthusiasm (*Enthusiasmus*). Revolution, in a moment of enthusiasm, is no longer overturning; revolution is occupation.

Marx's shift in language seeds an important transformation in revolutionary political thinking on enthusiasm. Not simply the desire for abstraction or revolutionary overturning, now enthusiasm-as-*Begeisterung* has become the affect of revolutionary occupation. As discussed in the last chapter, Arendt points us in the dangerous direction where enthusiasm commingles with relief. Through Marx, an alternative "enthusiasm" emerges; an affective threshold, residing on the boundary between the religious fantasy of human reality, the affective motivation of true human emancipation. In this way, we can read Marx's thought as a new beginning for political enthusiasm.

If we hope to rethink enthusiasm beyond the dead end of relief, we should follow the pathways that enthusiasm-as-*Begeisterung* opens up. Building on Marx, Walter Benjamin offers us a way of sensing this political enthusiasm in action. Though Benjamin never takes up the question of enthusiasm explicitly, I argue that we can read his efforts to understand the pathologies of progress and the state as a radical Marxian inheritance of Kant's "Old Question Raised Again" essay, one that engenders and performs enthusiasm in action.

Shooting at clocks

In the last days of July 1830, Paris became the site of immense civil unrest and extreme rioting.[14] Crowds, composed of mostly shopkeepers and skilled artisans – masons and carpenters and printers and tailors and shoemakers – formed and swelled, facing well-trained batteries of troops, deployed by Charles X in defense of the failing French monarchy. High rates of unemployment for skilled labor, coupled with unbearable increases in taxation rates for shopkeepers, had created desperate conditions for a large percentage of the population. Most of those involved in the fighting were old enough to be employed, and yet not so old as to have fought in the Revolution of 1789.[15] They were the generation born in the wake of the revolution; what more than a few witnesses poetically labeled as the *nouveaux Josués* – the new Joshuas.

Such a reference might seem a mere lyrical flourish to describe that post-revolutionary generation, the children who were raised in a world after the collapse of the *Ancien Régime*. But this name actually calls our imaginations to a more specific behavior of the July revolutionaries, aligning them, beyond mere generational affiliation, with the Hebrew prophet Joshua. In the fifteenth thesis of his essay "On the Concept of History," Walter Benjamin helpfully reflects on these "New Joshuas" in revolution:[16]

> In the July Revolution, an incident occurred which showed (a revolutionary) consciousness was still alive. On the first evening of fighting, it happened that clocks – standing in towers throughout Paris – were being shot at simultaneously and independently from several locations. An eyewitness, who may have owed his divination to the rhyme, wrote as follows: "Who would have believed it! It is said that there were new Joshuas who, incensed at time itself, were standing at the foot of every tower and firing on clock faces to make the day stand still."[17]

Joshua, the biblical figure, was politically famous for his military campaigns. One of the most crucial moments in his command, and a constituent moment of violence for the Hebrew people after the death of Moses, came during an ensuing conflict with the city of Gibeon. So as to facilitate this victory, and perhaps to demonstrate the transcendental power that accompanied the Hebrew army, Joshua was said to have commanded time to stop: " 'Sun, stand still over Gibeon, and you, moon, over the Valley of Aijalon.' So the sun stood still, and the moon stopped, till the nation avenged itself on its enemies."[18] Historical – or poetic – reference to these July revolutionaries as "New Joshuas" seems to point to a parallel action in attempting – no longer mythically – to arrest time.

What is this desire to arrest time – to make time stand still? Why, on the first day of intense political turmoil and civil unrest, would a supposedly random assortment of proto-revolutionaries (more bourgeois citizens than soldiers), scattered throughout the city, take it upon themselves to shoot at clock towers? What is the symbolic power embedded in the materiality of these clocks, such that their physical desecration and destruction would be the first act of a burgeoning revolution?[19] These questions all point to the political significance of time, and modalities of time in occupation.

Time, however metaphysical it may first appear as a concept, is crucially central to social and political life as an ordering mechanism. The July revolutionaries' act of shooting at clocks points to the centrality of time – how we consider it, how we measure it, and how it orders our daily existence. As Giorgio Agamben asserts, "Every conception of history is invariably accompanied by a certain experience of time which is implicit in it, conditions it, and thereby has to be elucidated."[20] These revolutionaries seem to have been attempting first – before anything else – to separate themselves from the ordering of daily existence that had been imposed on them by the previous political order.[21] As Benjamin remarked, "[This] very awareness of exploding the continuum of history is characteristic of the revolutionary classes at the moment of their action."[22] How we think about the political significance of time has clear implications for how we understand political order, as well as the act of its rupture.

Affect and interruption

My aim here is to consider what happens when enthusiasm starts to become enmeshed in ideology, and how to begin to distinguish it in action. Here I highlight an alternative pathway for a more radical manifestation of political enthusiasm. Walter Benjamin's essay *Critique of Violence* (1921) offers important examples of acts of enthusiasm, and especially the general strike.[23] Benjamin's discussion of the general strike draws the political imagination to what he named a "pure" politics, beyond mediation. This chapter reads the strike as a principle of political intrusion – one that is a lurking, though sublimated, enthusiasm. This reading productively problematizes the force of the strike. It extends Benjamin's thesis, beyond any historical imagination of the general strike as the mere force of labor, instead reading the strike as an act of enthusiasm that extends and complicates Kant's thinking, and in different ways from the Arendtian inheritance. This chapter also moves to more contemporary examples of enthusiastic acts, considering immolations, hunger strikes, and other "suicides" as similarly "general" politics, rupturing the violence of the state according to its own pathways of power.

As a guiding question, we might reasonably ask how the timing of events – the temporal ordering of events, and their rupturing – might matter to us politically. And, as we have seen in previous chapters of this book, the temporal horizon has profound affective consequences, especially for politics. The political enthusiasm that begins to take shape in Kant's reflections on the French revolutionaries, especially in comparison to the ancient Levites, crafts an affective landscape, where radical rebellion originates in political self-possession. That "taking hold of oneself" that Kant introduces us to, has a complicated history, inherited by Benjamin through Romantic thought as a radicalizing variability. If Kant's rethinking of political enthusiasm refocuses the language of enthusiasm away from derogations such as fanaticism and swarming (*Schwärmer*), it does so by shifting to a language of specialized experiences of political affect, resulting in a reading of enthusiasm as a revolutionary "passage" through political order. Kant's surprising move away from the derogated identity of the enthusiast, and towards a descriptive theory of activities that align enthusiasms affect, proves a trenchant critique of underlying secular prejudice within Enlightenment discourses since Hobbes, while beginning to explain a new form of radical political behavior against order.

At root in this radical tradition that Kant inadvertently initiates, is a critique – even against Kant's more famous reflections – of progress, and the temporal horizon of revolution. This move between the special languages of revolution and new temporal languages, and the overlapping intersections between the two, compose the majority of this chapter. My aim throughout has been to show how a Kantian rethinking of religious enthusiasm as a political concept that underlies revolution opens a complex set of arguments that get taken up and theorized in both sublime and pedestrian registers. In this chapter, I turn to Benjamin's critical inheritance of the form of Kantian enthusiasm to explain how certain modes of temporality – ways of understanding and using time – become politicized.

Specifically, how might political enthusiasm affect the temporal register of a politics that resists it?

There has been much theorizing of late that *how* a political regime conceives of time may be at the core of its own self-understanding of the order that it imposes on the world.[24] Indeed, much of modern Western political thought reveals a progressive view of time, grounded in a uniform chronology. (This is what we might refer to as "standard" time or "clock" time.) Time, thought of in this way, is always already related to space, for it is the uniform movement across space that comes to define the parameters of time as an experienced chronology. Imagine the hands of the clock sweeping through space as denoting the real changes in time. Such mechanized time became increasingly significant in the capitalization of labor and the industrial revolution, where economic development was grounded in a regularized and predictable form of linear time.[25] In this linear ordering of the chronology of time, and its categorization into past, present, and future, economic and political institutions developed strategies of power and knowledge.[26]

While the conception of time as regular and uniform and always already connected to how subjects perceive spatial relations and the movements to traverse them, has become the dominant order of temporality associated with the West, this modality of time is beset with pathologies that seem to limit any associated politics.[27] (By pathology, I mean that sabotaging desire for a specific political effect that, in our desiring it, results precisely in the forestalling of that effect.) These pathologies are linked to the idea of progress, one in which the political subject is always separated from the temporal reality wherein progress can be assessed.[28] This is the underlying thesis revealed in Benjamin's "On the Concept of History." By his account, while progress – and the linear conception of time on which it relies – may have proved significant in structuring liberal conceptions of power and normativity, such polities remain unable to counter any formal challenge to such normativity if that challenge relies on a similar conception of time. This was, of course, the central danger that fascism posed to liberalism in the early twentieth century. As Benjamin explains, "One reason fascism even has a chance is the fact that in the name of progress its enemies regard it as a historical norm. The amazement that the things we experience in the twentieth century are 'still' possible is not philosophical. Such amazement is not the beginning of knowledge, unless we consider the effect as being that this idea of history, from which such amazement originates, is untenable."[29] A profound belief in progress – that social and political change will result in the improvement of humanity – also results in a paralyzing inability to counter moral and political dangers. Such continuity of progress stands as the fundamental problem of modernity, and results in a uniquely modern form of catastrophe (one always already linked to progress).[30]

As discussed previously, central to the pathology of such political conceptions of progressive time seems to be the agency of what we might call "the witness" or the "bystander" or "the spectator."[31] Western conceptions of progress depend on a notion of subjectivity capable of division, of viewing itself from the outside. This disassociated subject – "standing outside" itself as it engages in a kind of self-witnessing (what Arendt defended as the bystander's view) – becomes both progressive object and authorizing subject, gazing upon its own historical development. The act of "witnessing" progress seems to take place in such a way as to divide that subject, allowing it to become both (1) that person as object who has changed over time and is still becoming, and (2) that subject who is bearing witness to that change and remains stable in the act of witnessing that becoming. Indeed, the isolation of the modern secular subject as "witness" may, in part, originate in ancient religious testimonies as acts of martyrdom ("to martyr" was literally "to witness," but with connotations of anxiety and memory).[32] But the secularized division of the consciousness of the progressive political subject moves the source of anxiety beyond previous notions of divinity into a new register: The modern "witness" of progress is never able to confirm that being the witness is in fact the same subject who is part of the progressing history imagined.[33] This is the anxiety already apparent in that famous conception of time and flux attributed to Heraclitus: "It is not possible to step twice into the same river … or to come into contact twice with a mortal being in the same state." Benjamin's own work has aimed at engaging this problematic, expanding an argument on revolutionary political consciousness that might be capable of escaping the pathos of the witness; what Benjamin famously calls "constellations" in thinking. Yet, as I hope to make clear in this chapter, such constellations in thought may themselves still be too ill defined to clearly escape the logic of the witness. Rather, what is necessary is a materialist rethinking of temporality that is capable of grounding conceptions of temporality, separate from space, and also from the witness.

Engaging the psychology of temporality can appear far removed from the ordinary functions of daily politics. But my aim here is to show that attention to this other worldly matter of time has real consequences for how we understand more imperative normative concepts, such as progress and its related politics, and the place of enthusiasm within that understanding. In the early sections of this chapter, I engage a complex set of philosophical languages on the concept of time, so as to begin to disentangle the political stakes of how we understand certain temporal frames. I then turn to the unusual site of the revolutionary general strike, and especially Walter Benjamin's radical theorizing of the strike, as an opportunity to see an act of enthusiasm – a concrete political manifestation of a revolutionary break with what I take to be some of the pathological undercurrents of progress. Ultimately, my aim is to delineate a conception of the general strike that might specifically respond to such pathologies, tracing the evolution of the revolutionary general strike beyond Benjamin, into a present resistant politics.[34] In this way, my thinking here follows Spivak's recent call in her work to take up "the continued rethinking of the concept (of the general strike) even as it has seen varying expressions in practice throughout its development."[35]

Stations

Ordinary time, what we might best call the time of clocks and calendars, stands as a fundamental ordering of a sequence of happenings along a continuum that can be identified relative to itself. This is what Paul Tillich refers to as *chronos* (χρονος "clock time, time which is measured."[36] The clock originally acted to physically measure time through tracing the regular passage of its hands across intervals. (Calendars originated as that by which to count those periods of time that exceeded a single day.) Past, present, and future become the categories for comparing events that occur within such measurements. The duration of such events could be calculated, as the division of time allowed for a regular manifold of units and their sequencing.

At first glance, such ordering might reveal itself as absent any normative conditionality. If this were the case, time would appear to us, but without affecting our consciousness. This is what Jean-Jacques Rousseau, for instance, has argued about clock time. As he explains, "I perceive the order of the world, though I have no knowledge of its purpose … I am like a man who one can imagine seeing for the first time a watch with its back taken off and who cannot help admiring the intricacy of its works though he has no idea what the machine is for."[37] Yet this analogy between the ordering of the world and the watch is misleading, for it assumes that the content of the analogy denies the normativity of time itself. The clock can impose order, as was the case, for instance, in the new revolutionary clock and calendar in France. The first generation of revolutionaries in France adopted both a new calendar and a new clock.[38] The division of time there was isochronic – literally meant to instill equality in the very ordering of the day. Each "day" was divided into ten hours, each hour being made up of a hundred minutes, and each minute being made up of a hundred seconds. The results of this transformation were that 1 second under the new Republican isochronic clock was equal to 2.4 seconds under what would now be regarded as "standard" time.[39] Rousseau's analogy misses the power of this ordering. As Tillich argues the point, "There is something mysterious about the clock. It determines our daily timing. Without it we could not plan for the next hour, we could not time any of our activities."[40] The very way in which we measure time signifies the value we place on it and how we measure our experiences in and of the world.

The normativity of time goes beyond the mere ordering of the day, providing a frame through which life itself can come to be measured. Again, following Tillich, "the clock also reminds us of the (fundamental) fact that we are timed. The voice of the clock has reminded many people of the fact that they are timed. In an old German night-watchman's street song every hour is announced with a special reminder. Of midnight it says: "Twelve – that is the goal of time, give us, O God, eternity.' "[41]

The song of the watchman reveals the implicit structure of this conception of time as teleological. The measuring of time helps frame a structure of our consciousness of duration as always already eliding toward some end. Inevitably, so Tillich argues it, we collapse the idea of time ending and our own mortal ending into each other. Here the emphasis on time is one on ends – what will happen to me, to the present, to the world. The normativity latent here regards what should be done between the now of this present and the inevitable final present that time – my time on earth – will become. That this normative conception of time – what should be done with *this* present as it transcends into a future present – is linked to clocks is not insignificant. Such a view of time regards it as a means of witnessing the movement of things through space, with the anxiety that space itself is an end in its appearance ending for me.

Revealed in this view of time is the centrality of time to our understanding of the appearances of the world. As Kant famously argued,

> Time is a necessary representation that grounds all intuitions. In regard to appearances in general one cannot remove time, though one can very well take the appearances away from time. Time is therefore given a priori. In it alone is all actuality of appearances possible. The latter could all disappear, but time itself, as the universal condition of their possibility, cannot be removed.[42]

At issue in the normative conception of time and the possibility of the end of a particularly human subjectivity is linked here by Kant to our sense perception of the world. How the world appears to us, our very senses of things in the world as the world, are directly set in a frame that we call "time" – an intuition that is necessary for us to even apprehend the world. Here, I trace a link between Kant's representational view of time as an a priori grounding of intuition as a coding of clock-based progressive time. Time, read this way, is not a thing, but that which we employ as we engage the things of the world. This explains at least part of the power requisite to the political ordering of time, and extending from this Kantian view of time, the political (and economic) use of such time has evolved as a necessary feature of the industrialized West.[43]

The political economy of the modern industrial nation state depends on ordered conceptions of time and a deep sense of time-liness. Predictions of the future, both economically and politically, depend on an ability to determine when things – goods and services, steel and soldiers – will be "delivered." As many have observed, the factory of the nineteenth century becomes the centerpiece of this normative employment of time.[44] Goods delivered off schedule cost in delayed production and market fluctuations. Indeed, even the very concept of a public may be linked to this notion of time. If we want to do something, if we want to catch an event (a train, for instance), we need clocks and a measure of time that can be shared in public with others. This shared time can come to order our existence – and matters a great deal for the legality of contracts made and promises kept. Such strategies for ordering time and predicting events have become central to the contemporary political experience.

The railroad is an especially potent illustration of the industrial West's employment of this normativity through time. As one historian observes, "The twenty-four-hour day and the three hundred and sixty-five-day year are as necessary to the railroad as to the calendar. There are no holidays. Christmas day in Chicago is two days before Christmas in Los Angeles, if you are moving east, and two days after Christmas if you are move west."[45] The railroad became a means in the West for organizing and initiating the employment of this normativity chronological time.

Crucial to this conception of chronological time is the desire for, and pathos of, mastery. As Martin Heidegger explains it,

> We pass the time, in order to master it, because time becomes long in boredom. Time becomes long for us. Is it supposed to be short then? Does not each of us wish for a truly long time for ourselves? And whenever it does become long for us, we pass the time and ward off its becoming long! We do not want to have a long time, but we have it nevertheless.[46]

The ordering of time in chronology turns time into an instrument with a use-value. Yet our experience of this instrument is not strictly instrumental. The mastery of time – to be capable of ordering it – leaves open the space wherein mastery fails. This failure, by Heidegger's account, takes the form of boredom (*langweilig* – almost literally "long while"), an affect that elicits the strange pathology of increasing our desire for mastery (the same desire where boredom originated initially). To illustrate this experience, Heidegger gives the example of waiting for the train in a station.

> What do we expect of the station? That it be a station in general? No – but rather that we can use it as a station, i.e., that at this

station we can immediately enter the train and depart as quickly as possible. It is a proper station precisely whenever it does not force us to wait. The station at hand refuses itself to us as a station and leaves us empty because the train that belongs to it has not arrived, so that there is such a long time that drags on until the arrival of the train. Thus it does not yet offer us what it properly ought to. To do so, however, it must be precisely a railway station and as such be at hand, in order to allow us to wait. Why else does it have a waiting room?[47]

The station becomes a cultural site of boredom. By Heidegger's account, the experience of the station is one that demands that it counter itself. It is a place that acts as a stopping point (either a beginning, middle, or end), and in so doing, is not itself a place that wants any person to remain. It is a place of waiting, and in that way, it is the cultural institution that may best exemplify the lived experience of chronological time, dividing the subject between being and an ideal becoming, where the subject's becoming takes precedent. This division, consequent to the normativity of chronological time, and embodied in the boredom of the train station, presents us with a portrait of the modern progressive human subject, always divided from themselves in their experience of time.

Such a divided progressive subject, by Walter Benjamin's account, faces the fundamental danger requisite to contemporary political life, namely that of alienation through boredom.[48] In this doubling of the modern divided progressive subject, a sort of blindness ensues. By Benjamin's view, all that is desired by the modern subject is progress, and for progress, everything will be sacrificed. The problem Benjamin asks us to face is how we are to confront the very idea of injustice in our present experiences of political life with such a notion of progress. A real consequence of contemporary notions of progressivism may be the very inability to respond to an emergency we recognize as wrong, especially if we experience that emergency as perfectly in conjunction with the progressive development of things as usual – that is, if the emergency can be predicted. The emergency Benjamin has in mind is fascism. In this reading, while fascism may have once been easily recognizable as a threat to the West, it was also pathologically fueled by the progressive hope that perhaps this emergency was really a mere stepping-stone, on the way to some more "progressive politics."

Vulgar historical materialism and historicism, the two current temporal modes of addressing contemporary political life in the West, present us with this problem of pathological hopefulness. Vulgar historical materialism acts in such a way as to always ask us to conceive of history as part of a conflict, there to help us transcend to a new moment. By this view, anything that happens in this world can be subjugated to the necessary historical conflict that must take place on the path to the accomplishment of world history. Historicism, by contrast, focuses in on the details of a historical moment, always desiring the perfection of the world available in that instant from which we must (as part of an ulterior present) remain isolated. Such isolation is only ever possible for a distant (too distant) past. *Chronos* – the ordinary time associated with a temporal and political conception of progress – becomes limited by these normative frames that besiege it.

Here we must return to Kant's understanding of time as an intuition to help explain the logic of chronological time that Benjamin (and Heidegger) seems so concerned with. For Kant, time (along with space) is a means by which we access our sense perceptions of the world around us; each acts as a precondition on our ability to apprehend the world through our senses. Space and time are not things, or even events, but rather the means by which we encounter the material world. He explains this logic as follows,

> In order that certain sensations be referred to something outside me (that is, to something in another region of space and time from that in which I find myself now), and similarly in order that I may be able to represent them as outside and alongside one another, and accordingly as not only different but as in different places, the representation of space must already underlie them [*dazu muß die Vorstellung des Raumes schon zum Grunde liegen*]. Therefore, the representation of space cannot be obtained through experience from the relations of outer appearance; this outer experience is itself possible at all only through that representation.[49]

From this view, space and time are not things, but rather emptiness that subjects require in order to intuit things. We know this is the case because we cannot experience the pure representation of space or time. The consequence of this logic depends on what we, as modern rational critical subjects, are capable of apprehending. By Kant's view, such subjects are the centerpiece of our experience of sense perceptions, and the intuitions on which they depend.

Is such a subjective consciousness required in order to have the intuition that time only ever appears with things (and thus allows the object to appear to us at all)? Moreover, what does this time suggest of our time and our conceptions of us within and before and after our time? Does the modern human mind need to resort to space in order to represent time? We need to linger on these questions, especially if we hope to counter the logic of mastery (and oppression) implicit in chronological time.

The new Joshuas

The politics that emerges from a chronological theory of time divides subjects from themselves, leaving agents in the position of never being able to encounter the promise of progress, or to counter any political dangers that might emerge along the way.[50] Crucial to the political pathologies of chronological time is the regularity and uniformity set by such experiences of duration. Chronological time is always set according to a notion of waiting (thus the boredom that Heidegger observes). And this waiting – waiting for death and/ or redemption, results in a constant instability in the normative experience of time itself.

But what if time is not regular? What if time is, as we might say, out of joint?[51] What does it mean for time to be irregular? How might we recognize time through its irregularities – and what might the political consequences of this other sort of time entail? One of the notable characteristics of chronological time is how easy it is to forget it and that it is even happening. It is so regular, so uniform, so omnipresent, that it is easy to imagine time's insignificance. This is the source of its normative power; that it is so easily forgotten even as it is employed in the structural ordering of subjectivity. The political stakes of time being out of joint, as Jacques Derrida worried, are that the sorts of justice claims that we make when politics has gone rotten – when the very frame in which we might make justice claims is itself corrupted against hearing such claims are revealed to us through our experience of time. This worry parallels Benjamin's regarding the emergency that we may recognize, but to this we may not be able to respond, at least if we are truly subject to modern progressive logics.

How does this joining and unjoining of time appear to us? One important illustration of such a notion of time occurs in the Christian experience of the event of redemption. Ancient Christians conceived of an alternative form of time, which at the right time would interrupt *chronos*. This other time, *kairos*, was a moment of opportunity. It offered a rupture – a critical time – in the empty time of the void of chronology. As Tillich explains it, "*Kairos* is the feeling that the time is ripe, mature, prepared – the right time. Something has happened – a time has occurred, a moment has come when something is now possible or impossible."[52] *Kairos* is the time of the decision, wherein an agent feels the capacity and the impetrative to act. It is the only moment when redemption is possible.

Such a rethinking of time as not merely uniform and sequential, but also as a disruption – as the right time – invites us to reflect on an alternative normativity. One crucial aspect to *kairos* seems to be the experience of the end as disruption of chromos. How are we to understand the sort of time that begins to finish and come to an end? What sort of time is this? This conception of time as central to the event has come to be interpreted as principally that time, which is the transition between *chronos* and eternity, a transition that is only possible (at least in Judeo-Christian contexts) through the Messiah. Messianic time is the time of redemption; a time where we are purportedly ourselves, and not merely spectators of ourselves. Following this logic, Agamben claims that "every conception of history is invariably accompanied by a certain experience of time which is implicit in it, conditions it, and thereby has to be elucidated."[53] Such elucidation is made clear in the temporal experience of *kairos* – the right time. Much of Agamben's own conception of history and time draws upon Benjamin's insights, who makes the profound point regarding Western conceptions of history that they are invariably linked to a notion of progress that constantly destabilizes them, leaving Western politics incapable of defending itself against political dangers such as fascism. Benjamin held the view that only in response to these ethical and political dangers can one begin to establish an agency that is freed from the confinements of the chronological theory of progress. As he explains,

> Articulating the historical past does not mean cognizing it "as it actually happened." It means to take possession of or to seize a memory as it flashes up at a moment of danger. Historical materialism hopes to capture the image of the past as it presents itself to the historical subject suddenly in a moment of danger. The danger threatens and menaces (*droht*) both the very existence of the tradition and its recipients.[54]

It is precisely this feeling of danger that cannot be ignored and helps ground the new aspects of normativity latent in an alternate conception of time, which might be grounded in the event. The messianic event reveals itself in chronological time as such an emancipating rupture, and the time of this interruption itself is what we might refer to as *kairos*.[55]

The time that appears in such a moment of danger is what Benjamin asserts is "now-time" (*Jetztzeit*).[56] What constitutes this now-time? The important question Benjamin raises for us is how might we face the emergency now? The solution that Benjamin offers is a second conception of time, beyond mere chronology, in which the past and the present escape their shared linear definition. Instead, time is experienced as part of a constellation of moments, which draw normative connection from the subject in the present who is recuperated and redeemed in such a moment. Such a conception of time has, at least in the secular liberal West, received much definition from the political theology of Judeo-Christian conceptions of time, wherein time is experienced as a regularized and uniform unfolding of the same divisions of temporal existence (*chronos*), punctuated by events that disrupt the regularity of time as experienced in its manifold form (*kairos*).[57] Indeed, while Benjamin does not use the word "*kairos*," there seems to be some profound similarities to his idea of now-time.

Much of the similarity may come from the experience of disruption latent in both conceptualizations of time. As Benjamin explains,

> To think involves not only the flow of thoughts, but also their arrest. Where thinking suddenly stops in a constellation (*Konstellation*) saturated with tensions, it gives a shock, by which it crystalizes into

a monad. The historical materialist engages a historical object only where it encounters such a monad. In this structure he recognizes the sign of a messianic arresting position of the event (messianic cessation of happening/messianic still-standing of the event), or put differently, a revolutionary chance to fit the oppressed of the past.[58]

The experience of rupture is an ethical experience of opportunity. The tensions of thought revealed in a moment of danger help the subject constitute the modality of a live history. Therein, time takes on a new form, one recuperated with the release of those tensions that only appeared in the messianic sign. Here time is standing still so as to allow for the possibility of redemption. This "still-standing" of the event points to the experience of an ulterior mode of temporality.

While Benjamin's conception of now-time offers some important correctives to a politics of chronological time, it may also risk the limitation of its own grounding in human subjectivity that it may have aimed to avoid. Implicit in Benjamin's notion of the constellation is the fundamental premise that the human subject is now part of a history that stands alongside other moments in the history before and after the present now. This "being alongside" and immersed in the tension of the now allows for the formation of a constellation of development (as opposed to linear progression). This constellation accounts for the instant of the now in which a redemptive reorientation of time is possible, but draws grounding of that instant in the requisite preceding and following moment that help give it meaning as a fundamental source of normativity. This is not a regularized chronology of sequential units of time, but a still-standing of time wherein distinct moments come to be infused with hope that events can be set in relation to one another.

While this conception of temporality breaks from the pathologies of progressive linear time, for here one is capable of acting in the moment of "danger," it is not clear that it necessarily avoids the logic of the witness. In this model, it seems the witness is now simply complicit in, as opposed to isolated from, the historicity of the event. Again, consider Benjamin's reflections of the July Revolution:

> In the July Revolution, an incident occurred which showed (a revolutionary) consciousness was still alive. On the first evening of fighting, it happened that clocks – standing in towers throughout

Paris – were being shot at simultaneously and independently from several locations. An eyewitness, who may have owed his divination to the rhyme, wrote as follows: "Who would have believed it! It is said that there were new Joshuas who, incensed at time itself, were standing at the foot of every tower and firing on clock faces to make the day stand still."[59]

The eyewitness is central to this conceptualization, being the one who testifies to the peculiar reality taking place.[60] The constellation of revolutionary consciousness formed here is one beset by the authority of the eyewitness who perceives a revolutionary moment unfolding in the action of the destruction of the clocks – the physical manifestation of time established by the ruling regime. This act of destruction was said to take place at a single moment from all around the city, and yet from discrete agents, all shooting simultaneously at the towers. Just as the stars of a constellation might appear to shine at the same moment to an astrological observer, so too did these bullets seem to fire in an exact instant. That the "eyewitness" is present to help crystalize the event-ness of this destruction seems to follow a similar logic as that which plagued progressive linearity. Everything about this conception of time and the events that take place within it still depend on the witness who is separated from the action that defines the instant of the event.[61] Here the question becomes, how, if at all, can we find a way for this witness to escape that alienation – to become both constitutive and involved in the "kairotic" event? I believe we find such a turning within the logic of the general strike.

Setting the strike

It is worth pausing to ask what might be meant by the phrase "revolutionary general strike." Is this strike an example of a political practice, one strategy – among many – in revolt against the state? Or, perhaps, is the general strike itself a principle of political action, always demanding that the logic of the strike itself become revolutionary?

Walter Benjamin's essay *Zur Kritik der Gewalt* (1921), translated as "Critique of Violence," famously offers a consideration of the general strike as a limit to the violence of state law. Made anxious by the pathological mythic violences of the state, Benjamin endeavors to explain justice beyond mere law and the mediated determinative logics of existing political institutions that administer the law. In Benjamin's view, law is either prohibitive (and thus able to cognize what must always already be prohibited) or moral (and thus applicable to all), always risking a violent abstraction through mediation. But what politics, if any, might stand beyond such law? Benjamin finds an answer in the general strike.

As Benjamin considers it, the legality of the strike authorizes it as an interruption of the law. The logic of the strike that Benjamin develops perfectly performs the revolutionary enthusiasm that Kant names.[62] Benjamin uncovers the logic of the general strike as a Romantic political practice that initiates the enthusiastic political event. This is the profundity of the strike, and Benjamin's thinking here has traditionally been read as an example of a particular political practice, revealing where and when politics escapes mere instrumentality.

Extending the claim that the true general strike escapes mere instrumentality, Benjamin's discussion of the general strike draws political imaginations to what he named as a "pure" politics, an enthusiastic politics beyond mediation. If that is right, how could we consider the general strike as an "example"? What does the general strike suggest about law and justice generally, that it avoids the mediacy of abstraction (a mediacy that may itself be present in "example")? Rather than limit the general strike by logics of the "example," my chapter reads the strike as a principle of political intrusion (both material and temporal). In this way, I argue that there is much evidence to suggest that the general strike has taken on new forms (some subtle, some not so subtle) in its long history. And, while different manifestations have appeared over modern history, there has been a fundamental principle that clarifies these phenomena. I read Benjamin as helpful here for considering the very principle of the general strike (in form, not merely content). And I hope to show how Benjamin, in his "Critique of Violence," offers an annunciation of the general strike as a principle that operates on a logic of self-possession as self-annihilation.

While we find much historical evidence for explicit manifestations of the general strikes of labor, limiting ourselves to this example may rupture the very power of the "general" that the strike allows us to encounter. Instead, by drawing comparison between the general strike and political suicide, we may productively problematize the force of the strike, extending's Benjamin's thesis, beyond our historical imagination of the general strike as the mere force of labor. Considering political suicide – immolations, hunger strikes, and other "suicides," for example – as "general" politics should allow for a rethinking of the general strike as a category of political practice, rupturing the violence of the state according to its own – always changing – pathways of power.[63] In short, the general strike is the suicide of the state.

The origins of the revolutionary general strike can be traced back to the labor movements of industrializing Western state economies.[64] The epigraph that begins this chapter comes from William Benbow's dedication to his radical pamphlet from 1832, "A Grand National Holiday."[65] Benbow is often credited with the invention of the "general strike" as a means of unifying labor forces to confront economic injustices and perverse inequality. The original ideal of the strike, at least as Benbow conceived it, took the form of the holiday – but maybe not as we would normally use that term today. As Benbow explained, "A holiday" in the sense he meant it

> signifies a *holy* day, and ours is to be *of holy days* the most holy. It is to be most holy, most sacred, for it is to be consecrated to promote – or to create rather – the happiness and liberty of mankind. Our holy day is established to establish plenty, to abolish want, to render all men equal! In our holy day we shall legislate for all mankind; the constitution drawn up during our holiday, shall place *every human being* on the same footing. Equal rights, equal liberties, equal enjoyments, equal toil, equal respect, equal share of production: this is the object of our holy day – of our sacred day, – of our festival!"[66]

While the "holiday" may be unfamiliar expression of the practice we have come to refer to as a "general strike," we still can see much of a rhetoric to be commonplace in the general strike in Benbow's articulation. The general strike is commonly conceived of as a labor strike – though one that spans across industries and regions, unifying a plurality of workers in disparate industries against unjust work and/or social and political conditions that span society. There are many historical examples where such rhetoric applies: the industrial cities of England and Wales in 1842, the Midwestern United States (especially St. Louis) in 1877, most of the world in 1919, Oakland in 1946, France in 1968, and Greece and Spain (among other regions in Europe) in 2012.[67]

Yet Benbow's call for the sacredness of what came to be known as the general strike may give us some pause. Why would we refer to the strike – and to the general strike especially – as having sacredness? Perhaps this is merely contextual rhetoric – Benbow was a radical pamphleteer known for his flamboyant prose, as well as by his critics as being persistently drunk (which may have helped). But the logic of the sacred is notable in how we might distinguish this originary form of the strike from its later iterations. To refer to the recent strikes in Greece,[68] or the previous general strikes threatened in Iceland,[69] as "sacred" would ring false to our contemporary ear. Still, we might better consider the logic of the sacred as a call to question: What else, if anything, is the general strike, beyond the simple interruption of labor forces across markets and regions? Can we recognize the general strike as a consistent practice, even in changing economic and social conditions? No. Are all these historical examples of the general strike precisely the same? Yes, though only in their shared principle. All this points us to the most pressing question of all: What especially has the general strike become today? Or rather, what would it need to become today, in order to encounter the contemporary neoliberal pathologies of capitalist societies, the "fragility" (to use William Connolly's phrase) that permeates everything?[70]

The rhetoric of the general strike, no matter the historical time and place, has usually reflected a shared effort to confront logics of domination along class lines, with workers from various industries or regions or cities or countries unified through the event of their own repulsion to such domination. Consider, for example, the radicalizing language of the protest against the city of Oakland, California in 2011:

> The time has come to shut "their" city down for good and realize … the creation of radically democratic and self-determined communities – in a vibrant movement that involves people from every race and class – in the conscious pursuit of the destruction of the existing social structures of race and class, as well as every other axis of oppression, that divides and oppresses in this society – "All power to all of the People!"[71]

Less than a week after this call to strike was issued, the Oakland general strike succeeded in closing the Port of Oakland, one of the central shipping container facilities and ports of trade on the western seaboard of the United States. The rhetoric of the Oakland general strike is familiar. It deploys affective logics of inclusion along "democratic" entanglements, calling for direct action in response to oppression, and through such action, an appropriation of the power of the people (all the people).

Yet despite how familiar this language of the "general strike" may have become, it is not clear that the very practices of the general strike have remained constant throughout the history of this phenomenon. (Benbow's call for a holiday is one expression; the occupation of the Oakland port is another.) It seems important then to consider how specific practices of general strikes might be shaped by unique contextual conditions.

Consider, for example, the strikes of 1919. If any general strike transcends the limits of a mere labor strike, beyond industry and region – as so many considerations of this phenomenon demand it must – it would be the various strikes of 1919, from the Spartacist uprising in Germany, on January 4–15, to Seattle on February 6–11, to Winnipeg from May 15 to June 21, among a grand coalition of other cities. Yet, despite the wide-ranging relations of these strikes, how should we consider their force? As one historian recently argued, the Spartacist revolt failed:

> The rebels did not manage to seize the symbols of power, not to mention its instruments. Once the revolt came to an end, it became evident that, to a considerable extent, it had served the very power it attacked. Not only because in 10 days of clashes in Berlin the proletariat had lost a great number of its activists and almost the entirety of its leadership, not only because the organizational structures of the class had ceased to exist, but also because there transpired the very suspension of historical time – indispensable for the holders of power seeking to restore a "normal time" which they themselves had suspended during the years of the great war.[72]

As potent as these strikes were, the reestablishment of dominant forces of power points us to a fundamental anxiety: The general strike always risks furthering the potency of purposeful law and law-preserving logics. The collapse of the mass proletariat uprising in Berlin was the upholding of those forces that succeeded its collapse.

But not all general strikes have had the same outcomes, or the same structures. Indeed, the various constituencies that composed "the proletariat" in 1919 (organized labor – skilled workers, and not unskilled workers or immigrant labor), as well as their demands, would be unrecognizable in later protests of the same or similar scale. Following Boltanski and Chiapello's analysis, consider the various strikes, and the actors involved, that marked the early part of the decade of the 1970s:

> The beginning of the 1970s was marked by a series of serious, long strikes … In a number of cases, the initiative lay specifically with semi- and unskilled workers not with skilled workers or craft workers, who had a longer and stronger record of unionization. Involved in the "front lines of social struggle" were immigrant workers, skilled and unskilled workers in automobile firms, unskilled workers in the electric ad textile industries, bank and insurance company employees, girocheque employees, packers at sorting centers, shop assistants in hypermarkets.[73]

These new workers found themselves in a social and political environment that left some of them with a different sort of power hierarchy, caught between the structures of skilled and unionized workers, on the one hand, and the state structures, on the other.

And, as, recent historical analysis would show, these strikes were only superficially successful. While we do not find the gross collapse of organized labor powers in these French protests (as we did in 1919), we do see a surreptitious reorganization of the very terms of labor as a result of this general strike. Again, as Boltanski and Chiapello remind us, "During the general strike in November 1974, for example, workers on the blast-furnace floor, who were demanding a revision of their grades, and the abolition of the category of laborer in particular, obtained satisfaction, but the corresponding duties were simply handed over to outside firms."[74] This satisfaction of strikers' demands, coupled with the outsourcing of the work that framed those demands, points to a new logic of the economic power of the firm. Indeed, we might regard this as the practical (as opposed to theoretical) beginning of the neoliberal transformation of the conditions that would demand a contemporary rethinking of the general strike.

Some recent theorists, William Connolly among them, have hope in a strike that would counter the most recent manifestations of these logics. As Connolly explains, a critical response to neoliberal logics today would depend on constructing "a pluralist assemblage by moving back and forth between experiments in role performances, the refinement of sensitive modes of perception, revisions of political ideology, and adjustments in political sensibility, doing so to mobilize enough collective energy to launch a general strike simultaneously in several countries in the near future."[75] But what would such a strike entail? Given Boltanski and Chiapello's concerns for the failures of the last set of strikes in response to the deployment of neoliberal policy in the 1970s, what would the strike need to become to complete such an insurgency? While Connolly ends his critique of neoliberalism in the *Fragility of Things* with a call for a strike, the form such a strike would take – would have to take – in order to short-circuit these new logics, is not clear. Here, I suggest we turn to Walter Benjamin for help.

To touch lightly

What is the revolutionary general strike for Benjamin?[76] In asking this question, I do not presume to isolate the revolutionary general strike from the context in which it appears in Benjamin's thinking, but rather to draw on it as a focal point around which the argument for a critique of violence takes its form. Benjamin is quite explicit that he hopes to find, through a critique of violence, the principle by which we might stand beyond the pathological structures of state violence. The principle – not the historical practice – that Benjamin poses for us to consider is the revolutionary general strike as a pure means.[77]

The question of the revolutionary general strike appears at a specific moment in Benjamin's critique, in relation to the specific question of the sorts of violence that might pose an existential threat to the phenomena of positive and self-preserving law. Benjamin here seems to have an important anxiety for a fundamental pathology in positive law, where the law itself is always employed for its own self-preservation – the German here is *"rechtszwecke"* – what we might read in English as "purposeful law" or "preserving law." Such law, which is already for a purpose, already designed with purpose, and thus an end in mind, will always aim to fulfill that end. The constitution of self, and the preservation of self, becomes the logic of such law and those who are subject to this law – the simple utilitarian logic of a law that finds justification in perusing ends, without a thought for means. Such self-preserving logics always already have the end of those logics, their death and destruction, as the counter-logic that resides outside of them. Positive law, in this view of its own self-preserving logic, always already aims to defend its own mortality.

Benjamin's critique of violence stands as a revelation of the internal dangers we face when confronted with such a law. We see this danger revealed through internal struggle – from the form of civil war and class conflict, to the mere supposed petty criminal – which all pose a problem for such legal logics. While positive law can constitute itself against the threat of destruction from outside itself, the inoculation of itself from itself is less obvious as a project, and thus more problematic. Here Benjamin points us to class struggle especially as the site where such internal conflicts would likely ensue. So as to preserve itself against itself, a "politics" grounded in positive law will find a need to preserve an internal inoculator – and do so through the legalization of the right to strike. As Benjamin explains, "The right to strike conceded to labor is certainly not a right to exercise violence, but rather to escape from a violence indirectly exercised by the employer." Here the logic of inoculation – "escape" – becomes evident. So as to *escape* the conflict of oppression internal to the economic sphere, the state authorizes that space where a refuge of violence might persist. The state, as Benjamin imagines it, is so concerned with self-preservation that it authorizes violence – a dose of that which it fears most – so as to stave off the more profound conflict. The medicalized condition of the healthy state that preserves itself through law faces its own limits in its ability to authorize itself through law, and violence becomes the means of that self-preservation (that pathological self-possession).

But, as Benjamin notes, the strike is not itself so obviously intended by law to be a site of violence. Something secret rests in its focus. As Benjamin argues, this is because the right to strike that has been legalized might rightly be read simply as "an omission of actions, a non-action ... which cannot be described as violence. Such a consideration doubtless made it easier for a state power to conceive the right to strike, once this was no longer avoidable. But its truth is not unconditional, and therefore not unrestricted."[78] That the strike can appear as both an action and a nonaction, and that it can be authorized as both an action and nonaction, is what follows from this mistaken judgment. As Benjamin famously argues,

> Organized labor is, apart from the state, probably today the only legal subject entitled to exercise violence. Against this view there is certainly the objection that an omission of actions, a non-action, which a strike really is, cannot be described as violence. Such a consideration doubtless made it easier for a state power to conceive the right to strike, once this was no longer avoidable. But its truth is not unconditional, and therefore not unrestricted. It is true that the omission of an action, or service, where it amounts simply to a "severing of relations," can be an entirely nonviolent, pure means.[79]

It is as though from the paranoid view of self-preserving logics the state cannot see this duality. The strike appears, not as a double force (and thus a possible counterforce), but simply as the means to an end – the staving-off of class conflict.

But what of the other view – the view of the strike? Here I am provoked by the idea of a "pure means" and the activity of the strike in Benjamin's thinking. Strike, both in German and in English, has its etymological roots in the Latin *stringere*, which means, "to touch," but specifically "to touch in a light way." (Imagine the spark of two stones produced from their strike – glanced together in such a way that they do not break each other, but instead produce a new light from their contact.) Here, Benjamin's thinking on the strike as an "omission" or a "nonaction" receives further force. As he explains,

> The antithesis between the two conceptions (that of the Law and that of the strike itself) emerges in all its bitterness in the face of a revolutionary general strike. In this, labor will always appeal to its right to strike, and the state will call this appeal an abuse, since the right to strike was not "so intended," and take emergency measures. For the state retains the right to declare that a simultaneous use of the strike in all industries is illegal, since the specific reasons for the strike admitted by legislation cannot be prevalent in every workshop. In this difference of interpretation is expressed the objective contradiction in the legal situation, whereby the state acknowledges a violence whose ends, as natural ends, it sometimes regards with indifference, but which in a crisis (the revolutionary general strike) it confronts inimically (and specifically an inimicalness from the state's view).[80]

What is the political thinking revealed in the strike that counters the inimical thinking of the law? The "strike" as pure means – as the revolutionary general strike – cannot imagine ends. How does such a strike begin? It begins in precisely the moment when those who would strike cannot imagine ends (when, we might say, the strike itself strikes). Here Benjamin points to a fundamental difference between the merely "political strike," which itself collapses under the logics of self-preserving law, and the general strike, which is truly political. The so-called political strike is "the strike *for*," already caught up in the end of its own thinking. This is the labor strike that works for particular actors and for particular ends. By defining itself by specific ends, the labor strike is blackmailed by exactly the legal logics that have authorized it. It follows the pathways of those legal logics, and imitates the inimical thinking that underlies the law. The true strike – the general strike – by contrast, is only ever a means. Its aim is only ever to strike. And, in this way, it has no vision of what would come next.

Here we see how the general strike becomes more than mere antithesis. The revolutionary general strike, by Benjamin's view, becomes emblematic of a unique form of violence, a form counter to *Gewalt*, the preserving violence of the state. The violence of pure means is what Benjamin terms "divine violence": "If mythical violence is lawmaking, divine violence is law-destroying; if the former sets boundaries, the latter boundlessly destroys them; if mythical violence brings at once guilt and retribution, divine power only expiates; if the former threatens, the latter strikes; if the former is bloody, the latter is lethal without spilling blood."[81] The general strike, seen in this way, is a fundamental negation of law-preserving logics, and indeed of the very notion of preservation. The strike, as pure means, negates the very notion of ends for which the law has directed itself.

Dating the past and future

In the strike as pure means, we see enthusiastic action within a shifting political time. For the state, means and ends appear in landscape of *chronos*; while the pure means of the strike interrupts the state through *kairos*. In the case of *chronos*, time is measured according to its relationship to space (where the movement of the hands of a clock literally traverse the sequential units of time). In the case of *kairos*, time is experienced an as interruption – the timeliness of the event, the right time to act.

And yet both conceptions of time here seemed plagued by two fundamental limitations. The first limitation is their relationship to becoming. Both *chronos* and *kairos* seem to derive their definition – and normative significance – from the unfolding of duration as it extends from the now of the present into the new now of the future.[82] *Chronos* depends on the constant unfolding of itself, and *kairos* – inversely to this – seems to rely on its normativity through the interruption of this unfolding. The second limitation, which establishes these notions of time, pertains to the witness who experiences this unfolding of becoming and its interruption. While Benjamin has problematized the progressive agent, who is subject to the always becoming of *chronos*, it seems there may also be inherited pathologies of the witness latent in his accounting of the messianic now-time as well.

While Benjamin aimed to make clear that the witness was in denial of itself in the chronological model of progressive time, the witness's presence in the messianic model of the constellation of time may still be structuring a limited conception of temporality. But how? Certainly, the limits requisite to the witness in the linear model of progress are not the same as the experience of the witness here. In the time of *kairos* the witness is self-aware of their own connection to history and that they remain in constellation with those other persons and moments and events that help compose the redemptive instant.

What remains limiting here is Benjamin's preservation of the witness's subjectivity as central to the formation of the constellation. For, while Benjamin's model may account for a mode of temporality that allows for a renewed agency, always able to respond to the dangers present in this ethico-political reality, it does not seem capable of accounting for temporality beyond the existence of humanity. Indeed, Benjamin himself seems anxious on this point. As he exclaims,

> "The miserable 50,000 years of homo sapiens," says a "new" biologist, "stands in relation to the history of organic life on earth as something like two seconds at the end of a 24-hour day." The history of civilized humanity would, according to this scale, fill one-fifth of the last second of the last hour. The Jetztzeit (now-time), as a model of messianic time, comprises the entire history of humanity in a tremendous abbreviation, coinciding together with the character which such a history of humanity has in the universe.[83]

Benjamin's interest is with that abbreviation, for only there can such now-time, and the messianic possibility it holds, persist. But this may be more politically limiting than readers of Benjamin would want. By confining the political agency Benjamin is able to articulate through this new "constellation" thinking, he may risk ignoring those moments of danger that reside outside of human witnessing (including climate change over extended periods, the origin of the earth, mass destruction, or terrestrial annihilation).[84]

Enthusiastic acts

How might this discourse on agency allow us to reconsider Benjamin's counter-logic of the strike – the logic of pure means and of the strike as divine violence against the logic of preservation? As Arthur Jacobson has wondered, "The unanswered question in the 'Critique of Violence' is whether God commits suicide, that is, whether divine violence is divine self-violence."[85] Johnson's focus is on the Judeo-Christian divinity and whether such violence is what leaves the human in the condition of their malformed and tragic life. But here I would ask that we turn his question around – rather than limiting the self-violence to God in divine violence, we might reasonably ask whether all divine violence (including the general strike) doesn't take the form of self-violence? Or, put another way; is suicide the principle of the general strike? And, while a common critique of Benjamin's notion of divine violence is that it authorizes political modes of irrationality, a closer examination of the principle of self-violence that underlies his theory may reveal an important potency. Divine violence is, above all else, violence without threat. This crucial claim gets misread too often, with the result that such "pure means" becomes an all too violent end.

What might we mean by reading suicide as a principle of the revolutionary general strike? There is, to be clear, no explicit mention of suicide within Benjamin's critique itself. And yet the logic remains lurking. Consider Benjamin's reflections on sacredness and bodily life in the critique:

> Man cannot, at any price, be said to coincide with the mere life in him, no more than with any other of his conditions and qualities, not even with the uniqueness of his bodily person. However sacred man

is (or that life in him that is identically present in earthly life, death, and afterlife), there is no sacredness in his condition, in his bodily life vulnerable to injury by his fellow men.[86]

Such views on the body – the body of the individual, and we might also wonder, the collective body of the politic – point us to that which lies beyond the preserved and preservable. If self-preservation is an extortion that allows the law to extend itself into the thinking and actions of legal subjects, it may do so – from a Benjaminian perspective – in such a way that it forecloses an agency of pure means.

Suicide itself seems to be an extreme expression of such agency: Suicide is – as Jean Amery referred to it – perhaps best thought of as death by one's "own hand" – the act of turning the hand against one's self and one's own body.[87] The "sui" (self) in suicide engages in an act of "cide" – a killing or slaying. This is a particular form of self-violence. From the Latin *caedere*, this violence is literally a cut, to kill through cutting, to engage a separation, a decision. What does it mean to make a decision on and for one's own self? Historically, cutting as *caedere* is a cutting down, especially a cutting of something that is standing. Read through this etymological logic, divine violence as self-violence seems to ask us to bear witness to such a cutting – violence without threat, a violence that cuts itself down. As opposed to the mythic violence that builds up the law (Benjamin uses the example of Apollo and Artemis who create the law that Niobe violates through their punishment of her), divine violence cuts down the law and the law-maker. Here, in the hand of divinity, is a different sort of law, one that is self-destroying.

How do these logics of suicide – of self-annihilation, as contrasted with self-preservation – helps us orient ourselves to the condition of the general strike? So long as the general strike remains misread as merely driven by a logic of ends – read as a strike for – the Benjaminian reading reveals a fundamental blackmail: The general strike will always already collapse under the weight of the self-preserving law. It would, in this way, act to uphold the very terms of that law – the preservation of certain ends. To consider the "suicide" as the counter to this upholding points us in a different direction, and not simply a metaphorical one. Benjamin's project, as I have suggested, has its focus on the principle of the general strike, not simply the strategy, but the logic. Written in the wake of the failures of the Spartacist uprising in Berlin, we might read

Benjamin as expressing an anxiety that the mass strike, on its basic terms, is not enough to overcome corroded political logics of the state. Thus, even without bearing witness to the variety of manifestations the general strike has taken on historically, Benjamin points us to a principle that might have to be present within the general strike itself.

And what if that principle became the strategy? What if suicide was not merely the metaphoric language of the logic of the general strike, but became the specific practice of the revolutionary general strike? Rather than mass protest, larger and larger numbers of activists standing against the ever-present largeness of the state, the revolutionary general strike would appear in specific "suicidal" and enthusiastic acts. Attention to their potency, and to the ever-changing conditions of economic form, may highlight for us the beginning of a new sort of general strike – a pure means against the behemoth of neoliberalism's constant logic of self-preserving ends.[88]

Notes

1 For an excellent and ranging history of this concept, see, for example, Peter Fenves, "The Scale of Enthusiasm," *Huntington Library Quarterly* 60, nos. 1–2, Enthusiasm and Enlightenment in Europe, 1650–1850 (1997): 117–52.
2 Recent work on the concept of revolution, especially that of Ypi, attempts to draw Kant and Marx closer together. See, for example, Lea Ypi, "On Revolution in Kant and Marx," *Political Theory* 42, no. 3 (2014): 262–87. I argue, counter Ypi, that Marx rethinks enthusiasm from within revolution, as opposed to that of the standpoint from without. This makes sense of Marx's changing language from "*Enthusiasmus*" to "*Begeisterung*," as I explain in what follows.
3 An earlier version of the research in this section appears in "Marx's Enthusiasm," *Krisis: Journal for Contemporary Philosophy* 2 (2018), Special Issue: Marx from the Margins.
4 Alberto Toscano, "The Open Secret of Real Abstraction," *Rethinking Marxism* 20, no. 2 (2008): 273–87.
5 Dominique Colas, *Civil Society and Fanaticism: Conjoined Histories* (Stanford University Press, 1997), pp. 337–42.
6 Jordana Rosenberg, *Critical Enthusiasm: Capital Accumulation and the Transformation of Religious Passion* (Oxford University Press, 2011), p. 60.

7 All translations of Marx are my own. Karl Marx and Friedrich Engels, *Zur Kritik der Hegelschen Rechtsphilosophie. Einleitung. Werke,* Band 1 (Dietz Verlag, 1976), pp. 378–91 at p. 380.

8 Ibid., p. 378.

9 Karl Marx, *Die heilige Familie oder Kritik der kritischen Kritikgegen Bruno Bauer und Kunsorten. Werke,* Band 2 (Dietz Verlag, 1972), pp. 3–223 at p. 86.

10 Marx and Engels, *Zur Kritik der Hegelschen Rechtsphilosophie. Einleitung Werke,* p. 388. Ypi is also concerned with this transformative affect in Marx's thinking on revolution. For instance, she claims: "In this moment of enthusiasm, Marx continues, the claims and rights of this agent 'are truly the claims and rights of society itself' and the actions it produces are those of society's 'social head' and 'social heart.'" Ypi, "On Revolution in Kant and Marx," p. 271.

11 Here I follow on Derrida's analysis. "What for the moment figures only as a specter in the ideological representation of old Europe must become, in the future, a present reality, that is, a living reality. The *Manifesto* calls it, it calls for this presentation of the living reality: we must see to it that in the future this specter – and first of all an association of workers forced to remain secret until about 1848 – becomes a reality, and a living reality. This real life must show itself and manifest itself, it must present itself beyond Europe, old or new Europe, in the universal dimension of an International." Jacques Derrida, *Specters of Marx: The State of the Debt, The Work of Mourning, and the New International* (Routledge, 2006), p. 126.

12 Karl Marx, *Manifest der Kommunistischen Partei. Werke,* Band 4 (Dietz Verlag, 1959), pp. 459–93, at pp. 464–5.

13 It was an important late German Enlightenment debate as to whether or how we might distinguish between *Enthusiasmus* and *Schwärmerei.* The worry here was that, without some affect of inspiration, the very notion of "Enlightenment" might collapse into a cold and calculating reason. Marx's language seems very attuned here to these historically informed worries.

14 For a historical overview of the concept of the "crowd" in the July Revolution, see David Pinkney, "The Crowd in the French Revolution of 1830," *American Historical Review* 70, no. 1 (Oct. 1964). On the context of the popular uprising and the July Revolution of 1830 (and its aftermath), see Francois Furet, *Revolutionary France, 1770–1880* (Wiley-Blackwell, 1995), pp. 269–384. For a recent theorizing on the complexity of constituent moments made evident in the crowd (though in a slightly different historical context), see Jason Frank, *Constituent Moments: Enacting the People in Postrevolutionary America* (Duke University Press, 2010).

15 See Pinkney, "The Crowd on the French Revolution of 1830," esp. pp. 6–7.

16 Walter Benjamin, "Über den Begriff der Geschite" [On the concept of history] originally published in *Neue Rundschau* 61, no. 3 (1950). Translations used are my own, though I make reference to Harry Zohn's, available as "Theses on the Philosophy of History," in *Illuminations*, ed. Hannah Arendt (Harcourt Brace Jovanovich, 1968), pp. 196–209.

17 Walter Benjamin, "Über den Begriff der Geschite," thesis XV, in *Illuminations*, p. 262. Benjamin's reference to "the rhyme" (*dem Reim*) here pertains to the ending of each couplet in this passage (l'heure/tour/le jour).

18 Joshua, 10:12–13, New International Version (NIV).

19 A parallel line of questioning appears in E. P. Thompson's "Time, Work Discipline, and Industrial Capitalism," *Past & Present* 38 (1967): 56–97.

20 Giorgio Agamben, "Time and History: Critique of the Instant and the Continuum," in *Infancy and History: The Destruction of Experience*, trans. Liz Heron (Verso, 1993), p. 91.

21 For an elaboration on the revolutionary sociology of time, see Eviatar Zerubavel, "The French Republican Calendar: A Case Study in the Sociology of Time," *American Sociological Review* 42 (1977): 868–77. Benjamin specifically references this reinvention of the clock and calendar in thesis XV, explaining, "The great revolution introduced a new calendar. The day with which the calendar begins acts as a historical time-lapse. It is this day, which always returns – in the form of holidays, and days of remembrance." My reading on Benjamin owes much to James Martel's recent work, especially *Divine Violence: Walter Benjamin and the Eschatology of Divine Violence* (Routledge, 2013).

22 Benjamin, "Über den Begriff der Geschite," thesis XV, in *Illuminations*, p. 262.

23 Walter Benjamin, "Critique of Violence" (1921), originally "Zur Kritik der Gewalt," in *Gesammelte Schriften*, ed. Rolf Tiedemann and Hermann Schweppenhäuser (Suhrkamp, 1977), vol. II/l, pp. 179–203.

24 Classic twentieth-century philosophical engagements with the concepts of time and temporality include Heidegger, Bergson, Levinas, and Benjamin, among others. Recent scholarly engagements with time and politics include, Reinhart Koeselleck, *Futures Past: On the Semantics of Historical Time* (Columbia University Press, 2004); Kim Hutchings, *Time and World Politics: Thinking the Present* (Manchester University Press, 2008); Nathan Widder, *Reflections on Time and*

Politics (Penn State University Press, 2008); David Hoy, *The Time of Our Lives: A Critical History of Temporality* (MIT Press, 2009); William Connolly, *A World of Becoming* (Duke University Press, 2011); Ashley Woodward, "The End of Time," *Parrhesia* 15 (2012); and Cesare Casarino, "Time Matters: Marx, Negri, Agamben, and the Corporeal," in *In Praise of the Common* (University of Minnesota Press, 2008), pp. 185–206.

25 Indeed, from the factory, to usury, to debt, modern practices of capitalism are directly tied to the productive torques generated by there being a standardization of time. For the classic portrayal of the relationship between capital and time, see Karl Marx, *Grundrisse: Foundations of the Critique of Political Economy* (Penguin, 1974).

26 Antonio Negri, "The Constitution of Time," in *Time for Revolution* (Continuum, 2003); and Casarino, "Time Matters."

27 Sheldon Wolin reveals a similar concern in his discussion of the radicality of the demos and its experience of time as it intends to reclaim the power, which justly belongs to them as requisite to their labors. See Sheldon Wolin, "Norm and Form: The Constitutionalizing of Democracy," in *Athenian Political Thought and the Reconstruction of American Democracy*, ed. Peter Euben, John Wallach, and Josh Ober (Cornell University Press, 1994), pp. 29–58.

28 For an elaboration on the history of this critique of progress and the Western conception of time, see Koselleck, *Futures Past*; Benjamin, "Über den Begriff der Geschite," thesis VIII, in *Illuminations*, p. 257. On Benjamin's conception of time, see Michael Lowy, *Fire Alarm: Reading Walter Benjamin's "On the Concept of History"* (Verso, 2006); and Peter Fenves, *The Messianic Reduction: Walter Benjamin and the Shape of Time* (Stanford University Press, 2010).

29 My translation builds from Benjamin, "Theses on the Philosophy of History," in Arendt, *Illuminations*, p. 257; *Gesammelte Schriften*, ed. Rolf Tiedemann and Hermann Schweppenhauser (Suhrkamp, 1972–82), vol. I, 2, pp. 691–704.

30 We might associate this other view of progress with the "Old Kant."

31 As I hope to make clear in the later portions of this chapter, Benjamin's "On the Concept of History" seems designed to invoke the specter of the witness, even as it problematizes this experience.

32 See, for example, the various notions of martyrdom discussed in Margaret Cormack ed., *Sacrificing the Self: Perspectives on Martyrdom and Religion* (Oxford University Press, 2002).

33 For a discussion of Heraclitus on this point, see Daniel W. Graham, "Heraclitus: Flux, Order, and Knowledge," in *The Oxford Handbook of Presocratic Philosophy* (Oxford University Press, 2008), p. 173.

For further discussions on this point, see Rebecca Comay, "Benjamin's Endgame," in *Walter Benjamin's Philosophy: Destruction and Experience*, ed. Andrew Benjamin and Peter Osborne (Clinamen, 1994), pp. 251–91.

34 For a recent contextualization of the general strike in the neoliberal era, see William Connolly, "The Fragility of Things and the General Strike," *Theory & Event*, 18, no. 3 (2015).

35 Gayorti Chakravorty Spivak, "General Strike," *Rethinking Marxism: A Journal of Economics, Culture & Society* 26, no. 1 (2013): 9–14.

36 Paul Tillich, *A History of Christian Thought: From Its Judaic and Hellenistic Origins to Existentialism* (Simon & Schuster, 1968), p. 118.

37 Jean-Jacques Rousseau, "Profession de foi du Vicaire Savoyard," in *Oeuvres complètes 1959–1995*, vol. 4. p. 578. Translation excerpted Mario Viroli, *Jean Jacques Rousseau and the Well-Ordered Society* (Cambridge University Press, 2003), who also offers a more sympathetic reading of this text.

38 See, for example, Sanja Perovic, *The Calendar in Revolutionary France: Perceptions of Time in Literature, Culture, Politics* (Cambridge University Press, 2012).

39 See Eviatar Zerubavel, "The French Republican Calendar: A Case Study in the Sociology of Time," *American Sociological Review* 42 (1977): 868–77.

40 Paul Tillich, *The New Being* (University of Nebraska Press 2005), p. 166.

41 Ibid.

42 Kant, *Critique of Pure Reason*, ed. and trans. Paul Guyer and Allen Wood (Cambridge University Press, 1998), p. 162. The standard pagination A31/B46, which I will use throughout.

43 See Marx, *Grundrisse*; and Negri, "The Constitution of Time."

44 Ibid.

45 W. F. Cottrell, "Time and the Railroad," *American Sociological Review* 4, no. 2 (1939): 194.

46 Martin Heidegger, *Fundamental Concepts cf Metaphysics* (Indiana University Press, 2001), p. 80.

47 Ibid., p. 103.

48 See Benjamin, "Über den Begriff der Geschite."

49 Kant, *Critique of Pure Reason*, A23/B38.

50 See Agamben, "Time and History."

51 Derrida, *Specters of Marx*.

52 Tillich, *History of Christian Thought*, p. 118.

53 Agamben, "Time and History," p. 91.

54 Benjamin, "Über den Begriff der Geschite," thesis 6.

55 See Lowy, *Fire Alarm*, p. 87.

56 Benjamin, "Über den Begriff der Geschite," thesis XIV and appendix A.

57 Agamben offers a profound analysis of the political theology of time in his "Time and History" essay. For critical analysis of Agamben's conceptions of *chronos* and *kairos*, see Casarino, "Time Matters." For earlier elaborations on this division, see Paul Tillich's lectures on Christian his conceptions of time.

58 Benjamin, "Über den Begriff der Geschite," thesis 262.

59 Benjamin, "Über den Begriff der Geschite," thesis XV, in *Illuminations*, p. 262. Benjamin's reference to "the rhyme" (*dem Reim*) here pertains to the ending of each couplet in this passage (*l'heure/tour/le jour*).

60 Comay's "Benjamin's Endgame," p. 264.

61 As Cessara notes, Negri is especially critical of Benjamin on this point, and calls (though without a clear answer) for a corporeal model of temporality that might correct this reestablished authority of the witness.

62 As a reminder, I read enthusiasm – as Immanuel Kant puts it – as the feeling that accompanies "the idea of the good," and in so doing, acts as "a straining of our forces by ideas that impart the mind a momentum whose effects are mightier and more permanent than are those of an impulse produced by the presentations of sense." It is the feeling that commingles inspiration and conviction, giving the sense that what one will do is also what one should do. While a diverse constellation of emotions and passions certainly play a part in the functioning of political engagement, for good or for ill, I show how enthusiasm offers a central focal point for understanding the affective functioning of such action.

63 The most recent theoretical engagement with such activities is Banu Bargu's excellent *Starve and Immolate: The Politics of the Human Weapon* (Columbia University Press, 2014). My reading here extends her thinking and follows the unexplored opening she acknowledges on p. 18 regarding the logics of sacrifice and destruction in Benjamin's political thought.

64 For a recent historical overview of the concept of the strike, see Jeremy Brecher's *Strike!* (PM Press, 2014).

65 William Benbow, *Grand National Holiday, and Congress of the Productive Classes* (Journeyman Press, [1832] 1977).

66 Ibid., p. 8 (original emphasis).

67 Again, see Brecher, *Strike!*.

68 The two most significant Greek labor unions, GSEE and ADEDY, held general strikes on May 6–8, 2016.

69 Workers for the Federation of Special and General Workers in Iceland planned a general strike on May 26, 2015, which would have frozen the national economy.

70 See Bill Connolly, *The Fragility of Things: Self-Organizing Processes, Neoliberal Fantasies, and Democratic Activism* (Duke University Press, 2013). For Connolly's reflection of the strike, see p. 195. For further contemporary theorization of the strike, see, for example, Kevin Duong, *The Virtues of Violence: Democracy against Disintegration in Modern France* (Oxford University Press, 2020), esp. chap. 4.

71 George Ciccariello-Maher and Mike King, "Oakland on Strike!" *Counter Punch*, October 27, 2011.

72 Furio Jesi, *Spartakus: The Symbology of Revolt* (University of Chicago Press, 2014), p. 55.

73 Luc Boltanski and Eve Chiapello, *The New Spirit of Capitalism* (Verso, 2007), p. 238.

74 Ibid., p. 237.

75 Connolly, *The Fragility of Things*, p. 195.

76 For the most recent reflection on Benjamin's political thought, see James Martel, *Divine Violence: Walter Benjamin and the Eschatology of Sovereignty* (Routledge, 2012).

77 The difference between principle and practice is crucial here, as Benjamin hopes to break his readers from the historical examples of what had been named as "general strikes," finding something of the principle of the strike there, in such actions, but in other – more revolutionary – acts as well. Here his theory breaks with the historical frames that aim to capture it.

78 Walter Benjamin, "Critique of Violence," in *Reflections: Essays, Aphorisms, Autobiographical Writings*, ed. and trans. Edmund Jephcott (Schocken Books, 1978), p. 281.

79 Ibid.

80 Ibid., p. 282.

81 Ibid., p. 297.

82 See Henri Bergson, *The Creative Mind* (Citadel Press, 1992).

83 Benjamin, "Über den Begriff der Geschite," thesis XVIII.

84 See Ray Brassier's *Nihil Unbound: Enlightenment and Extinction* (Palgrave Macmillan, 2010).

85 Arthur J. Jacobson, "Suicide and Justice," 13 *Cardoza Law Review* (1991–92), p. 1333.

86 Benjamin, "Critique of Violence," p. 299.

87 Jean Amery, *On Suicide: A Discourse on Voluntary Death*, trans. John D. Barlow (Indiana University Press, 1999), p. 8.

88 Two recent examples help to illustrate the possibility of this change in strategy of the strike in a neoliberal era: (1) In 2010, the Hon Hai Precision Industry Co. Ltd, otherwise known as the Foxconn Technology Group, a mass contract manufacturer of electronic devices and gaming systems, and also the proprietor of the single largest factory plant in the world, comprised of over 430,000 workers, reported 14 suicides by workers. While this may be a relatively low percentage of suicides in relation to the general population, what stands out as unique is the directedness of these suicides: Each explicitly stated their actions were in protest to the extant conditions of life in the factory city of Foxconn. (2) We find similar conditions within Orange S. A. (formerly France Telecom). There, over 60 suicides were reported between 2008 and 2011, within a company of just over 100,000 employees. Again, the rate of suicide is lower than the overall rates for France, but the directedness is the same – against the conditions of work and life within the corporation itself. These two cases, among others, point us to the possibility of changing tactics in the form of the general strike under neoliberal conditions. Not "general" in the sense of spanning across industries, but general in their representative character, these suicides – despite their low number – became conditions understood as fundamental assaults on the neoliberal logic of the firm, and the state power that endorses such structures.

5

Stirring emotion: hatreds in democracy

> We strive to further the occurrence of whatever we imagine will lead
> to joy, and to avert or destroy what we imagine is contrary to it, or
> will lead to sadness.
>
> – Baruch Spinoza, *Ethics* (1677)

A resisting politics

If political enthusiasm becomes the breaking of the mediatory power
of the state – through, for example, the general strike – the question still persists whether or if such an enthusiastic act can form the
basis of a politics. At issue here is whether the very force of resistance that Benjamin cultivates in his thinking on the enthusiastic
political act can transform into a politics that continues over and
through time. Is such resistance merely momentary, or can enthusiasm become the beginning of a sustained political engagement? If
we leave the genealogy of enthusiasm to the narrative that it was
once the religious affect thought to be the unmediated experience of
divinity, and paradoxically – through the purported forces of secularization – transformed into the unmediated objective experience
of state power, such questions of a counter-politics of resistance
would be mute.[1] But Benjamin's thinking opened up the possibility that within this secular fantasy, and the legal structures that
uphold it, there are opportunities for engagement that transform
that enthusiastic energy, and redirect it.

What is a resistant politics that might counter such a secularized
or secularizing state? Jacques Rancière gives us a unique pathway
into this problem.[2] Rancière's accounting of an anarchic democracy that exists only insofar as it "holds open" the question of who
should rule and how they should rule, inherits the logic of a resistant

political enthusiasm developed in the previous chapters, and extends this thinking into political form and formlessness. Rancière explores the resistant power of democracy (resistant against claims to rule by those hierarchical forces that claim the legitimate authority to rule over another, rather than "share" in power). Rancière avoids the collapse into the secularizations of enthusiasm that disappear divinity, or the condemnation of the secular over the religious and the religious over the secular.

Specifically, in his critique of the pathologies of the hierarchy of rule, Rancière implicitly directs us away from such binaries, and towards an understanding of democratic power that only exists in resistance. This move follows his investigation of rule. And, as I hope to make clear later, the problem of a politics of enthusiasm only appears through the question of the binaries rule (the ruler and the ruled). While the question of rule is itself always seemingly formally a question of binaries, democratic rule deconstructs this framework, making the question of rule explicit. As Patchen Markell explains, "To say that democracy is a form of rule ... is just to say that it is one distinctive way of arranging the institutions and practices through which authoritative decisions are made and executed in a polity. Of course, there has been fierce disagreement about what, exactly, makes rule democratic."[3] That logic of disagreement is what is so central to Rancière notion of politics, though not intuitively so. Rancière traces a movement between those who would claim a hierarchical potion of rule against those who would work against it. That "working against" results in a political formulation that is seemingly void of a claim to rule – and, as we shall see, only exists if it can work directly against such a claim. In this way, Rancière's thinking on democracy – which embodies this formless form of rule – avoids the paradox of who democracy is for. Rancière purports a democratic politics that works against the trap Markell describes as, "the ideal of popular sovereignty, in which the people jointly exercise control over their collective destiny, and the ideal of popular insurgency, in which the people spontaneously shatter the bonds of established political forms."[4] What results instead, so long as it resists, is a form of rule that has no more claim to power than another, and yet is capable of persisting.

The resistant enthusiastic democracy that resists external claims to power is importantly something other than the state. Politics here is not simply a set of institutions reified to retain such power (for the authorization of those institutions would turn the abstraction of enthusiasm into a structure that could then work as a resource for alienation). Here I follow Alberto Toscano, when he claims, although "it might transcend religious content by separating itself from any confessional determination, the state maintains religious form by embodying the alienated freedom of man in something external to him."[5] Rancière moves us past the question of such statist claims. What requires clarification is whether a resistance is possible that would disrupt that externality? Reflecting on this problem, Jordana Rosenberg has argued: "This informal integration of religious and civil abstractions makes its appearance not only in the ideology of the sovereign state, but also in the historicization and aestheticization of this state in the discourse of enthusiasm."[6] Extending their historical reading, I think Rancière helps frame an argument where we might turn such enthusiasm against the state.

As a means to trace this overturning, I focus here on enthusiasm in democracy and especially the contemporary affective strategies and conditions faced in democratic life. As an entry into the contemporary view of democracy, I turn to Rancière's book *Hatred of Democracy*, as a site to begin to consider these affective dimensions.[7] At the heart of this affective life, according to Rancière, is the condition of hatred. I hope to show how Rancière, sometimes explicitly and sometimes implicitly, deploys a "democratic" rhetoric, which does not seek to destroy this logic of hatred, but rather seeks to find a means of existing in a world where hatred(s), including hierarchies and xenophobia, are a profound reality to be resisted (and exist as a spring to take energy from). This move, from the hatreds that plague democratic life (hatred of democracy), to a political engagement with hatred that acknowledges its reality (hatred for democracy), depends on developing a grammar that begins to reflect these democratic forces between subjectivities. At the heart of this grammar, lurks an enthusiasm that remains unnamed.

Hatred of Democracy has, at its core, the anxiety that democracy has become fundamentally confused. What goes by the name "democracy" today is covered by a veil of hatred – a hatred *of* democracy (a grammar of that affective logic that is especially significant to Rancière). The task of the text seems to be how to uncover a democratic politics, a formless politics through language that takes that hatred seriously. For my purposes, what is so interesting now is how to conceive of that hatred and respond to that hatred, without simply rejecting it as a profound ignorance or antidemocratic impulse. It seems crucial that we ask how, if at all, can a democratic populace become pathologically antidemocratic without cognizing that very shift. As we will see, the hatred that has sometimes driven democracy comes with a loss of the concept of enthusiasm, a loss that haunts even Rancière's own argument. In what follows, I lay out the framework for this problematic of hatred, explicating Rancière's thinking on binaries and the grounds of such hatred, followed by his translation of that energy into a democratic claim to rule. I conclude with a discussion of the place of enthusiasm within this argument, and the contrast to joy.

Hatreds

Rancière's theorizing of the "hatred of democracy" begins with a contemporaneous recounting of the many manifestations of hated democratic objects. In Rancière's telling – at least in 2005 – such objects include demands for gender equality, religious pluralism, gay marriage, and social security. They also include changing reading habits among the populace, protests over retirement packages, and the neoliberal university. Apparently, we find "democracy" in reality television, gossip magazines, and blockbuster films, as well as the desire for artificial insemination. While we might add, or reflect on, the odd omissions of certain additional problems (protests over police violence and racial inequality in the United States, xenophobia, the migration crisis, etc.), the list is, in some ways, meant to be endless – a start to a reflection on the plurality of forms that make up the formlessness of the contemporary grammar of democracy. Rancière's aim seems, simply put, to draw highlights of democracy.

But what sort of democracy is revealed in reality television, or the opinion that such tastes are "democratic"? Do I find the same idea of the "democratic" in Donald Trump's *The Apprentice*, as that which appears in collective protests over police killings across the United States? Rancière seems more interested in showing the very diversity of what goes by the name democratic. As he puts it, all of these are really "symptoms" – "manifestations of the same illness."[8] All these democratic objects are democratic because they all share a cause called democracy. Meaning that the democratic has moved from some – even if fictionalized – originary desire for individual political engagement to individual desire as the form of that engagement (including opinion, preference, speech, and taste).

"Democracy," as Rancière introduces us to it, gets read as the cause of various illnesses – defined by the voice of the nondemocratic other. This defining voice – a voice we inherit at the beginning of the text – before we shed it – is one that inflects a hatred to anyone of these many manifestations of democracy. In the rhetoric of his opening, Rancière is ventriloquizing such hatred, initiating its normalization, and inventing us to share in its voicing. The voice that condemns this cause ("this democracy," as exhibited by example of fabricated sensational news, failing social security measures, changing curriculums, economic protest, cultural transformation by mass desire, etc.) gets the name of the affect of hatred.

Hatred usually gets read as aversion or extreme dislike for someone or something: "An emotion of extreme dislike or aversion; detestation, abhorrence, hatred."[9] But the etymology – of both the English "hate" and the French "haine" – points specifically to the old German "*hatoz*," (from the pre-Germanic *kodos*). This closely parallels the Greek meaning of the term, something close to "rancor," or the feeling that accompanies the recognition of "social rupture," which draws hatred closer to anger.[10] Hatred, in the sense of "*kodos*," becomes reactionary. This hatred identifies a rupture to be overcome or repaired, pointing the direction to fulfillment, as well as that which denies fulfillment.

The presence of such hatred in democracy, and the casting of hatred towards democracy by its enemies, is – as Rancière reminds us – nothing new. Ancient hatreds of democracy appear in the very word "*demo-krasis*" – literally the "force of the village/tribe," but often read as the "force of the people" or the "rule of the people" as a translation.[11] The ancient hatred originates in the objection posed by those who claim a right to rule by birth. (Those who claim that birthright initiate a genetic aristocracy, where "rule by the best" becomes inherited.) This hatred, by Rancière's account, is one that we cannot engage because we cannot stand in common with it (at least part of the joke of the word "democracy" is that its origins in the hatred of the people as unable to rule, revealed in the word itself, is so structured as to deny any "standing in common" or "share" of rule).

The ancient contrast between *arche* and *krasis*, and especially the rightful and healthful (as opposed to illegitimate and unhealthful) experience of *krasis* is significant for making sense of this "joke." The joke contrasts "*Aristo-krasis*" with "*Demo-krasis*." But additionally, it contrasts *arche* and *krasis*, both being forms of rule, though with significantly divergent expectations and understandings. As Josh Ober helpfully reflects,

> The word *arche*, in Greek, has several related meanings: beginning (or origin), empire (or hegemonic control of one state by another), and office or magistracy. A Greek magistracy was an *arche*, the public offices as a constitutional body were (plural) *archai*. An *archon* was a senior magistrate: the holder of a particular office with specified duties (in classical Athens, for example there were nine *archons* chosen annually – along with several hundred other magistrates).[12]

Any modifiers to *arche*, by this reading, then, are simply meant to explain the number of people ruling (mon-arche = one ruler, for example). The question of legitimate authority is revealed by the concept of "*arche*" itself, and not by the number of office holders. *Krasis* is something altogether distinct. As Ober explains, "-*kratos* terminology seems not to be about offices as such. Unlike *arche*, the word *kratos* is never used of 'office.' *Kratos* has a root meaning of 'power'– but Greek linguistic usage of the noun *kratos* and its verbal forms ranges widely across the power spectrum, from 'domination' to 'rule' to 'capacity.' "[13] Significant here is that *kratos* would never be modified by a number of persons ruling, but always by a type of person ("the best," "the wise," etc.). The old hatred, the aristocratic hatred of democracy made apparent in the word itself, was a hatred of institution, and especially what could reasonably count as the legitimate political intuitions, contrasting rule by office (oligarchy) with rule by capacity (aristocracy). The old hatred of democracy hated the idea of democracy as that which could ever have the capacity to rule (thus *krasis* collapses from the noble "capacity" or "power" to the ignoble "force" with the attendant derogation). At play in the joke of democracy is the funny idea that power and people could ever be linked together. This is the first joke of democracy, as the root *krasis* can also be read as force – democracy is not the power of the people but the force of the people, meaning democracy is a mob, and not a form of government or an ordered system of legitimate power.

This original hatred of democracy has historically propelled a series of reactions as democracy has come in and out of holding power. Rancière is especially interested in these reactions as pathways for us to consider a critical genealogy of the contemporary democratic. The first in the logic Rancière hopes to concern us with is that of the republican compromise. Saving democracy from itself, the Roman republic and later the US constitution sought to preserve a form of democracy that also allowed for government by the best and a preservation of property. This compromise with democracy was one grounded in an always already unstable notion of the democratic, eager to overcome "democracy" and "the populace" or "the masses." But, as a compromise, there was a commingling of structures. This is significant, from Rancière's view, for what we start to notice in the history of democracy is an odd spreading of the revolutionary overturning that operates within democracies. Just as democracy originated in a political system that deconstructs continuing aristocratic rule in favor of the alteration of rulers, so too has the intuitional compromise with the "democratic" had to purport a sharing and an alteration. If we read the democratic as mere alternation of ruler and ruled (a reading Rancière will disagree with), then we start to see the compromise of republican logics as caught in a similar alteration (senate over people and the people over senate). As this history progresses from an originary moment of the democratic, to institutional compromises with the democratic, an odd reification of "who rules" begins to take hold, with the hierarchy of "ruling" reasserting itself. This reassertion, we will see, is the pathology at the core of democracy. And nowhere does the danger of this pathos become more apparent than in the second compromise of democratic structures – beyond the originary compromise of shared power between rulers and ruled, aristocrats and democrats, and the republican compromise between aristocratic virtues and democratic principles, comes the new compromise between democratic institutions and democratic tastes. And it is this compromise for which, according to Rancière, democracy might not survive, for it has also elicited the new hatred of democracy.

The new hatred is distinct from the ancient form of the best and these transformative critiques. The new hatred is a hatred of the people (not of institutions), and the taste of the people as the driving force behind this new democratic life. As Rancière explains it,

> The new formula of the hatred of democracy is as such: democratic government is bad when it is allowed to be corrupted by democratic society, which wants for everyone to be equal and for all differences to be respected. It is good, on the other hand, when it rallies individuals enfeebled by democratic society to the vitality of war in order to defend the values of civilization (which is to say, the values pertaining to the clash of civilizations). The thesis of the new hatred of democracy can be sufficiently put: There is only one good democracy, the one that represses the catastrophe of democratic civilization.[14]

Here Rancière shows us that, over time, democracy has become a multiplicity of forms, both governmental and societal, ordering and living. The old hatred of democracy was a hatred of the governmental form and its illegitimacy. But in that hatred – the way that hatred operated (that particular form of the hatred of democracy) – we see the beginning of discourse wherein democracy becomes more than mere government. Remember the old hatred of democracy hated it through the joke that it was not actually governmental, neither *arche* (office), nor capable of the virtues of holding power authoritatively (true *krasis*). The historical compromise of Roman thought and its inheritances was that such societal forms might be preserved reasonably, while allowing other governmental forms – republican forms – to present themselves. This compromise produced yet a third stage into his history of the hatred of democracy – the current stage, where elected officials, or those who believe they should rule, defend an institutional arrangement named democracy as a means to overcome democratic society and its various idiosyncratic perversions. This is, in short, the history of democracy's revolution – from governmental to society to intuitional bureaucracy. This revolution, as Rancière offers it to us, has carried and magnified the desire for hierarchy in how it preserves the value of the ruler. The pathology here is revealed in the idea of this as revolution rather than progression (that defenders of democracy today defend it against another form of democracy – a "democratic" civil war). The democracy of the new haters of democracy (democratic government) fasces two enemies – the external enemy of democracy (the tyrant, dictator, totalitarian) and the so-called internal enemy (democratic life).

Democratic life – anarchic life – is characterized by a "feverish energy"; democratic government, by contrast, seeks to control or curtail that energy, directing it towards "material prosperity, private happiness, and the formation of social bonds."[15] As Rancière explains,

> The new antidemocratic sentiment gives the general formula a more troubling expression. Democratic government, it says, is bad when it is allowed to be corrupted by democratic society, which wants for everyone to be equal and for all differences to be respected. It is good, on the other hand, when it rallies individuals enfeebled by democratic society to the vitality of war in order to defend the values of civilization, the values pertaining to the clash of civilizations. The thesis of the new hatred of democracy can be succinctly put: there is only one good democracy, the one that represses the catastrophe of democratic civilization.[16]

The new democratic haters' "good" view of democracy is one that is always able to manage the double excess of democratic life – the excess of democracy on the streets, and the excess of the social lives of individuals who withdraw from social life for private happiness. Through this hatred of democracy as democratic society, the "democracy" becomes hierarchical and self-destructive.

Democracy's vistas

What is our stance, as readers and thinkers, toward this new hatred? Does Rancière hope we will reflect on this hatred, or that we will give it up? In order to explore these questions, I put forth that it will be helpful to consider the performance of hatred through the text, and especially Rancière's thinking on performance. By considering the text as itself a reformulation of the pathways of hatred, and the performance of – rather than merely an argument for – that reformulation, we can attune ourselves to the power Rancière claims in representations and in the ruptures of representations.

Rancière's central argument regarding representations presents itself in his discourse on spectatorship and the politically of theater in his essay "The Emancipated Spectator."[17] By Rancière's account, theater is "the purifying ritual in which a community is put in possession of its own energies" – it is "the living community" because of this logic of self-possession.[18] Theater, especially radically critical

theater that works to rethink theater – to rethink the community –
is of special interest to Rancière, for this theater is caught up in
the political project of calling the community of the theater into a
space to question that calling. Just as enthusiasm, as was discussed
through Benjamin, must ask itself the question of pleasure and happiness, so to must theater ask itself and its audience the question of
its accomplishment.

And yet this question risks a lot, especially if it is productive of
a dispossession. What Rancière seems so moved by in the theater,
and the coming together to take possession of energies that will be
shared, is that of self-possession. If possession is the "taking hold of"
something – seizing it, or occupying it, depending on our internal and
external relations to that which is possessed – then self-possession of
a community is the "taking hold of self" that confirms both the existence of the self-standing community, as well as the agency of that
self through holding. Theater is the opportunity, and the risk, for
that very possession. The risk here comes through the sense experience of the theater, and how we might interpret or privilege a sense
like vision. Rancière, impersonating one version of Arendt, pretends
"the spectacle is the reign of vision, and vision is exteriority – that
is, self-dispossession. The malady of spectating man can be summed
up in a brief formula: the more he contemplates, the less he lives.'"[19]
But here, Rancière argues, critics misunderstand the spectacle and the
spectator, placing too much emphasis on the binary between the two,
and the passivity of the spectator (rather than the ordinariness of
spectatorship). The consequence of this fundamental misunderstanding is a profound alienation; consider the spectacle as the view of that
which the audience has become "dispossessed."

The logic of separation – between spectator and actor, subject
and experience, community and world – performs alienation, driving apart the subject and the world, and reducing the agentic qualities of both on each other. This follows the familiar exclusionary
binary I discussed in earlier chapters (especially my critique of
Arendt). Separation is then a fundamental danger – and not just an
aesthetic one – to how subjects conceptualize the world and themselves. As Rancière explains,

> [Why] identify gaze and passivity, unless on the presupposition that to
> view means to take pleasure in image and appearances while ignoring
> the truth behind the image and the reality outside the theatre? Why
> assimilate listening to passivity, unless through the prejudice that

each is the opposite of action? These oppositions – viewing/knowing appearance/reality, activity/passivity – are quite different from logical opposition between clearly defined terms. They specifically define a distribution of the sensible, an a priori distribution of the positions and capacity and incapacities attached to these positions. They are embodied allegories of inequality. That is why we can change the value of the term, transform a "good" term into a "bad" one and vice versa without altering the functioning of the opposition itself.[20]

The problem here is that of variability of the binary, as opposed to its transcendence. The alienated subject finds themselves productive of further alienation through a mode of spectatorship that depends on the binary of viewer and viewed, spectacle and spectator. The "allegories of inequality" paralyze both parties, for even as one becomes dominant over the other, the inequality persists, alienating both. This logic of the allegories of inequality is as political as it is aesthetic: The fundamental problem of the binary (and this is as true for spectator and actor as ruler and ruled) is that "the term can change their meaning, and the positions can be reversed, but the main thing is that the structure counterposing two categories – those who possess a capacity and those who do not – persists."[21]

The pathological element that rests at the core of the separation of spectators from the spectacle is a self-alienation that is also a world alienation. Just as a certain mode of hatred maps the rupture of a norm broken or a self lost, and desires for its return (the new hatred of democracy desires democracy's purification of itself from democratic taste and society, and a whole self that is again secure), the spectating self may very much desire this return to self, and yet also produce the very terms of its alienation (or even annihilation). What Rancière proposes as a counter is a mode of spectatorship that moves through such manifestations: "Emancipation as re-appropriation of a relationship to a self, lost in a process of separation."[22] But the *how* of this emancipation, and the *where*, is not clear here. Only through his politics does Rancière's thinking on such an emancipation (and an emancipation for the living community) become apparent.

At issue, both in the politics of spectatorship, as well as the hatred of democracy, is a logic of domination that haunts. As Rancière explains, "Domination works through the distinction of the public, which belongs to everyone, and the private, where the liberties of all prevail. These liberties each person has are the liberties, that are the domination, of those who possess the immanent powers of society. It is the empire of the law of the accumulation of wealth."[23] The distinction, and the boundary of distinction, works to uphold the "power over" and dominion over another. Just as the spectator removes themselves so as to engage the spectacle as spectacle, that removal produces a loss of self that becomes self-alienating. It is equivalent for the new haters of democracy. As Rancière continues, "The public sphere allegedly purified of all private interest is also a privatized, limited, public sphere, one reserved for the play of institutions and the monopoly of those who work them to their advantage. These two spheres are only separated in principle the better to be united under oligarchic law."[24] Exactly the desire for purification of democratic society results in the production of a purified space for such society to persevere.

The question then becomes how to think past these logics of domination – how to think beyond the binary of the ruler and the ruled, spectacle and spectator, so as to slip the knot of such entangled power. Rancière makes it clear, such a release cannot result in one over another (a new ruler overruled, a new alienated self). In order to resist domination, we must resist it fully, both internally to ourselves and externally as well. The release from logics of domination requires some shift (not a break), some movement (not a freezing), some stir …

The stir

On December 17, 2010, at about 11:30 a.m., Mohamed Bouazizi – a produce vendor in the small Tunisian city of Sidi Bouzid – stood in the street that lay in front of the gates to the provincial government headquarters, poured petrol over his head and body, and lit himself on fire. His body burned in this fire, even despite the efforts of bystanders to put the blaze out (one even attempted to douse Bouazizi with water, but mixed with the oils of the petrol, this simply made the fire spread faster). The fire was hot enough to melt his clothes and his body together. And, by the time the ambulances arrived, the fire had burned off his lips. The burns were bad enough, covering over 90 percent of his body, that the local hospital in Sidi Bouzid could not adequately care for him. He was transported first to the coastal city of Sfax – some 80 miles to the east – and then later 160 miles north to Ben Arous Hospital, near the outskirts of the capital in Tunis. He died there on January 4, 2011. On January 14, President Ben Ali's government collapsed. Bouazizi's suicide – perceived as a desperate protest of self-sacrifice against the corruption of the government and the deepening inequality of Tunisian life – was regarded by many as the precipitate for both the collapse of the Tunisian government, as well as the initiation of other successful protest movements across the Maghreb and the Arab world, known collectively as the "Arab Spring." We recognize such change by the very affect that seemed to characterize these protests – this was a moment of political enthusiasm, a stirring.

Rancière begins his argument on the hatred of democracy in earnest with analysis of a deceptively simply phrase: "democracy stirs." Excerpted from *The Economist* on March 5, 2005 (the complete phrase of the title he engages is "Democracy Stirs in the Middle East"), the article, along with the rest in this magazine, itself is – as Rancière describes it – a celebration of "the flame of neoliberalism."[25] What strikes Rancière as so important about this phrase – now almost commonplace – is that internal to it is a rhetoric that belies a serious critique of contemporary democratic hatreds and desires. The voice that celebrates "democracy stirs in the Middle East" is, by Rancière's account, triumphant, specifically because democracy has been "brought" to the Middle East. Foreign coalition forces, let by the United States and the United Kingdom, have established democracy through elections, and the ostensible subject of the article is the celebration of this moment as an event. Rancière explains,

> One will recall the statement issued by the American Secretary of Defense concerning the pillaging that occurred after the fall of Saddam Hussein. We have, he basically said, brought freedom to the Iraqis. And yet, freedom also means the freedom to do wrong. This statement is not merely a circumstantial witticism. It is part of a broader logic that can be reconstituted from its disjoined elements: it is because democracy is not the idyll of the government of the people by the people, but the disorder of passions eager for satisfaction, that it can, and even must, be introduced from outside by the armed might of a superpower, meaning not only a State disposing of disproportionate military power, but more generally the power to master democratic disorder.[26]

Rancière calls our attention here to the problem of imposing order under the name if democracy, even as the rhetoric that accompanies that imposition is fraught with disorder. That desire to "master democratic disorder" is especially troubling, for it seems to fundamentally undermine the democratic. It is the foundational act of a new hatred of democracy – the intuitional democratic order that forces itself through military power so as to cover over democratic disordering. The voice of the triumphant *Economist* rings out, "Democracy stirs!"

But "stirs" is a very specific word choice, and one that Rancière uses to highlight a competing notion of the democratic lurking in this grammar. "Stirs" – in the example of the title of the article: "Democracy Stirs in the Middle East" – sounds like a benign description of those democratic elections brought about by force of arms and not by the protests of the people. But if democracy is not simply government for the people by the people but a "disorder of passions eager for satisfaction," can that disorder be brought by a foreign military power? What would it really mean for democracy to stir then?

One way of reading the phrase "democracy stirs" is that democracy is that which is stirred. Here democracy is the object, acted upon by outside forces (meaning forces that are outside the democratic stir it). We might say, "once, democracy slumbers, but now it stirs, and soon it will be awake."[27] Here are echoes of the stirring of the slumbering horse that Socrates thought democracy might have become. This sense of "stirring" is hopeful, and seems to persist so long as those external forces initiate force, and maybe a little longer after (think of the gadfly). The democracy that stirs when it is stirred is those removed from the stirring – separated and alienated from the forces that act upon it,

Another reading of "democracy stirs" is that democracy is that which stirs. Here democracy is the subject, the actor that does the stirring. This self-subsisting, independent democracy works to uphold that which it stirs. And what is it that it stirs, that it mixes up, or disorders? This stirring may be something altogether undemocratic – something beyond democracy (imagine the headline: "Democracy Stirs Hatred Against Imperial Invaders"). Here the stir becomes the action of democracy, but one that may work to "hold open" or "foreclose."

A third reading of "democracy stirs" may work between these previous two. Democracy is neither simply that which is stirred (object), or that which stirs (subject), but the very performance of the stirring. Here "democracy stirs" is an ideational statement: democracy is that which stirs. Read this way, democracy becomes both that which is stirred and that which does the stirring, and remains so (remains democratic, remains subject and object) as long as it stirs. Democracy becomes a force, but one that is self-possessed and in motion because of itself.

In these cases, we see a multiplicity of democracies, all of which are in an ordered disorder, both internally to themselves, and with regard to each other. The grammar of the stir, as Rancière points out, opens up these possible critical interpretations, even as the rhetoric deployed is simply meant as blind triumphalism.

But I want to argue that this logic of the stir runs far deeper into Rancière's thinking on democracy than might be immediately apparent from this opening. It is not simply that this is a cute introduction to his critical thinking on the democratic, but rather this logic of the stir is that which is essential to the democratic and constitutive of it. Unlike other modes of political ordering (monarchy, aristocracy, totalitarianism, etc.), democracy receives its condition from itself and through itself. Only so long as democracy stirs can we call it a democracy.

If that observation holds true, how might we join this thinking with Rancière's concern regarding hatred, and specifically the hatred of democracy? Is the stir against hatred, or do they operate on similar planes? Following this thesis on the self-stirring of democracy, I want to argue that here Rancière proffers an opening to consider the hatred of democracy as somehow a moment for the pervasive of the stirring. If the self-possessed democracy, the self-stirring democracy requires itself to be disorder even as it disorders itself, as Rancière seems to suggest, then it may require competing notions of itself so as to persist. The new hatred Rancière described – institutional hatred for the democratic society – may best be viewed as a relationship that stirs democracy, so long as both forces remain in motion with each other (and one does not overturn the other). The move to the stir is, it seems, meant to take seriously hatred as constitutive of democracy, as helping to shape it, but taking the result of that hatred of democracy as a form of action (stirring) as the real focus of democratic life. What we have seen so far in the logics of hatreds is really the view of democracy from another vista (or a singular vista). The stir allows us to begin to consider democracy from within.

Shared power

Rancière's accounting of the stir of democracy draws close parallels with the historical origins of Athenian democracy, and especially Sheldon Wolin's accounting of democratic Athens as a fugitive politics. Wolin's description of democracy as fugitive has a multiplicity of meanings that fall into two distinct groupings: (1) Extralegal: Fugitive democracy appears against the law it exits; fugitive democracy exists beyond any legal system whatsoever; fugitive democracy exists as a fugitive legal system, etc. (2) Temporal: Democracy is also fugitive in the way that it appears – almost as though the "democratic" is not a lasting form of institutional governance, but rather a pause between institutional forms – a fleeting, fugitive moment in-between. These senses of fugitiveness (the legal and the temporal), are not precisely congruous, and Rancière's notion of the stir maps much closer to one (extralegal) than the other (temporal). Following Wolin a bit of the way down the path of his thinking should help in clarifying the stakes for both authors with and against one another.

Athenian democracy of the fifth century originates among a shipbuilder. Quoting the Old Oligarch, Wolin relays,

> It is right that the poor and the ordinary people (in Athens) should have more power than the noble and rich, because it is the ordinary people who man the fleet and bring the city her power; they provide the helmsmen, the boatswains, the junior officers, the lookouts, and the shipwrights; it is these people who make the city powerful much more than the hoplites and the nobles and respectable citizens.[28]

By Wolin's reading, these origins make sense of the particularities of the instability of democracy in its first appearance (and every marking since). Athens was beginning to define itself as a naval power (indeed, this would become the basis for its imperial power in the following century). Faced with a diminishing elite, and a populace more and more mobilized, conditions were prepared for a conflict. As Wolin explains,

> The political challenge of the demos inevitably overflowed the customary and institutional boundaries within which elites were attempting to fix politics. Consequently, democratic politics appeared as revolutionary and excessive, irregular and spasmodic. The response of Greek constitutional theory was to attempt to suppress the eruptive character of demotic politics, but it became necessary to incorporate it selectively as a preliminary to conceptualizing the "problem": of politics as a contest involving competing claims to rule and conflicting views of equality.[29]

These competing notions of rule and equality could have formed the basis of a civil war.

And yet the invention of democracy can, according to Wolin, be seen as a unique response to this problematic. Rather than rethinking the conflict through a legal framework, or even an economic one, the shipbuilders and other advocates offered aristocrats a rethinking of political power. Wolin continues, "The push toward democracy during the fifth century was not, as it was and still represented to be, a simple demand for 'equality before the law.' It was an attempt to redefine the terms of ruling and being ruled by insisting on a share of power."[30] That demand issued not from a leveling impulse but from a realization by the demos that the power of the polis was, in large measure, their power. Crucial here is the idea that power, which had been held by one over another, transformed into power that could be shared. It is that single transformation – not equality before the law, or even the sharing of power itself through the system of alteration of ruler and ruled, but the rethinking of power – that comes to mark democracy. Democracy is that politics defined by its own capacity to rethink power. When we would think that these shipbuilders would take power and hold it over their oppressors. Rather than holding power over, these new democrats rethink power as that which is to be shared (so power itself becomes something to be shared). This is the origin and fleetingness of democracy – democracy is only ever the momentariness of shared power, when power does not rest as a hierarchical ruler-over-ruled, but as the sharing-of-power-with.

That democracy is caught in its own rethinking of power points to its historical instability, as well as its fugitiveness. So long as that power itself transforms, and democracy thus remains in a fugitive status with itself, the originary source of political enthusiasm that was lurking in the shipbuilders' revolt rejuvenates. But this rejuvenation only appears, by Wolin's reading, in those moments of transgression. As he argues the point,

> Revolution might be defined for our purpose as the wholesale transgression of inherited forms. It is the extreme antithesis to a settled constitution, whether that constitution is represented by documents ("basic laws") or by recognized systems or practice. Democracy was born in transgressed acts, for the demos could not participate in power without shattering the class, status, and value systems by which it was excluded.[31]

The limit to Wolin's claim becomes temporal, and democracy is not so much a politic here as a set of transgressive acts.

For Rancière, democracy is best thought of as a motion (the stir), rather than a moment (the moment of transgression where power is rethought and reconstituting itself). Part of this difference may be set by the very projects each sets out. Wolin is much more concerned with the originary moments of democracy; Rancière, by contrast, has attuned himself to the contemporary democratic frame, and especially the history (and thus perhaps revolutionary motion) of democracy through time.

Rancière's genealogy offers an important corrective that Wolin's project may miss. The transformative qualities of the originary fugitive moment may be limited by distinct historical contexts in the future. If we simply limit democracy to the sharing of power, and not the rethinking of power (in this original case as shared), then we may become too prescriptive – blackmailed by a conservative fantasy of the shipbuilders' democracy.

Rancière's tracing of that historical transformation reveals a covering over that is crucial for our reading of political enthusiasm. While I have been arguing throughout that Rancière offers us a democratic logic that may move us towards a politics of political enthusiasm, what I have not yet explicated is why we would especially think of enthusiasm as the frame for such a politics. Rancière offers us a hint towards this thinking, in a brief annunciation of enthusiasm within a discussion of changing historical conditions. As Rancière explains (via Marx),

> The Bourgeoisie has drowned the most heavenly ecstasies of religious fervour, of chivalrous enthusiasm, of philistine sentimentalism, in the icy water of egotistical calculation. It has resolved personal worth into exchange value, and in place of the numberless indefeasible chartered freedoms, has set up that single unconscionable freedom – free trade ... The bourgeoisie has stripped of its halo every occupation hitherto honoured and looked up to with reverent awe. It has converted the physician, the lawyer, the priest, the poet, the man of science into its paid wage labourers.[32]

The only other mention of enthusiasm comes in Rancière's conclusion to his argument on hatred, and through a critique of progressive faith. As he argues,

> Regarding all this, regarding those years around '68 that saw the last great eruption in the West, their enthusiasm has transformed into resentment. They have not for all that given up on the things that form their triple inspiration: reading signs, denunciation, and rupture. Simply, they have shifted the target of condemnation, and changed temporal rupture. In a sense they are still subjecting the same thing to critique: for what is the reign of consumerism, if not the reign of commodities? And the principle of limitlessness, is it not that of capitalism? But the resentment puts the machine into reverse gear, inverting the logic of cause and effect.[33]

In both accounts we see enthusiasm trapped in modes of closure, either condemned in its religious form as the failed counter to bourgeois calculation, or the conservative source of the ideological pathologies of progressive faithfulness. But, through Rancière's thinking on democracy, we start to see the glimpse of another sort of politics all together, and one wherein we might wonder by what affect the stir can originate. While Rancière does not and cannot name it, I want to at least plant the seed that we might reasonably call this affect enthusiasm, a name that was once – even by Rancière's account – quite meaningful, but that bourgeoisie society has disappeared. Rancière's "stir" works in such a way that, within the contemporary frame, he can develop a politics that releases itself from the logics of calculation and the conservative pathos of progressivism, resulting in a unique democratic politics that depends on a logic of political enthusiasm.

Holding politics open

If the working thesis is that enthusiasm haunts the stir, but goes unnamed, how do we see this manifest? Why turn to enthusiasm at all? The history of enthusiasm goes further than such definitions might superficially reveal.[34] Enthusiasm was originally the state Greeks would describe of their priests, and especially of their occupying a heightened place of consciousness during religious practices. It was literally perceived as a god entering inside them and speaking through their mediated presence to the audience. As Plato describes it, "The best things we have come from madness, when it is a divine gift. The prophetess of Delphi and the priestesses at Dodona are out of their minds when they perform that fine work of their for all of Greece, either for an individual person or for a whole city, but they accomplish little or nothing when they are in control of themselves."[35] Enthusiasm was not a common experience to have felt, but rather something that one witnessed as part of the interaction between the gods and humanity – an immediate experience of divinity. Because a "divine presence transfigured consciousness" of the priests, their particular kind of religion was made possible.[36] And, for the Greeks anyway, this kind of transfiguration was not something that could or should be made available to everyone. Instead, mediation by priests and seers was important so as to maintain a boundary between the human and the divine.

But what if that boundary itself was what was to be occupied? How would anyone reside at that perimeter between God and human, between omnipotence and impotency? Here we begin to see the complex relation between having and not having political power. Rancière's exposition of the right to rule, and the desire of the right to rule, help with this elaboration.

From Rancière's view, the link that lies at the heart of all forms of democracy (and the centerpiece that provokes all hatreds of democracy) is its fundamentally political character. Rancière claims that democracy is "the very principle of politics, the principle that institutes politics in founding 'good' government on its own absence of foundation."[37] Meaning democracy is precisely that principle which allows a collectivity to make a decision without foundation, and call it a good one. Part of this account relies on us understanding what Rancière might mean by "without foundation" and here some account of the logic of *arche* is useful.

Following Arendt, Rancière exalts the idea that *arche* is both command and commence. "*Arche* is the commandment of he who commences, of what comes first. It is the anticipation of the right to command in the act of commencing and the verifying of the power of commencing in the exercise of commanding." In the ancient notion of rule, the very ideal of government "consists in realizing the principle by which the power of governing commences."[38] Those who would be capable of rule, capable of holding the office to rule, are those with a disposition to *arche*.

Rancière defines these capacities for rule among seven titles, four of which are genetic (by birth), including the rule of parents over the young, the old of the young, masters over slaves, the rich over the poor; two are according to natural disposition, including the rule of the strong and the rule of the knowledgeable; and the last, the seventh title, is what interests Rancière most, and is the rule of chance (the rule of lots). While all the other titles depend on an abstract notion of legitimacy, as well as a notion of ruler overruled, democracy according to chance is in a unique position, for it places no subject higher than another. This very claim works to scandalize the other modes of ruling, and positions itself already as a stirring force in friction with their energies. As Rancière explains, "The scandal (of democracy) is simply the following; among the titles of governing there is one that brakes the chain, a title that refutes itself; the 7th title is the absence of title; such is the most profound trouble signaled by the word democracy."[39] Read this way, democracy works to deconstruct the very notion of legitimacy, breaking with hierarchies and the other notions of superiority. This "breaking" is not an absolute rupture, but a stirring free, or a release, from the hierarchies that uphold the other "legitimate" claims to power.

Here, in his accounting of the titles to rule, we find that democracy is only ever itself (only ever stirring), when it is holding open the claim to power against every other legitimate claim. The force of democracy comes from this ability to stand against all other claims. It is a breaking, but a rupture with what we would expect form other modes of authority, for it stands in resistance to their claims. As Rancière describes it,

> In this way democracy is a rupture of kinship (consider Cleisthenes rule). The power of the divine shepherd and the government of divine chance are the two governments that come from the

heavens – democracy is the power of those who have no more entitle-
ment to govern than to submit (and this title is always present as an
extra to the other forms of politics that exists, if those forms are to
establish rule against the cross currents of the other forms – rich ruling over stung, for example).[40]

"No more power to rule than not to rule, to submit than not to
submit." It is on this precipice that Rancière locates democracy, not
as a set of institutions, or even an event or a movement, but, I would
argue, as an affective condition, and one that is set by the prescience
of institutions and the possibility of power, evinced through the
action of such resting of power from those who would hold it over
another. This affective strategy operates as enthusiasm. Not as the
immediacy of the state, in place of divinity, but in the immediacy
of the claim against other legitimate modes of governing, arche.
As Rancière continues,

> If politics means anything it means something that is added (some-
> thing extra) to all of these governments of paternity, age, wealth,
> force, and science, which prevails in families, tribes, workshops and
> schools and put themselves forward as models of the construction of
> larger and more complex human communities. Something additional
> must come; a power, as Plato put it, that comes from the heavens.[41]

The additional force, which once would have been described as enthusiasm by Plato, Rancière will not name. But this power – this affective
force – works as a "holding open" of the space where this "something
extra" might persist. A power evinced in political enthusiasm.

Joy and enthusiasm

In his conclusion to *Hatred of Democracy*, Rancière reintroduces
us to a pithy and profound account of democracy, beyond form
or order:

> Egalitarian society is only ever the set of egalitarian relations that
> are traced here and now through singular and precarious acts.
> Democracy is as bare in its relation to the power of wealth as it is
> to the power of kinship that today comes to assist and to rival it. It
> is not based on any nature of things nor guaranteed by any institu-
> tional form. It is not borne along by any historical necessity and does
> not bear any. It is only entrusted in the constancy of its specific acts.

> This power can provoke fear, and so hatred, among those who are used to exercising the magisterium of thought. But among those who know how to share with anybody and everybody the equal power of intelligence, it can conversely inspire courage, and hence joy.[42]

This distinction in formlessness has become characteristic of Rancière's thought. It seems to me that in this space he offers us an opportunity to consider democracy without subjecting that idea to conceptual frames that would block it. In this way, he asks us to ask the question, "What do we mean by democracy?" and to take seriously that, in the asking, we are transformed in our account of the meaning of the democratic and ourselves.

But why joy?[43] Why end this treatise on hatred and democracy as caught in the logics of those hatreds, with the idea of joy? I want to suggest that this offering is meant to be an opportunity for us as readers and thinkers of democracy. That joy appears felt within as a resolution of the hate that stands in the view of democracy from outside. By offering joy, Rancière offers us the chance to move away from that hatred. But move to where and for what? Are we meant to reside in joy or in some other site? It is here where I would argue the absence of the answer is significant. A democratic opportunity – where there is no rule for how to move and how to think and how to act. And if we move from that point, move from joy to somewhere new, to the procedure of democracy that takes chance seriously, and holds open the power to take chance seriously – especially as opposed to the other potentially legitimate rules that might always want to rule, we might reasonably call this new immediacy a kind of political enthusiasm.

Notes

1 For the most recent history on these logics, see Jordana Rosenberg, *Critical Enthusiasm: Capital Accumulation and the Transformation of Religious Passion* (Oxford University Press, 2011), especially the section on "Religion, or Secularization: Dialectical Method for the Literary Study of Secularisms." On the trajectory of the forces of secularization, see Talal Asad, *Formations of the Secular: Christianity, Islam, and Modernity* (Stanford University Press, 1993). For an account of the pathologies of secularism regarding political engagement, see William Connolly, *Why I Am Not a Secularist* (University of Minnesota Press, 1999).

2 I use Jacques Rancière's *Hatred of Democracy* (Verso, 2006), as the central text to develop this argument.

3 Patchen Markell, "Rule of the People: Arendt, Arche, and Democracy," *American Political Science Review*, 100, no. 2 (2006), p. 1.

4 Ibid., p. 2.

5 Alberto Toscano, "Beyond Abstraction: Marx and the Critique of the Critique of Religion" *Historical Materialisms*, 18, no. 1 (2010), p. 21. Cf. Rosenberg, *Critical Enthusiasm*, p. 5.

6 Rosenberg, *Critical Enthusiasm*, p. 5. See also Rosenberg's further discussion of this point in her introduction to *Critical Enthusiasm*.

7 The most relevant recent literature on Rancière's democratic politics includes G. Rockhill and P. Watts, eds., *Jacques Rancière: History, Politics, Aesthetics* (Duke University Press, 2009); Todd May, *Contemporary Political Movements and the Thought of Jacques Rancière: Equality in Action* (Edinburgh University Press, 2010); Todd May, *The Political Thought of Jacques Rancière: Creating Equality* (Duke University Press, 2009); Sam Chambers, *The Lessons of Rancière* (Oxford University Press, 2012), esp. chap. 1 "Politics"; Davide Panagia, "Rancière's Style," *Novel* 47, no. 2 (June 20, 2014); and Ian Anthony Morrison, "Rancière, Religion and the Political," *Citizenship Studies* 17, nos. 6–7 (2013): 857–71.

8 Rancière, *Hatred of Democracy*, p. 1.

9 From A. Simpson and Edmund S. C. Weiner, eds., *The Oxford English Dictionary*, 2nd ed. (Oxford University Press, 1989), entry for "hate." On the German "*kodos*," see Friedrich Kluge and John Francis Drake, *An Etymological Dictionary of the German Language* (Bell, 1891), entry for "Has," p. 137.

10 See Thomas Walsh's discussion in *Fighting Words and Feuding Words: Anger and the Homeric Poems* (Lexington, 2005), esp. pp. 91–3.

11 See Josiah Ober, "The Original Meaning of 'Democracy': Capacity to Do Things, Not Majority Rule," *Constellations* 15, no. 1 (2008): 3.

12 Ibid., pp. 5–6.

13 Ibid.

14 Rancière, *Hatred of Democracy*, p. 4.

15 Ibid., p. 8.

16 Ibid., p. 4.

17 Rancière, *The Emancipated Spectator* (Verso, 2009).

18 Ibid., p. 6.

19 Ibid., p. 6. The quotation here is from Guy Debord, *The Society of the Spectacle*, trans. Donald Nicholson-Smith (Zone Books, 1994), p. 23.

20 Ibid p. 12.

21 Ibid p. 13.

22 Ibid., p. 15.

23 Rancière, *Hatred of Democracy*, p. 57.

24 Ibid.

25 *The Economist*, "Democracy Stirs in the Middle East," March 5, 2005, www.economist.com/leaders/2005/03/03/democracy-stirs-in-the-middle-east (accessed May 14, 2021).

26 Rancière, *Hatred of Democracy*, p. 6.

27 Thanks to Tom Dumm for the suggestions that stir here could relate specifically to sleep, and especially to the sleep that is sometimes broken.

28 "Old Oligarch" (pseudonym of Xenophon), "Constitution of the Athenians," in *Aristotle and Xenophon on Democracy and Oligarchy*, ed. and trans. J. M. Moore (University of California Press, 1975), p. 2. Cf. Sheldon Wolin, "Norm and Form: The Constitutionalizing of Democracy," in *Athenian Political Thought and the Reconstruction of American Democracy*, ed. Peter Euben, John Wallach, and Josh Ober (Cornell University Press, 1994), p. 46.

29 Wolin, "Norm and Form," p. 48.

30 Ibid., p. 46.

31 Sheldon S. Wolin, "Fugitive Democracy," *Constellations* 1, no. 1 (1994): 11.

32 Rancière, *Hatred of Democracy*, p. 18.

33 Ibid., p. 87.

34 On the Greek conception of ἐνθουσιασμός, see Walter Burkert, *Griechische Religion der archaischen und klassischen Epoche* (1977), translated into English by John Raffan as *Greek Religion: Archaic and Classical* (Harvard University Press, 1985), see esp. Burkert's discussions of "*Enthusiasmos*," "The Art of the Seer," and "Oracles," on pp. 109–18. For more recent historical elaborations on Burkert's survey, see Pierre Bonnechere's chapter "Divination" in Blackwell's most recent *Companion to Greek Religion*, ed. Daniel Ogden (Blackwell, 2010), especially the section titled "Inspired Divination Through the Mediation of a Religious 'Magistrate,'" pp. 154–5.

35 Plato, *Phaedrus*, 244b, trans. Alexander Nehamas and Paul Woodruff (Hackett, 1997).

36 This parallels how Burkert describes it. See Burkert, *Griechische Religion der archaischen und klassischen Epoche*, p. 111.

37 Rancière, *Hatred of Democracy*, p. 38.

38 Ibid., pp. 38–9.

39 Ibid., p. 40.

40 Ibid., p. 47.

41 Ibid., p. 45.

42 Ibid., p. 97. The original French passage reads as follows: "*La démo-cratie est nue dans son rapport au pouvoir de la richesse comme au pouvoir de la filiation qui vient aujourd'hui le seconder ou le défier. Elle n'est fondée dans aucune nature des choses et garantie par aucune nécessité historique et n'en porte aucune. Elle n'est confiée qu'à la con-stance de ses propres actes. La chose a de quoi susciter de la peur, donc de la haine, chez ceux qui sont habitués à exercer le magistère de la pen-sée. Mais chez ceux qui savent partager avec n'importe qui le pouvoir égal de l'intelligence, elle peut susciter à l'inverse du courage, donc de la joie.*"

43 For an excellent genealogy of joy, see Adam Potkay, *The Story of Joy: From the Bible to Late Romanticism* (Cambridge University Press, 2011), esp. pp. 220–36. For a political accounting of joy and enchantment (discussed earlier in this chapter), see Jane Bennett, *The Enchantment of Modern Life: Attachments, Crossings, and Ethics* (Princeton University Press, 2001).

Conclusion: misrecognizing current enthusiasms

> I'm terrified at the moral apathy, the death of the heart, which is happening in my country.
>
> – James Baldwin, interview (1963)

Mass partisan feelings

Political enthusiasm is the affect that allows us to recognize new beginnings – when political transformations are taking place, and when those transformations are progressive or reactive. Political feeling in general, and enthusiasm in particular, has long been problematized in contemporary democratic politics as a fundamental danger. But the place of enthusiasm in contemporary democratic politics has become more complex as democracies face a crisis of internal cohesion.

Accompanying the recent rise of populist movements in Western democracies has been the analogous aura of fascism.[1] Most current democratic understandings of enthusiasm point to its internal logics as leading to fascism and antidemocratic authoritarianism. But what if the exclusion of enthusiasm is leading to its pathologization in democratic politics? In this brief conclusion, I offer some reflections on how the energies of enthusiasm may be necessary for democratic reforms, and how to recognize the boundary between a progressive democracy and its decline into fascisms.

While once it would have been unnecessary to ask, one might now have to inquire what historical relation, if any, continues to persist between fascism and democracy? The early histories of fascist movements, and their defeat, are well known. As Simone Weil explains,

Politically speaking, it is the essential characteristic of totalitarian regimes that they prolong, year after year, a situation which is only natural in a state of general excitement. Every people is liable occasionally to what one might call totalitarian moments. At such moments there are unanimous and cheering crowds and even the passive elements in the population, including those who were formerly hostile to what is being acclaimed, feel a vague admiration and sense of satisfaction, some of the active opposition are lynched or executed, to no one indignation, and the remaining opponents find themselves reduced in a way that cannot understand, to importance. Such moments are intoxicating.[2]

But we would be right to wonder, what happened to the subterranean political affect of fascism once unleashed – the "intoxicating" excitation of mass feeling in fascism as it carries through the genealogy of this political from, even in its exhausted condition? Understanding the affective logics raised through fascism might be necessary for preserving democratic forms of life, as well as the risks posed in mixing these forms of politics together.

Nowhere is the boundary between democracy and fascism less clear than in the contemporary United States. This is most apparent in the horrific rise of white supremacist groups, and the reflection of that ideology in the rhetoric of former US president Donald Trump. One important example that illustrates this interconnection, and the risk posed to democracy, is available in Trump's reflections on events that transpired in Charlottesville Virginia on August 12, 2017. In his public remarks on the conflict that ensued between white supremacists and their leftist critics, Trump struggled to condemn acts of extreme violence, including when James Alex Fields drove a Dodge Challenger into a crowd of peaceful protestors, injuring nineteen, and killing Heather Heyer. As Trump explained,

I think the driver of the car is a disgrace to himself, his family and this country. *You* can call it terrorism. *You* can call it murder. *You* can call it whatever you want. *I* would just call it as the fastest one to come up with a good verdict. There is a question. Is it murder? Is it terrorism? Then you get into legal semantics. The driver of the car is a murderer. What he did was a horrible, horrible, inexcusable thing.[3]

The specific language Trump uses here to refer to these violent acts is unnerving, not least in part because what he offers is specifically *not* a denial. The word he uses to describe the actor is "disgrace"; a disgrace, to fall out of favor, the affective condition of lost grace. Trump's comments highlight his deep trepidation. Almost stumbling in an effort not to condemn this violence, his words circle around how we should name the violence, and how we should feel. He sees himself as the one to come to a verdict, the "fastest one" to come up with a good verdict – though not a legal verdict. In this extralegal, popular, imaginary verdict, Trump claims, "The driver of the car is a murderer." And yet, he still struggles to condemn him.

Even more unnerving, within moments of this "verdict," Trump's trepidation transforms into an "excitation." On August 15, 2017, in what was intended to be a conference updating the press on the Trump administration's efforts to *renew infrastructure*, Trump went on to say these now famous words: "You had a group on one side, and you had a group on the other and they came at each other with clubs and it was vicious and horrible. And it was a horrible thing to watch. But there is another side. There was a group on this side."[4] Trump's remarks were meant to renew the underlying structure of a Manicheanism – a partisan construction, taking stock of many "sides." His use of the phrase "another side" is especially disturbing – as though there is always "another side" to every political action, always a justification that can be used, no matter how vile or abhorrent the act might seem. By his view, there is not just one side; there is a boundary, and one side, and another side. Here, in Trump's language, we find the very structure of violence.

The onetime US president's unwillingness to condemn white supremacy, creating an equivalence between what he later contrasts in this same press conference as the alt-right and the alt-left, worked to magnify racial and political tensions within the United States. The "other side" that he continues to emphasize distracts from the void of his judgment – the extralegal, nonverdict he names as "verdict" and seems to maintain. That void, and the further opening of that void, on August 15, has real political consequences.[5]

The first European fascist movements triggered an affective political energy, attractive to large populations of alienated workers living under conditions of modern anomie. The histories of these movements, and their defeat, are well known. But what happened to the subterranean political affect of fascism once unleashed? How does the "excitation" of fascism carry through other forms of politics once fascism was defeated? With the rise of recent conservative populisms, it seems especially necessary to revive an investigation of this phenomenon.

Here I raise a lurking anxiety. Trump, through his rhetoric, has managed to begin a project of coopting subaltern vocabularies for the right. Part of the contemporary renewal of fascism may depend on this appropriation, and the fundamental misrecognition of the subaltern – a kind of playacting, where white supremacists pretend to be a new subaltern. Here I offer a speculative reading of the dangers of that playacting, counter to more nostalgic interpretations.

Trump's comments on the violence at Charlottesville raise a number of serious worries regarding his politics and intent. One submerged current I would call our attention to is the classification of groups, and the claim to be subaltern counter public. I use the language of the subaltern counter public specifically.[6] Nancy Fraser, in her essay "Rethinking the Public Sphere: A Contribution to the Critique of Actually Existing Democracy," surely had another conception of the subaltern in mind, at least in her early defense of counter publics. Conceiving of the subaltern as those excluded from dominant modalities of the public sphere, Fraser reads counter publics as micro discursive sites, residing beside dominant public spheres. Such sites, as she explains, are "where members of subordinated social groups invent and circulate counter discourses to formulate oppositional interpretations of their identities, interests, and needs,"[7] pointing us to the emancipatory potential of alternative publics. By Fraser's account, counter publics form in those spaces and languages that are excluded from dominant publics. She describes these as "parallel discursive arenas where members of subordinated social groups invent and circulate counter discourses to formulate oppositional interpretations of their identities, interests, and needs."[8] For Fraser, subordination is the central tenet the orients a counter public. This parallels Fanon's claim that "enthusiasm is par excellence the weapon of the weak."[9] One wonders how versatile the self-perception of subordination might really be. Can any group within the political spectrum organize itself around an affect of subordination?

Here my worry is both with self-identification, as well as appropriation. Can one misrecognize oneself as subaltern? Can white supremacists utilize those counter publics for ruptures of the democratic? Fraser certainly admits this possibility, claiming there need not be any criteria that prevents subaltern counter publics from becoming antidemocratic. But I pose a deeper concern; perhaps the very form of the counter public is itself productive of those dangerous confusions, wherein the subaltern becomes weaponized by antidemocratic forces in surprising and offensive ways.

We might wonder whether these counter publics, which are supposed to lie on the outside – that is "beside," but not exactly the other side – escape the logics of what Habermas once named as "nonpublic" opinion.[10] For Habermas, nonpublic opinion is constructed opinion – made, as opposed to there (public opinion that appears in a place or is that which allows a site of appearance as public). But that dyad does not fully capture Habermas's concern. He worries that nonpublic opinion is indistinguishable from public opinion, because it is unclear whether it originates in "public communication or through opinion management."[11] The result, Habermas elaborates, is that "it must remain undecided ... whether the latter (opinion management) refers merely to the enunciation of a mass preference incapable of articulating itself or to the reduction of a plebiscitary echo of an opinion that, although quite capable of attaining Enlightenment, has been forcibly integrated."[12] It seems to me that Fraser does not take Habermas's worry about the group seriously enough, and thus her argument on counter publics actually leaves open the return to the previous dominations that she aims to avoid.

That, even as they aspire to alternative discourses, the structure of thought in mass society is such as to always already collapse these discourses into their preceding interests (and also the preceding worlds of domination that conditioned these interests). In other words, the danger I worry about here is that modes of domination continue to persist because of and through these counter publics, at least as Fraser describes them.

Perhaps Fraser's public "beside" is not so different from Trump's "other side." Evidence for this presents itself in mass society always incorporating the logic of counter publicities. Consider, for example, the rhetoric of the contemporary conservative American right, and how closely it corresponds with the individualism of the new left in 1960s. If we follow Fraser here, do these counter publics always return to the energy and patterns of the previously exist-ing circuit – as she notes, "reducing, although not eliminating, the extent of our disadvantage in official public spheres"?[13]

Democracy's excitement

How can we learn to distinguish between democracy and this new fascism? Fascism is the politics that depends on exclusions, and pathologically so.[14] Its "unification" leaves absent the anxiety of unification for what and how. The hope of union as the centerpiece of a politics may itself motivate affective logics of exclusion.

Georges Bataille is especially useful here. In his essay "The Psychological Structure of Fascism," he offers us an understanding of the affective logics raised through fascism. Bataille was especially interested in how close fascism could come to manifest forms of democracy, and thus attention to these affective registers that he names may be especially useful for democratic resistances to fas-cism. Whether, or how close, contemporary populism lies within the sphere of a resurgent fascism may depend on highlighting the formal structures of that dangerous transition. What are the mecha-nisms that might allow us to identify part of that boundary?

Democracy, as discussed earlier, is that politics defined by its own capacity to rethink power. In its origins, at exactly the moment when we might think the demos would take power and hold it over their oppressors, rather than holding power over, these new demo-crats rethink power as that which is to be shared. In this way, we said that power itself becomes something to be shared, as opposed to a project of domination. This is the origin and fleetingness of democracy – democracy is only ever the momentariness of shared power, when power does not rest as a hierarchical ruler-over-ruled, but as the sharing-of-power-with.

Compare this with the latencies of fascism. At least as Bataille understands it, fascism is an "acute reactivation of latent sover-eign agency." That reactivation comes from a "shared dejection – between mass and leader" and a celebration of "impoverished life" and with "a character purified by the fact that the paramilitary groups substituted for the army in the constitution of power imme-diately have that power as an object." While democracy may originate in a rethinking of power as that which could be shared, fascism may originate in a sharing of dejection – a "throwing" down, an "under" power. The narrative Bataille offers is one where fascism appears as the "unlimited actualization of imperative forms through a negation of humanity as a value." That negation results in "sudden formation of total power" – a new group that sees itself as beyond human.[15]

Importantly, that newness seems formed and caught in a nostalgia, as a re-activation. Again, Bataille explains, "fascism renews historical existence, once again uniting military and religious authority to effect a total oppression."[16] That it *renews*, is an "acute *re-activation*." What grounds the affective potency of fascism appear as "counter discourses" motivated by – again to transplant Fraser's language – "oppositional interpretations" of "identities, interests, and needs." That oppositional force relates to a structural social pathology that he names "the homogenous." Counter readings of fascism as that which aims to achieve total homogeneity, total unity, Bataille understands fascism's psychology as arising out of a peculiar admixture of homogeneous society and heterogeneous impulses. His vocabulary is specific to him, but may prove helpful for diagnosing the dangerous subversion of anti-public counter publics. As Bataille argues, "Homogenous society is productive society namely useful society. Every useless element is excluded," this is because "production is the basis of homogeneity." "Homogenous" here should *not* be read as the same kind of status identity but of the same kind as function. A vibrantly liberal society with a capitalist economy would still be ruled by homogenous elements, even if pluralist in identity. It is the notion of kind, not identity, that Bataille focuses on. As he continues, a "heterogonous world includes everything resulting from unproductive expenditure," meaning that the heterogonous is anything that cannot be productive or fit within the logics of productions. Bataille reads the heterogonous as "all rejected as waste," this includes "the waste of body, the waste of living – trash, and those who exist in waste – vermin, unwanted persons – unproductive acts – the erotic, dreams – unproductive groups – mobs, the impoverished."[17]

In order to preserve its function of production – which Bataille reads broadly as the function of economy and social relations – the homogenous *kind* seems to elevate itself over the heterogenous, no matter the form. Again, Bataille claims "homogenous society excludes every heterogeneous element, whether filthy or noble; the modalities of the operation vary as much as the nature of the excluded element."[18] Homogenous society seeks to preserve itself, and that logic of preserving motivates exclusions of that which cannot produce preservations. His worry is that homogeneity is "incapable of discovering in itself a meaning and purpose for action and consequently enters into dependency upon imperative forces it has excluded." He does not hope to turn the heterogonous society into the homogeneous society. Rather, he sees a dangerous potency and tension in their division. Indeed, the transformation and cooption of heterogonous elements may define homogeneity's power, but the heterogeneous cooption of homogeneity is what we might understand fascism to entail. The potency of heterogeneity, both for itself and for homogeneity, is crucial to Bataille's reading. "Heterogonous reality" is a force or shock. As that which is excluded from the productive, the presence of that which is nonproductive to a world normalized by the productive, presents a potency of in its manifest negation. Bataille claims here that "it – heterogeneity – presents itself as a charge, as a value, passing from one object to another. A force that disrupts the regular course of things."[19] The value of the excluded could be read as emancipatory.

The fascist leader pathologically "utilizes" the force of the heterogeneous, which is to say those who identify as the excluded, to preserve the heterogeneous within the homogeneous. This should strike as a dangerous formulation – to use the useless, and to then make the useless the center of utility. The capacity to perform this political miracle, depends on "the affective flow that unites the leader with his followers – which takes the form of a moral identification of the latter with the one they follow (and reciprocally) – it is a function of the common consciousness of increasingly violent and excessive energies that accumulate in the person of the leader and through him become widely available."[20] The fascist leader, by this reading, sets a political impulse to renew, displaying more and more violent energies, and justifying the heterogonous as manifesting of the potency of excluded. It must preserve the excluded as excluded – as misrecognized. This is enthusiasm misrecognized.

Building new circuits

We can now point to a delicate and urgent line of contemporary questioning: If democracy begins to collapse into fascism, can the enthusiasm of that movement be deployed for the stirring of democracy? How else is enthusiasm? Is there a charge that avoids weaponization?

This line of questioning seems, at first glance, certainly contra Habermas. Habermas of course worried that Bataille's notion of heterogeneity led to the preservation of fascist logics. But I actually want to read Habermas as closer to Bataille than he was perhaps willing to admit. If Fraser's notion of counter publics risks the perpetuation of misrecognized logics of fascist reawakening, Habermas's language points to another possibility, wherein a radically new intra-organizational public presents itself – with a logic distinct from previous conceptions of the public because it lies beyond, between the damaging conformities of mass society.

Here, in a way that is neither nostalgic, nor particularly Habermasian, I suggest a turn to *The Structural Transformation of the Public Sphere*, as a site of uncovering a resistance to fascism. There, Habermas famously documented the evolution of the mechanisms of publicity in the changing social and economic conditions of modernity. Habermas argued that the rise of specifically private opinion in the guise of public consensus was the most recent – and devastating – evidence of a condition of erosion. By his account, contemporary logics of administration result in elite private opinions that aim to cover over the private, secret space of such views through the public acceptance of them as "public opinion." Here private opinion works to dominate the public through the very use of the logics of publicity, limiting authorship of such opinion to an increasingly shrinking elite, and employing a "pastoral authority" over the populace. In this way, the ideal of democratic consensus finds its functional limit; for though these opinions are made visible to the public, it is in such a way as to mollify the significance of their origins as private.

As I mention above, Habermas makes a crucial distinction between opinions made and opinions there. As Habermas himself puts it, "Caught in the vortex of a publicity that is staged for show or manipulation, the public or non-organized private people is laid claim to not by public communication but by the communication of publicly manifested opinions."[21] We may come to live in horrible world when we use taste and aesthetic judgment to ground an insurgent force against status, only to watch that insurgency become pathological through logics of consumerism.

But is there a promise of critical publicity, beyond this decline of the public sphere? In the concluding chapter of his study on the public sphere, Habermas oddly describes this perversion in terms of circuitry, comparing this pathological development of consensus to the flow of electricity. As Habermas himself argues, "In the same proportion as informal opinions are channeled into the circuit of quasi-public opinions, seized by it, and transformed, this circuit itself, in being expanded by the public of citizens, also gains in publicity." Transformations of circuits may point us to the means of this resistance. As Habermas continues, the "communicative interconnectedness of a public can be brought about only in this way: through a critical publicity brought to life *within intra-organizational* public spheres, the completely short-circuited circulation of quasi-public opinion must be linked to the informal domain of the hitherto nonpublic opinions."[22] Why describe the consensus of public opinion in terms of a circuit? Why employ the metaphor of the stream of electricity, channeled by the material utilization of such electricity, for industrial means?

I think there may be good reason to read Habermas's metaphor of the short circuit as a means to rethink public consensus. An electrical short circuit results when there is low resistance. Given another, more obvious, avenue of flow, electricity finds a means of correcting this low resistance in the circuit, traversing a shorter path through the circuit. Following the logic of this metaphor, the conveyance of public opinion itself poses a constant risk to democratic consensus as a political ideal. The correction that a short circuit offers can result by the failure of design in the original circuit. One important result of this shorter path can be a surge of power, disrupting the very purpose of the circuit itself (to contain the flow). (Recent historical examples of whistleblowing illustrate precisely this outcome.) I would argue that, just as the circuit of electricity can sometimes break with its own established pattern through a short circuit, so too should we start to consider the means by which consensus might require short-circuiting of the logics of political power.

But this raises another question: How do these intra-organizational public spheres relate to subaltern counter publics? Two divergent readings of the public sphere may help here. The first notion of the public sphere is one performed through a debating public sphere, productive of a sort of communicative rationality. The other was a deranged version of this, where logics of consumption transformed the public sphere into something always already "made." But, I wonder, is there a more progressive possibility than either of these? Perhaps a new, iterative, public sphere, one that, while "made" under conditions of consumption, radically disrupts the logics of consumption, through our very experiences of it as a space of publicity.

The reawakening and renewal and reactivation of fascism point us to the excitation present in the force of homogenous societies' exclusion of the heterogonous. As Bataille explains, "The fact of fascism ... demonstrates what can be expected from a timely recourse to reawakened affective forces. An organized understanding of movements in society, of attraction and repulsion, starkly presents itself as a weapon."[23] Exclusions prove the tensions to excite, to stir, to set in motion, as a weapon. As Foucault himself puts it: "The twentieth century will undoubtedly have discovered the related categories of exhaustion, excess, the limit, and transgression – the strange and unyielding form of these irrevocable movements which consume and consummate us."[24]

Preservations of counter publics may not be enough to counter the fascist cooption of subaltern logics of exclusion, and the subsequent fascist risings, unless they are coincident with itinerant intra-organizational publicities that rethink the flow of such excitations, however temporarily. We should be anxious of and watchful for languages of nostalgic renewals that are totalizing, and hopeful for rhetorics of fugitive transgressions as signs of such coincidence. There are certain moments of political despair, when it seems that nothing is possible. Democracy falls down under such constraint. But the energy manifest in moments of political enthusiasm, when all seems possible, are absolutely necessary for democratic transformations.[25] This explosion of political energy may not happen today. It is too soon ... or perhaps too late. But this energy is what makes enthusiasm such an affective force.

New enthusiasms

From its origins in religious discourse, to its condemnation as a bodily disease, enthusiasm has had a long and tumultuous history. Many have long viewed enthusiasm as a danger to be avoided at best, and better yet cured. But in political life, and especially the lifeworld of democracy, such hopes prove misleading. Democratic politics, with an ever-changing sense of sharing in power, relies on affective resources to help motivate and recharge that sharing. As dangerous as enthusiasm can be, it also proves necessary for exactly the impossible project that underlies that democratic sharing. Viewed in this way, enthusiasm is always a radically contemporary political phenomenon, constantly operating to disrupt and restructure modern politics.

Political enthusiasm is itself a resource that we can use to make sense of the grammar of democratic power. The feeling that arises to foreshadow political change, drawing us in its current towards political action, enthusiasm helps invest us in those actions that will transform the lifeworlds we exist within. This is why it is so often said that nothing at all can be accomplished without enthusiasm.[26] But the place of enthusiasm is not just a sign of political change. It can also help motivate that change, and help us make sense of the affective structures on which political transformations rely. By moving political imaginations into the hypothetical space of "as if," enthusiasm works to invest us in the possible politics we can imagine. In democracies, where the sharing of power is so essential and so tenuous, a constant reimagining of possible political worlds becomes necessary in preserving that logic of sharing, as opposed to reifying pathways of domination and hierarchy. Only insofar as democratic actors can manage to motivate their sharing in rule can democracy avoid collapsing into more insidious politics.

Enthusiasm has always been crucial to democratic politics. My aim in this book has been to make sense of that significance, as well as the threats posed in not understanding it. Democratic actors are committed to democracy through enthusiasm as a resource to continue to imagine how else democratic power can be. This does not necessarily lead away from partisanship, but it does work to refocus political energies on sharing power, rather than on the domination of another. Read this way, enthusiasm is a performance of an opening, a resistance within hierarchical power that acts as a release of authority.[27] We might once have regarded this opening "between" as a religious experience – an opening *between* the human and divine, but it can now take on a very different tone.[28]

We can imagine enthusiasm before fanaticism. For, while the two ideas so often seem to come close together, their relation need not be regarded as contrasting. Instead, each may best be viewed as forms of related political feelings. What enthusiasm allows is an openness to the new and the possible. We feel enthusiasm as the possibility of an ever-renewing politics. Fanaticism, by contrast, seems to appear when the pathway to preserve the new replaces the desire to initiate it. A sure sign of this collapse occurs when we realize that the logics of constitution and revolution have vanished into a policing logic of self-preservation.

When directed to the openness on which democracy relies, enthusiasm helps hold the seemingly impossible space of democratic sharing. When directed at preservation, that openness becomes an empty signifier. Rather than focusing on how to confirm and hold onto political power perpetually, democracy survives only when the sharing of power becomes the focus. In this way, democracy truly becomes enchanted by political enthusiasms.

Notes

1 Benjamin Moffitt, *The Global Rise of Populism: Performance, Political Style, and Representation* (Stanford University Press, 2016), chap. 8, "Populism and Democracy."

2 Simone Weil, "Cold War Policy in 1939," in *Selected Essays, 1934–1943: Historical, Political, and Moral Writings*, trans. Richard Rees (Oxford University Press, 1962), p. 189.

3 Donald Trump, "Remarks by President Trump on Infrastructure," August 15, 2017 (original emphasis), www.whitehouse.gov/briefings-statements/remarks-president-trump-infrastructure/ (accessed May 17, 2021).

4 Ibid.

5 Here I extend on some of Bill Connolly's thinking on "aspirational fascism." See, for example, his essay "Trump, the Working Class, and Fascist Rhetoric," *Theory & Event* 20, no. 1 (2017): 23–37. There, Connolly aims to link a "Trumpian politics of persuasion" with a kind of "shock politics." This, "to think more closely about the rhetorical power of the Trump phenomenon" and "to explore counter-rhetorical skills needed today."

6 See, famously, Gayatri Spivak, "Can the Subaltern Speak?" in Cary Nelson and Lawrence Grossberg, eds., *Marxism and the Interpretation of Culture* (University of Illinois Press, 1988), pp. 271–313. See also Judith Butler and Athena Athanasiou, *Dispossession: The Performative in the* Political (Polity, 2013), esp. chap. 12, "Dispossessed Languages, or Singularities Named and Renamed."

7 Nancy Fraser, "Rethinking the Public Sphere: A Contribution to the Critique of Actually Existing Democracy," *Social Text* 25, no. 26 (1990), p. 67.

8 Ibid.

9 Frantz Fanon, *Black Skin, White Masks*, trans. R. Philcox (Grove Press, 2008), introduction, p. xiii. For a detailed and insightful discussion of Fanon's complex thinking on enthusiasm, see George Ciccariello-Maher, "Decolonizing Fanaticism," *Theory & Event* 17, no. 2 (2014).

10 Axel Honneth raises a worry about the exclusionary logic of the language of the subaltern in his critique of Nancy Fraser's reliance on particular social movements to structure her thinking on the counter public. Honneth explains, "The different movements ... can only be tied to the common aim of non-exclusive, democratically-oriented demands for cultural recognition when we abstract away from those that militantly try to assert their 'particularity' with the threat of violence by tacitly applying a normative criterion." Axel Honneth, "Redistribution as Recognition," in Nancy Fraser and Axel Honneth, eds., *Redistribution or Recognition? A Political-Philosophical Exchange* (Verso, 2003), p. 121. Here, Honneth follows Craig Calhoun's worry, that "without much theoretical rationale (new social movements theory) groups together what seem to researchers relatively 'attractive' movements, vaguely on the left, but leaves out such other contemporary movements as the new religious right and fundamentalism, the resistance of white ethnic communities against people of color, various versions of nationalism, and so forth. Yet these are equally manifestations of 'identity politics' and there is no principle that clearly explications their exclusion." Craig Calhoun, "The Politics of Identity and Recognition," in *Critical Social Theory: Culture, History, and the Challenge of Difference* (Oxford University Press, 1995), p. 215; cf. Honneth, "Redistribution as Recognition," p. 121.

11 Jürgen Habermas, *The Structural Transformation of the Public Sphere: An Inquiry into a Category of Bourgeois Society*, trans. Thomas Burger (MIT Press, 1992), p. 239.

12 Ibid.

13 Fraser, "Rethinking the Public Sphere," p. 67.

14 See, for example, Bill Connolly, *Aspirational Fascism: The Struggle for Multifaceted Democracy under Trumpism* (University of Minnesota Press, 2017).

15 Georges Bataille, "The Psychology of Fascism," in *Visions of Excess: Selected Writings, 1927–1939*, ed. Allan Stoekl (Manchester University Press), p. 149.

16 Ibid.

17 Ibid., p. 138.

18 Ibid., p. 146.

19 Ibid., p. 143.

20 Georges Bataille, "The Psychological Structure of Fascism," in *Visions of Excess: Selected Writings, 1927–1939*, ed. Allan Stoekl (University of Minnesota Press, 1985), p. 143.

21 Habermas, *Structural Transformation*, p. 248.

22 Ibid. (emphasis added).

23 Georges Bataille, "The Structure of Fascism," in *The Bataille Reader*, ed. Fred Botting and Scott Wilson (Blackwell, 1997), p. 145.

24 Michel Foucault, "A Preface to Transgression," in *Language, Counter-Memory, Practice: Selected Essays and Interviews*, ed. Donald F. Bouchard (Cornell University Press, 1977), p. 49.

25 On "all that is possible," see Aristide Zolberg, "Moments of Madness," *Politics and Society* 2 (1972), p. 183.

26 See, for example, Ralph Waldo Emerson, "Circles," in *Essays & Lectures* (Library of America/Penguin Books, 1983), pp. 401–14.

27 Again, Lyotard has argued that the concept of "passage" is crucial to Kant's idea of enthusiasm, but for Lyotard the passage is between phases of critique. Lyotard is helpful here, for he finds in Kant a speculative rationality at odds with the old Kant so often identified with the first critique and what Nietzsche reflected on as the cold rationality of the Enlightenment imaginary. The "new" speculative Kant, Lyotard explains, thinks according to the "as if." Jean-Francois Lyotard, *Enthusiasm: The Kantian Critique of History* (Stanford University Press, 2009), p. 12.

28 See Michel Foucault, *Security, Territory, Population: Lectures at the Collège de France, 1977–1978*, ed. Michel Senellart, trans. Graham Burchell (Palgrave Macmillan, 2007), p. 195.

Appendix: C.M. Wieland,
"Schwärmerei und Enthusiasmus" (1775)

[A]   Mit den Worten muss es so genau nicht genommen werden – pflegt man zu sagen und hat sehr Unrecht. Freilich sollten sich gescheite Leute nie zanken, wenn sie nichte wenigstens wissen worüber. Uber eben damit dies nicht so häusig geschehe, wäre sehr zu wünschen, dass man sich einmüthiglich entschliessen möchte, allen Wörtern, deren Bedeutung noch schwankend ist, auf immer und allezeit eine festgefezte und Jedermann klare oder klar zu machende Bedeutung zu geben.

[B]   Ich finde, das viele Gelehrte noch immer Schwärmerei und Enthusiasmus als gleichbedeutende Wörter gebrauchen und dadurch Begriffe, die mit äusserster Sorgfalt auseinandergeseßt werden sollten, dergestalt verwirren, dass sie immer Gefahr laufen, ihren Lesern halb wahre Sässe für voll zu geben und in ohnehin übel aufgeräumten Köpfen noch mehr Unordnung anzurichten.

[C]   Ich nenne … Schwärmerei eine Erhißung der Seele von Gegenständen, die entweder gar nicht in der Natur sind, oder wenigstens das nicht sind, wofür die berauschte Selle sie ansieht. So schwärmt z. B. horaz, wenn ihn Bachus, von dessen Gottheit er voll ist, in ubekannte haine und Felsenhöhlen fortreißt – und Petrarca, wenn es ihm vorkommt, das die Seufzer und Klagen seiner Laura Berge verseßen und Flüsse stehen machen könnten. Dem Worte Schwärmerei, in dieser Bedeutung genommen, entspricht das Wort Fanatismus ziemlich genau; wiewohl dies leßtere durch den Gebrauch einer besondern Gattung von Schwärmerei, nämlich der religiosen, Schwärmerei ist, sondern die Wirkung des zugeeignet worden ist. Uber es giebt auch eine Erhißung der Seele, die nicht unmittelbaren Unschauens des Schönen und Guten, VollKommenen und Göttlichen in der Natur und unsern Innersten, ihrem Spiegel! Eine Erhißung, die der menschlichen Seele, sobald sie mit gefunden, unerschlafften unverstopften, äussern und innern Sinnen sieht, hört und fühlt, was wahrhaft schön und gut ist, ebenso natürlich ist, als dem Eisen, im Feuer glühend zu werden.

[D]   Diesem Zustande der Seele weiss ich keinen schicklichern, angemessnern, Namen als Enthusiasmus. Denn das, wovon dann unsre Seele glüht, ist göttlich; ist (menschenweise zu reden) Strahl, Ausfluss, Berührung von Gott; und biese feurige Liebe zum Wahren, Schönen und Guten ist ganz eigentlich Einwirkung der Gottheit, ist (wie Plato sagt) Gott in uns.

[E]   Hebet Eure Augen aus und sehet: was sind Menschenseelen, die diesen Enthusiasmus nie erfahren haben? Und was sind die, deren gewöhnlichster, natürlichster Zustand er ist? – Wie frostig, duster, unthätig, wüst und leer jene? Wie heiter und warm, wie woller Leben, Kraft und Muth, wie gefühlvoll und anziehend, fruchtbar und wirksam für Alles, was edel und gut ist diese!

[F]   Schwärmerei ist Krankheit der Seele, eigentliches Seelenfieber; Enthusiasmus ist ihr wahres Leben! – Welch ein Unterscheid in wesentlicher Beschaffenheit, Ursach und Wirkung!

[G]   Ich vergesse hier gar nicht, das die Grenzen des Enthusiasmus und der Schwärmerei in jedem Menchen schwimmen; das der Enthusiast oft schwärmt; das weder Under noch er selbst allemal mit Gewissheit sagen können, was von Allem, was in ihm vorgeht, der einen oder der andern Ursache zuzuschreiben ist. Uber soll uns dies abhalten, den grossen wesentlichen Unterschied und (woran bisher noch so wenig gearbeitet worden ist) diesen Unterschied so genau als möglich zu bestimmen?

[H]   Uber wie kann dies geschehen, so lange man die Wörter Schwärmerei und Enthusiasmus für gleichbedeutend nimmt?

[I]   Beiläusig merk' ich noch an, dass Enthusiasmus – wenigstens niemals, wo man sich ganz bestimmt auszudrücken hat – durch Begeisterung überseßt werden sollte. Dies leßtere Wort hat eine weitere Bedeutung; denn der Geister sind mancherlei.

Der Schwärmer ist begeistert wie der Enthusiast; nur das diesen ein Gott begeistert und jenen ein Fetisch.

[J] Endlich solit' ich kaum hinzuseßen dürfen, dass es, was man auch über den wesentlichen Unterschied zwischen Enthusiasmus und Schwärmerei und den verschiedenen Gebrauch dieser Wörter festsessen will, immer hohe Zeit wäre, die Namen Enthusiast und Schwärmer nicht länger als Schimpfwörter zu gebrauchen.

[K] Ein Schwärmer sein, ist nicht schimpflicher, als ein hißiges Fieber haben; ein Enthusiast sein, ist das Liebenswürdigste, Edelste und Beste sein, was ein Sterblicher sein kann.

[L] Uber freilich, wer wird die frostigen, lichtlosen, öden und leeren Seelen jemals dahin bringen, dies zu fühlen?

[M] Ich besorge also – doch nein! Ich will nichts besorgen. Helfe, was helfen kann! Wenn wir immer besorgen, immer daran denken wollten, dass wir in die Luft bauen, ins Wasser säen, den Fischen predigen u. s. w., so würden wir zuleßt gar nichts mehr thun; – und das taugte noch weniger!

C. M. Wieland, "Fanaticism and Enthusiasm" (1775)

[A] In everyday speech it need not always be true that what we *say* a word means and what that word actually *is* should always coincide. Of course intelligent people should never disagree, especially when they know what is right and what is not. But still – at least so as to mean what we say – it remains highly desirable that we should try to decide unanimously on meanings for all words whose definitions remain unclear. Therein, at least, we may begin a foundation by which to always be sure of our own meaning when we do speak.

[B] As an example, I find that many scholars still use *Schwärmerei* and *Enthusiasmus* synonymously. The costs of this particular confusion are especially great, for these scholars remain in perpetual danger of giving their readers the sense of one idea, hoping to relieve mental fantasies, when they really mean the other (which in this case could literally produce them). Thus, the meaning of these terms should be delineated with extreme care.

[C]   As I define it ... *Schwärmerei* appears as a kind of divine
        infestation of the soul, which is unnatural to it, but which
        the intoxicated soul still seeks out. Consider a fanatic such
        as Horace, and for him it was Bachus, of whose divinity he
        always remained full, causing him to range aimlessly among
        groves and caves; or another, such as Petrarch, when he found
        himself made content by lamentations professed to Laurel
        mountains and rivers. Here *Schwärmerei* should be under-
        stood as roughly equivalent to fanaticism (although up until
        now this was just a special kind of *Schwärmerei*, namely the
        religious kind). Yet we can also consider another kind of occu-
        pying of one's soul which itself is not *Schwärmerei*, but rather
        something consequent to the immediate presencing of the
        beautiful and the good, the perfect and the divine in nature
        acting as a mirror to our innermost being. That kind of occu-
        pying of the soul can be identified by disruptions that yet still
        allow for both external and internal senses to see, hear, and
        feel what is truly beautiful and good, and just as naturally as
        an iron glowing in the fire.

[D]   This state of mind is, I believe, reasonably described as
        Enthusiasmus. This state, where our soul is ignited, is itself
        god-like. It is as though (so many claim) the enthusiast effuses
        that which they received by contact with God. Such deeply
        infused love of truth and beauty and goodness is the very real
        influence of the deity; it is (as Plato says) God within side us.

[E]   Lift up your eyes and see: What is the state of the human soul
        which has never experienced such enthusiasm? What is their
        natural state? – How frozen, dull, passive, formless and empty
        are their lives? Could we ever say, "How bright and warm
        (like a life wrapped in wool), powerful and magnanimous,
        affective and magnetic, fruitful and effective for all, noble and
        good is this?"

[F]   *Schwärmerei* is a disease of the soul – a real "soul fever";
        Enthusiasmus is the real *life* of the soul. What a difference
        essential nature in cause and effect can make!

[G]   I do not mean to pretend here that such clear boundaries pre-
        sent themselves everywhere *Enthusiasmus* and *Schwärmerei*
        swim. The enthusiast really does seem to rave (like a fanatic),
        and he himself may not be certain what it is that stirs him.

But it is precisely because of that mistake that – one way or another – reason is due. We should not be discouraged by such confusion, and instead should take up the task of defining the differences (so little of which have been identified) of these two very disparate states.

[H] Yet how could any such definition be achieved when the same concept continues to find confused expression in the two words *Schwärmerei* and *Enthusiasmus*?

[I] Incidentally, I have yet to ever notice where enthusiasm – at least where that word is employed correctly – could be replaced by the word delusion. Obviously this latter word has more particular meanings, for there are many kinds of ghosts in this world. Indeed, the *Schwärmer* is as excited as the enthusiast, yet the one (enthusiasm) is inspired by God, while the other (*Schwärmerei*) is a fetish.

[J] At last I am beginning to find hope that there is a means of distinguishing the substantial difference between enthusiasm and *Schwärmerei* – that we can, over time, begin to mean different things with these two words, and yet also that neither of the names enthusiast or *Schwärmer* will continue to hold derogatory connotations.

[K] To be a *Schwärmer* need not be shameful, for it is the result of an illness; and to be an enthusiast, well … this is to be the most loved, the noblest, and the best that any human could be.

[L] So who now will drag those frigid, unenlightened, dreary, and empty souls towards such warmth?

[M] Is it me? Have I resolved this confusion? – of course not! I have resolved nothing. Help! What can help here? If we always try to resolve everything, always try to recollect, then we are building things in air, sowing seeds in the water, preaching to the fish, etc. Here, now, we have done nothing more than gather – though perhaps that is good for even less!

Acknowledgments

Enthusiasm arises in a special kind of solidarity. This book, like all political theory, was born from generosity. It has grown through collective enterprise, in being together with others. Thanks are due to so many who have helped make the wilds of political thinking welcome, without whom this work would not have been possible.

I began this research at the University of California, San Diego, under the direction of Tracy Strong. It is not an exaggeration to say I learned to think politically alongside Tracy. His thought has always seemed to me to be at the edge of things, and I've have tried my best to further the example. He was a true *Doktorvater*, offering to me what felt like undue care and attention. Tracy is, in the very best sense, full of multitudes. He has guided me to think in the "with" and the "without." And it is because of him that I find true joy in contradiction and wonder.

Much of my early thinking on enthusiasm developed in conversation with friends and colleagues at the *Institut für Sozialforschung* in Frankfurt and at the *Institut für Philosophie* at *Goethe-Universität*. Axel Honneth invited me to serve as a research fellow there in the 2009–10 academic year, and for many visits thereafter. At a crucial moment, in a smoked-filled office at *IG Farben Haus*, he asked whether I had considered exploring political enthusiasm further. This book is my reply to his urging. I hope he hears the echoes of those conversations. My thanks too to Daniel Loick, Julia Ng, and especially B. Rousse, for their questions, both personal and professional. Beginning friendships and research projects can often intertwine, and theirs have been crucial in moving my thinking forward from the start.

My arguments have been made all the better over the years by many key interlocutors. At UCSD, these include Tracy Strong, Fonna Forman, Harvey Goldman, Phil Roeder, and Patchen Markell; thanks to you all for all pushing this project towards the question of how enthusiasm works in contemporary politics. Many friends and colleagues have asked serious questions for which I have not always had good answers. I hope they see their efforts reflected on these pages. These thinkers include Philip Michelbach, John LeJeune, B. Rousse, Sayres Rudy, Jonathan Nedeau, Keven Schnadig, Nancy Luxon, Theo Christov, Banu Bargu, John McGuire, James Ingram, Sylwia Chrostowska, Robyn Marasco, Ben Schupmann, Simon Stow, Lasse Thomassen, James Martel, Jennifer Culbert, Davide Panagia, Alex Livingston, Simone Chambers, Steve Johnston, Char Miller, Libby Anker, Christian Thorne, Robin Celikates, Derek Denman, Anders Berg-Sørensen, and Lars Tønder.

In Massachusetts, I found much support and encouragement from friends and allies, including David Jones, Boris Wolfson, Adam Sitze, Mike Stein, Nick Xenos, David Hall, Monica Ringer, Chris Dole, and John Drabinski. Colleagues in the Political Science and the Law, Jurisprudence, and Social Thought departments at Amherst College all lent valuable support, especially Lawrence Douglas, Martha Umphrey, Nasser Hussain, Amrita Basu, Pavel Machala, Kristin Bumiller, Javier Corrales, and Jonathan Obert. All made me feel these thoughts were worth defending. The "Theory Corridor" in Clark House was a constant inspiration. Adam Sitze pushed me in every which way to learn to think differently about political ideas. He is a model scholar, and his voice reverberates here. Tom Dumm read too many drafts of this book at so many stages. The words "thank you" are not enough to express my esteem for all his support. Tom's advice has shaped nearly every page, and only for the better. Austin Sarat has guided me through every aspect of thinking through these arguments. He has been the kindest friend and most generous colleague. These debts are not so easily repaid. At a crucial stage in the development of this text, Mark Reinhardt, Kennan Ferguson, and Bill Connolly all participated in a critical workshop that helped to shape the direction of this text. Their critiques helped me to work the manuscript into a political theory of enthusiasm. I am very much obliged for their care.

Many thanks are due to students who have pushed my thinking into new avenues of thought, especially those that took part in seminars on democratic theory and fanaticism. Thank you to Nica Siegel, Alex Diones, Sam Rosenblum, Jeff Feldman, Siraj Sindhu, Andrew Lindsay, Stefan Yong, Jane Berrill, Tiffany Wong, Annika

Ariel, Erik Petrie, Matt Debutts, Mike Milov-Cordoba, Emma Saltzberg, Josh Mayer, Alex Deatrick, Deidre Nelms, Chun-Tak Suen, Joey Ramesar, and Meghna Sridhar.

My thinking has evolved in dialogue at several crucial moments. Once upon a time, Danielle Allen introduced me to political theory and political thought at the University of Chicago. She has been a source of constant inspiration along the way. Many recent conversations with Lasse Thomassen on enthusiasm and representation have changed these concepts for me. Lasse offered key advice as this book was just being finished, but his tone is reflected in my final revisions. A special thanks to Sayres Rudy, who continues to be the most honest, ruthless, thoughtful, and kind interlocutor I know. Simon Stow has been a dear friend, exactly when I needed one. He has read every word of this manuscript and offered the most outrageous and thoughtful encouragement. He is the model of a generous thinker, smoothing out the hard edges of my thinking. Thank you especially to Lars Tønder, for inviting me to Copenhagen, for braving all the darkness and the cold with me, and for reminding me to keep celebrating the democratic comedy.

At Manchester University Press, I have been assisted along the way with generous support by Jonathan de Peyer, Rob Byron, Lucy Burns, Jen Mellor, and Sophie Robinson. Manchester's history in radical politics makes this an ideal home for this book, and their attention has made it feel the ideal press.

I have received generous support along the way from many institutions and funding sources, including the University of California, the William Andrews Clark Memorial Library at UCLA, the *Institut für Sozialforschung*, Harvard University, DAAD, the Office of the Dean of the Faculty at Amherst College, and from the University of Copenhagen.

I would not have been able to write this book without the care and love of my family. Thank you to Christy and John, Scott and Lorri, Sue, and Brinton and Karen; to my nieces and nephews; to my in-laws Albert and Virginia; and thank you to my parents Bill and Freddi, who know more than most how much this book means to me, and how their care made it possible. Thank you to my daughter Stelle; she has been a constant lesson in the ways joy multiplies and becomes plural. Stelle has grown up alongside this book, forming it with every question she has asked and every hope she names. I have learned more from her than I could have dreamed possible.

More than anyone or anything, I offer thanks to Alivia Price. She has been my love, my greatest advocate, and a true source of enthusiasm. Alivia has helped me navigate every joy and disaster, no matter how big or small, with care and love. This book is only possible, and filled with possibility, because of her.

Andrew Poe
Copenhagen, Denmark

Index

EU authorised representative for GPSR:
Easy Access System Europe, Mustamäe tee 50,
10621 Tallinn, Estonia
gpsr.requests@easproject.com